What Others Are Saying about Pastor McAlester's Bride

"WE ARE SURROUNDED BY INVISIBLE ENEMIES who are out to destroy our lives, our marriages, and our happiness. Don't believe me? *Pastor McAlester's Bride* may convince you otherwise. With this unique blend of the movies *Ghostbusters* and *The Exorcist*, Ms. Walding crafts a story that rivals C. S. Lewis's *Screwtape Letters*, a story that allows the reader a peek into a realm beyond our five senses but a realm that is no less real. This book deals with so many topics and in such a real way—love, betrayal, marriage, spiritual warfare, sacrifice, pride, fear, and more—that I had a hard time putting it down each night! A refreshing and poignant look at a subject rarely addressed in Christian fiction."

—MaryLu Tyndall, best-selling author of the
Legacy of the King's Pirates series.

"I'd close the book momentarily, and look out the window—to absorb what I'd just read. Then plunge back into it. I JUST COULDN'T PULL MYSELF AWAY from *Pastor McAlester's Bride*."

—Faye Headrick, Christian evangelist.

"A PAGE TURNER that cannot be put down until the last page is read."

—Edith Chastain, lay missionary to
Guatemala, Singapore, and Thailand.

PASTOR

McALESTER'S

BRIDE

God bless you today
and always!

Lynne

Lynne Wills Walding

PASTOR

McALESTER'S

BRIDE

BY

LYNNE WELLS WALDING

RUTH & PROBITY PUBLISHING

ISBN 978-0-9853242-7-8

PASTOR McALESTER'S BRIDE

Originally published as *Handful of Demons*

All Scripture quotations are taken from the New American Standard Version of the Bible.

All of the characters and events in this book are fictitious. Any resemblance to actual persons, living or dead, or to actual events is purely coincidental.

It is the mission of Ruth & Probity Publishing Company to adhere to the principles of integrity and compassion in all our dealings, as required by our Christian beliefs. And to present Jesus Christ to our readers as Savior, Friend, and Redeemer . . . The Answer to every affliction.

PRINTED IN the United States of America.

DEDICATION

To my perfect little family—all gone to be with the Lord.
My daddy, Jim Wells, master of anything he'd put his mind to, who
thought that I, too, could do anything. Larry—my brother, my best
friend, and my hero. And my mother, Adele, who did more than any
other mortal to make me who I am. I'll see you all in the morning.

Acknowledgments

Where to begin? I owe so much to so many, for believing in my ability to bring this—my debut novel—to fruition.

First and foremost, I want to thank my husband, Dee, and my son, Billy, for their undying encouragement, even when I wanted to crawl into bed and cover my head.

I'm so grateful to my magnificent editor, book designer, and cover designer, Susan Lohrer, for her patience . . . her brilliance . . . and the friendship we've established.

My first readers—couldn't have made it without them. Thank you, Faye Headrick, Dixie Webb, Shauni Nix, Karen Bond, Edith Chastain, Diane Loftice, and my two stepdaughters, Kelly Gilbert and Kimberly Cornsilk. Your input was invaluable.

A great big thank-you to my awesome proofreader, Adam Blumer.

Thanks to my "Library Lady," Jann Smith, for her help when my computer was being mean to me, as well as the rest of the sweet ladies at McMillan Library in Overton for their helpfulness.

Always . . . always, the biggest thanks goes to my Lord and Savior, Jesus Christ, for all He's done for me. "He watches over me with eyes of mercy."

If I can write a story entertaining enough to keep my readers turning the pages, yet scriptural enough to make them aware the Enemy seeks to devour them—and Jesus is their refuge—then I've accomplished what I think God has called me to do.

Lynne Wells Walding

1

October 8, 1993
St. Michael, Arkansas

C asey stumbled blindly down the small-town sidewalk, encased in a cocoon of grief. White sneakers darted into her field of vision. Oooof! She collided with their owner. But for the quick thinking of a gentleman who'd stepped into her path, she would have run headlong into the opened door of a little shop.

He looked down at her. "You okay?"

"Oh, yes, I'm fine." She rubbed her forehead with her fingertips, trying to get a handle on her emotions, and lifted her eyes to glance at his kindly face. Then quickly looked away. "I'm sorry, I wasn't looking where I . . . where I . . . was going."

He tilted his head to one side and wrinkled his brow. "Forgive me, but you don't look at all fine. You look upset—no, make that bewildered. Are you sure you're all right?"

His intent expression reflected concern, and he appeared to look far beyond the inconsequential bump they'd just shared. Her insides trembled as his gaze seemed to touch the core of her soul and release the lock she'd so carefully placed on her emotions.

Much to her chagrin, the tears lurking just below the surface made their grand entrance, overflowing her eyes and spilling down her cheeks. Her shoulders began to shudder.

Then right there outside the doorway of Mrs. Anderson's little antique shop, this affable-looking stranger gently put his arms around her shoulders, drew her to him, and held her close. She didn't have the strength or the desire to pull away. For a long moment they stood there with his arms around her shoulders, and her arms dangling awkwardly at her sides. Her face was buried in his chest, and his clean-smelling, bulky gray sweater soaked up her torrent of tears.

Casey needed this small display of human concern. She'd known no gentleness in her life for nearly three years. Ever since Edward had begun to change. Of late, she felt like her heart was dead, and she was in mourning for it.

She became aware of the inappropriate intimacy of their embrace when she realized she could hear his heartbeat—or was it her own? She squirmed beneath the arms that encircled her.

"I'm sorry. That was very bold of me." He pulled away and broadened his stance, a grin lighting up his face. "I'm braced for a good, sound face slap now, if you're ready."

That coaxed a weak smile to her tear-dampened face, but Casey stood mute. She was afraid to say anything for fear of making a bigger fool of herself than she already had.

He touched her arm. "Okay, tell you what. There's a little coffee shop right down the street. Let me buy you a cup of coffee, and I'll tell you my life's story. You don't have to say a thing. You can get up and leave when you're ready. Just promise me you'll stay through my kindergarten experiences, because that's *definitely* the most exciting part." Something a dear old friend would say in jest. But to be totally realistic, it sounded more like she was about to let herself be picked up by a tall, attractive stranger.

2

"Please don't entertain the thought that you're being picked up," he continued, evidently a mind reader. "I've never picked up a girl and I don't plan to start now. But I could use a cup of coffee and I think you could too. For the sake of expedience, we'll sit at the same table. Think of it as a favor to the establishment. They won't have to clean two tables when we leave."

It sounded innocent enough. He was so kind, and he had a great sense of humor. And after all, what harm could the man do in a public place in broad daylight?

"Okay," she said warily. "I guess I do owe it to you to wait around until your sweater dries, to make sure it doesn't shrink."

He smiled and nodded.

"There is one condition," she added. "I have to pay for my own coffee, or it would officially be a pickup. And I don't want you to break your perfect record."

"You have a deal. Here." He handed her a handkerchief, and she dabbed her eyes.

She offered the hanky back, but he held his hand up, indicating she should keep it. Casey accepted, not wanting to be rude. As she stuffed the hanky in her purse, it occurred to her she should get rid of it before she went home. How would she explain, if Edward saw it? He would accuse her of awful things.

"So, you got the message from the home office on what to wear today!" he said, taking two long strides around her to be on the street side as they walked to the coffee shop.

She looked up at him, puzzled.

"I'm joking," he said patiently. "You didn't notice that we look like the Bobbsey twins? Except I don't have beautiful freckles."

He had a twinkle in his eyes and a funny little curl at the corners of his mouth, even when he wasn't smiling.

Casey had never considered her freckles beautiful. His remark spurred a twinge of excitement in her, and she suddenly felt a little more spring in her step.

"Oh, forgive me. I've been kind of out of it this morning." She leaned away from him to take a sweeping glance at his attire.

Noticing for the first time that his sweater was a close match to

3

her gray lamb's wool cardigan and he too was wearing blue jeans, she smiled.

"Yes, we do look like two old friends who decided to dress alike, don't we?"

Or two lovers out for a wonderful autumn day together.

Her cheeks flamed hot, and she turned her face away. She and Edward had often dressed to match until a few years ago. Now he said it was foolishness. Yet she had no desire for anyone but him. And certainly no inclination to repeat the mistakes of her youth. She just wished she had her old Edward back. Regardless, she had no mind to complicate their already chaotic life by having a relationship with someone. Except maybe a good friend. Someone to talk to.

But that should be a woman, shouldn't it?

The coffee shop was less than fifty steps away. A quaint, neat establishment with an intriguing smell. A unique blend of fresh coffee, pies baking, and eucalyptus.

As they worked their way down the single row of high-backed booths, her escort got a wave, a nod, or a handshake from every table they passed. And more than a few curious looks. When they were seated a little over halfway back, he asked if she'd like anything more than coffee.

"No thank you," Casey murmured as she surveyed, with interest, the adjacent brick wall. Painted forest green, it was adorned with every imaginable sort of memorabilia, from horseshoes to Elvis posters, antique clocks to ballet shoes, and old tin signs to ancient coffeepots.

"Are you sure? This place serves the best strawberry pie in the world," he cajoled.

"Just coffee, please. And I really want to apologize for crying like I did. I'm not usually that sensitive."

"I suspect you're one of the most sensitive people I've met all morning. And I've had a very busy morning. Been to my barber, my accountant, and my psychic," he bantered back at her. "Just kidding about the psychic," he added with a grin.

He obviously wasn't going to let the conversation get too maudlin, and she appreciated that. She could use some lighthearted chitchat with a friend. She'd been so long without a good friend. Her life was filled with many people she referred to as friends. But not one person she'd be comfortable calling at 2:00 a.m. if she was worried or frightened. That was Casey's rating system for a *real* friend.

Edward was a pastor, so her friends tended to be folks in the church. Wisdom prohibited sharing problems with her husband's congregation. Especially marital problems. And although she may be awakened by frightened or worried people in the wee hours of the morning on a regular basis, it wasn't wise to return the favor. She'd learned early in her marriage that in spite of the appearance of busyness and popularity, a pastor's wife leads a lonely existence.

When they first walked in, he'd held up two slender fingers. Now a friendly waitress in a crisp uniform brought two cups of coffee and set them down before them. She gave the man a quick peck on the cheek and winked at Casey, then she wordlessly turned and left.

"Thanks, Mae," he said, studying Casey's face as though memorizing it perhaps to paint it.

"Forgive me for staring at you. But, honestly—and this *is* going to sound like a pickup line—you really do look like someone I used to know. Well, actually, I didn't know her very well . . . I mean . . . I wanted to. I worked with her mother and she . . ."

He sighed and looked down at his coffee. "I'm sorry. Too much information."

"No," she said, leaning forward, "please, go on. I'd like to hear about it."

"Well." He fidgeted with the handle of his cup. "I was working and going to school. Didn't have much money, so I couldn't take her on an elaborate date. So I asked her mother if she thought she might go to the movies or the zoo with me. But she said her daughter was involved—said the word like it was profanity—with some jerk. No love lost there. Anyway, she assured me there was no way her daughter would ever go out with anyone else, as long as he was in the picture."

He paused as though to end the story there.

Casey propped her elbows on the table and cradled her face in her hands. "And?"

"And . . . the girl moved away with the jerk. End of story. I've often wondered if I could have made a difference had I at least tried. She always had a big smile for me . . . and . . . oh well, that's water under the bridge. She barely knew I existed.

"You can stop me anytime, you know." His eyes pleaded for reprieve.

Laughing, for the first time in a very long time, Casey exclaimed, "I did too!"

"You did too *what*?" His forehead rumpled.

"Me too. I had a mother *and* a jerk. But I didn't have a knight in shining armor who wanted to save me from the jerk. So I ended up with him . . . for a while. Head over heels in love. Not good. Didn't have a happy ending."

"Maybe you could tell me *your* story. Help me out here with the fool I just made of myself," he implored her.

"We'd have to know each other a lot better before I could do that." She twisted the corner of her napkin. "You'll have to settle for the scene I just made out there on the sidewalk."

She found herself feeling a fondness for this stranger. But she didn't even know him. And would *never* know him well enough to tell him about her past. Nonetheless her heart went out to him.

He was gazing down into his cup of coffee, fingering the rim.

"So," she asked, deliberately changing the subject, "do you live in St. Michael?"

He brightened and looked up from his cup.

"Yes, a few miles out. Had a practice here for about twenty years. Sold out to my junior partner not too long ago, and now I'm living off the fat of the land, as they say. I have a few acres where I raise things. You know—dogs, cats, horses, and assorted wild critters."

He hesitated, one forefinger against pursed lips. "Let's do names. That would be a good start. You tell me your name and a few words about yourself. Then I'll tell you mine. Okay?"

Casey sat erect and ceremoniously cleared her throat.

"Ahem. My name is Casey McAlester. I live in Sugar Bluff, Arkansas, and I'm a pastor's wife. I have a grown son, a bunch of dogs and cats, and one pet possum."

6

She could feel a smile tugging at her mouth.

"And I feel like I've just introduced myself at an AA meeting," she laughed, unable to maintain her solemn countenance any longer.

"That's more like it," he said. "Good sense of humor, and doesn't always cry when spoken to." They chuckled. "So you do wild critters, too?"

"Yes, except he's not wild anymore. He had a broken leg and couldn't be rehabilitated. But *you* are stalling." She pointed an accusing finger at him. "I've told you my name. Now it's your turn."

Casey folded her arms in a mock stern look. She was definitely loosening up. Why, she was acting almost like her old self. *Maybe my heart isn't dead after all.* Maybe, with God's help, she could find a way to connect with Edward and get their marriage back on track. She'd prayed a lot about it—but never felt like her prayers were being heard, much less answered. Until today . . . *just now.* This stranger from out of nowhere had ignited a flicker of hope in her spirit.

He took another long sip of coffee. "DeWitt. And that's not my last name, it's my first name. Family name. My mother's maiden name, as a matter of fact. Awful, isn't it? I couldn't even go by my middle name, because it's infinitely worse. Ogden! Another family name. DeWitt Ogden Gregory. Sometimes I wonder, when my folks chose those names, if they realized my initials would spell DOG. Therefore, was it fate that I become a vet? I really had to keep my initials a secret when I was in vet school. My friends would've made life miserable with dog jokes.

"But most folks call me Witt or Dr. G." He shrugged. "I prefer Witt."

A vet. Now that was a vocation she could be comfortable with. She was glad he wasn't an MD like she'd first assumed when he mentioned having a practice. No common ground. But a vet? Yes. They could be good friends.

In another life, that is.

"Okay." Casey tapped on her coffee cup with one fingernail. "You've been so honest about your whole name, I guess I'll have to be honest about mine. It's not really Casey."

Witt had his cup raised to take a sip. He held it there, his gaze riveted on Casey's face.

"I felt like I needed to change everything about myself after the jerk and I broke up. So I began using my initials. K. C. They eventually blended into Casey, and I've gone by that ever since. My real name is Katherine. Katherine Cecilia Morgan McAlester. Antiquated, isn't it?"

Witt drew in a ragged breath. His cup hit the table with a loud clatter.

2

AUGUST 30, 1963
SAN ANTONIO, TEXAS

D el Morgan peered through the plate glass window of the hotel dining room to watch for Allen's car. She eyed the darkening sky.

To the northwest somber clouds amassed and encroached on the sun's territory like a sinister black entity. In a losing battle to hold them back, the sun cast the foreboding yellow hue that often precedes a tornado.

She caught sight of his Cadillac slowing down in front of the building. The passenger door swung open and Katherine slid out before the vehicle had come to a full stop. There was little doubt in Del's mind Allen had told her to make it quick.

Dust and leaves swirled in tiny funnels and hit the window, making little tapping noises. The big front door flew open on a gust of wind and the glowing young lady burst in—all smiles. Del knew

Katherine was excited about Allen's grand plan, but wished she didn't have to feign enthusiasm about it.

"We're all packed, Mom. Ready to pull out."

A customer walked to the counter at that same moment.

"Hang on a minute, baby, I have a customer." Del turned her attention to the tastefully attired man at her register.

"That'll be $32.40 with tax, sir. Thank you. Please enjoy your stay."

She could always tell by his manner of dress whether a customer was a hotel guest or someone in off the street. People didn't pay an entire month's rent for one night's stay in a luxury hotel unless they had money. Lots of it.

The customer swept his change from the counter and walked toward the lobby. Then to the bank of elevators. Del wet the tip of her index finger on her tongue and drew an imaginary 1 in the air. Katherine giggled. Chalk up another one.

Del studied her daughter's face, seeing not the young adult that stood before her, but a freckle-faced toddler with a smudge on her cheek. Tears tried to surface in her eyes, but she willed them to stay put. She must not turn this into a solemn occasion. Katherine was too happy. Del wouldn't see her again until she could afford to take a few days off to make the drive in her raggedy old VW Beetle. But she knew mothers have to let go sometime, even when they know their kids are making a terrible mistake.

"Is Allen coming in?"

"Oh, you know him, Mom. He's out there with the engine running and the radio and air on. He didn't want to go to all the trouble of finding a parking place, locking up the car and so on, just to say goodbye. He said to tell you we'll see you soon."

Del doubted Allen said anything, but Katherine was the eternal peacemaker. Del knew how much she wanted the two of them to get along. She tried to be nice to him for Katherine's sake. But he remained aloof. She had his number, and apparently he knew it. So, theirs was a strained relationship at best.

"Okay, sweetheart. Gimme a hug. Can you stay a few minutes?" She held out her arms to receive Katherine and breathed in the fresh scent of her lavender cologne.

She had tried to talk her out of going. So often it became a sore spot between them. Better to keep the good-byes as pleasant as possible.

Allen was never going to do right by her baby and everyone knew it but Katherine. He was taking her to live in Houston. But he wouldn't be staying there. He traveled and kept an apartment in San Antonio, where his company was based. Somehow he'd convinced her to relocate to Houston because he did a lot of business there.

Del had heard rumors that Katherine was not his only love interest. He'd been seen in the company of several young women.

But every time she tried to warn her, Katherine was adamant. "He's required to entertain clients—men and women. I know he loves me and I don't want to hear any more gossip."

The way Del saw it, this move would free up his evenings here and give him somewhere to stay when he was in Houston. A good deal for him. A losing proposition for Katherine. Someday she'd wake up. When that day came Del would move heaven and earth to try to soften the fall.

"Can't stay, Mom. If we keep moving, we might be able to stay ahead of the storm."

She snatched the pencil from behind her mother's ear. "Before I go, do you have a little scrap of paper I can write a note on?"

Del tore about three inches of tape from the cash register. "Big enough?"

"Uh-huh."

A smiled creased Del's face at her little girl's habit of sticking the tip of her tongue out when she was concentrating. She wrote a few words. Then laboriously folded the note into a tiny square and slipped it into her mother's hand.

Katherine's auburn hair was swept up in loose curls on the back of her head with a few wisps the wind had worked free, teasing her cheeks and the nape of her neck. Her pale-yellow sundress, strappy little sandals, and lightly tanned, freckled shoulders made her look like a Monet painting come alive.

"Please give this to that nice boy who's always so sweet to you. I don't see him around right now."

"He was here a minute ago, honey. I'm sure he's back in the kitchen. Hang on, I'll go get him."

The color left Katherine's cheeks. "No, Mom. I don't want to see him. I was just trying to be nice. What if Allen decided to come in and caught me talking to some guy?"

"Would that be so . . ." Del bit her tongue.

Katherine couldn't even recall the young man's name, but he was completely smitten with her. She was all he could talk about when he and Del had lunch together. Handsome in a tall, lanky, almost underfed way, he had a head full of thick dark curls and kind blue eyes even Del—at her age—could get lost in. And he was such a hard worker. Putting himself through college and working long hours. If only Katherine had given him a chance. Gotten to know him.

"Mom, are you listening?"

Del drew a deep breath and let it out with a whimper. Wishful thinking. "Sure, baby."

"So, enough with the matchmaking, Mom. Allen and I are in love. And we're getting married soon. Case closed."

Del forced a grin and held up the note, waving it in a tiny circle. "Mind if I read this?" She raised her eyebrows impishly, her eyes darting from the note to Katherine and back.

Katherine shook her head and smiled indulgently. "You know I don't. But I'm thinking maybe the note is a mistake."

"I was only teasing. I wouldn't dream of reading it. And it's never a mistake to show a kindness."

"Well, I'm sorry if I was impatient with you, Mom. It's just that no one understands about me and Allen." She picked at a spot on the countertop with one fingernail. "They think because he's a little older he's going to take advantage of me. And he's not like that. I was hoping you, of all people, would understand."

Del reached over and gave her hand a squeeze. "I understand, baby."

Katherine glanced at her watch and then out to the Cadillac, still running at the curb. "I've got to go now. I love you. You know I hate for you to be here alone. But I'm twenty-one. It's past time I cut the apron strings. Allen's going to buy me a car and we're going to get married. Everything is going to work out great. You'll see."

The two women embraced for a long time. Swaying, as though to soft music. Del was glad business was slow this morning. She needed these few uninterrupted minutes. She and her daughter had been each other's best friend and confidante almost all of Katherine's life. More like sisters than mother and daughter. Until Allen.

"Please take care of yourself, Mom. I love you." Katherine took a step backward.

"Drive carefully and don't forget to call when you get there." Suddenly weak-kneed, Del leaned against the counter for support. "I love you too. So much."

Katherine eased away a few feet, her eyes locked on Del, before turning her back and heading for the exit. Pushing the door hard against the wind, she tried unsuccessfully to hold her skirt down with one hand. It whipped around her knees and thighs as she turned to wave with her free hand.

Through the plate glass window Del saw her dash to the waiting vehicle and reach for the door handle as a deluge fell from the skies. Like someone had tipped over the water jars of heaven. Only after the sleek white sedan disappeared around the corner did she return to her post, a lump in her throat the size of Texas.

From thirty feet away Witt had seen Katherine saying good-bye to her mother. He stepped away from the round window in the swinging door separating the dining room from the kitchen. Tears welled in his eyes. He blinked them back. He was twenty-two years old. A grown man. Grown men don't cry.

He'd loved Katherine from the first time they met, when Del casually introduced them over a year ago. She never called him by name. Chances were she didn't remember it, but a smile from her kept him high for a week.

He fought the urge to run out and grab her. Refuse to let her leave with that . . . that . . . phony.

He thrust his fist into his open palm. "Who do I think I am? What right does a hotel busboy have to a girl like her?"

He noticed the chef looking askance at him and relaxed his fist.

He was a fool to even ask Del about her. At the rate his schooling was going, it'd be years before he'd have anything to offer. And how did he plan take her out? On his bicycle? He shook his head. Now Allen, he was a jerk all right, but he had it under control. Had a good job. Drove a Cadillac.

Witt swallowed hard. He'd captured the vision of Katherine, pale-yellow skirt billowing in the wind, and stored it in his heart. He stood frozen for several long seconds, staring at the door she'd disappeared through. Then turned abruptly and busied himself at the long sink. There was work to be done.

"Dear God," he whispered from his private hell, "I will always love that woman."

3

Katherine stayed awake for as long as she could, waiting for Allen. He hadn't been home in three weeks and she had some things weighing heavily on her mind. When she couldn't keep her eyes open another minute, she scrubbed off her carefully applied makeup, trudged to the bedroom, and climbed into bed. She wouldn't get to talk to him tonight. Tears seeped between her lashes.

She was just drifting off when she heard his key in the front door. The door squeaked. Next, the sound of his suitcase opening. The soft thud of his shoes as he took them off and the jingle of keys on the coffee table told her he was undressing in the living room in order not to disturb her.

Moments later he slipped silently into bed and turned his back to her. She touched his shoulder.

"I went to the doctor Tuesday," she whispered.

"Oh? Something wrong?" Allen turned toward her in the dark and gave her a little smooch on the cheek.

"Not really."

"What do you mean, not really? Either you're sick or you're not. It's not something serious, is it?"

He sat up in bed and turned on the bedside lamp. She squinted against the sudden brightness and pulled a pillow in front of her so he wouldn't have to see the freckles that marred her freshly scrubbed face. She hated for him to see her without makeup—had ever since he told her she'd be really pretty if she didn't have so many freckles.

"Take that pillow down and talk to me," he said testily. "Why did you go to the doctor?"

"I . . . I . . ."

"Out with it! Why did you go to the doctor? Must you always be so melodramatic?"

"I'm . . . we're . . . we're . . . going to have a . . . a . . . baby, Allen." She forced the words past the tightness in her throat.

"We're *what*?" He leaped off the bed and jammed the wall switch on. Harsh light blazed over her.

"I'm sorry. I know you didn't want to have one yet, but it's not like we're too young to start a family." Katherine reached out to touch him.

He pulled away. "We can't have a baby now. It could cost me my job."

"What are you talking about, Allen? People get married and have babies every day. It's not grounds for getting fired."

"You don't know my boss. He wants us all footloose and fancy free. Wives and kids interfere with travel itineraries."

Something rose up in Katherine's spirit. She was getting so tired of his excuses. She'd hoped the baby would make him come around.

She threw back the covers and stood in front of him, shoving her naked face in front of his. "Is this why we haven't gotten married, because the guy you work for doesn't approve? Does he approve of our sleeping together?"

"What's gotten into you, Kat? You know we're going to get married when the time is right. This isn't the time." He turned his back to her and heaved a sigh, then slowly turned back. His eyes were blazing. "Read my lips. We *cannot* have a baby."

Pulling back, he began pacing. "I know somebody who can take care of it. But it's going to cost me. Man, it's always something!"

"Take care of it? What on earth are you suggesting?"

"Take care of it. You know . . . an abortion. Don't act so dense. What else would I be talking about?"

She'd known he'd be upset, but she hadn't expected *this*.

"No." Katherine sank back onto the bed, leaning back against the headboard.

"What do you mean, no?" He closed his eyes and pinched the bridge of his nose between his thumb and forefinger. His jaw clenched. "We have no choice. You can have a baby later."

"I can't have *this* baby later." She wrapped her arms around her waist. "I love this child and I want it."

She could scarcely believe her own voice. The naked truth had come to her as a pinpoint of light that grew larger and larger until it filled her soul. She loved this tiny, innocent embryo more than she loved Allen. His powerful magnetic field was no match for her God-given maternal instincts.

"Kat, please . . . please . . . don't go and get independent on me now, of all times." Suddenly his tone became wheedling. "I'm asking you . . . begging you . . . let me make the arrangements. It's perfectly safe. The guy's a doctor."

Her chin quivered. She looked down at the bed and rolled the edge of the quilt between her forefinger and thumb. "If you want to leave me . . . just leave. I'll raise the baby by myself." She sat up straighter and raised her eyes to look squarely at Allen. "I love you. But I love this baby too, and I refuse to abort it."

He stalked back into the living room and shrugged into his clothes. Without a word, he gathered up his suitcases and carried them to the front door. Katherine got up and leaned against the bedroom doorway, watching him. But she made no attempt to stop him. If she followed him and begged him to stay as she had so many times before, he'd won. She couldn't let him win again. Not when her baby's life depended on it.

He set his suitcases outside. Then turned and closed the door behind him, avoiding Katherine's steady gaze. She could see his car under the streetlight through the front window. He didn't go to it. He must be waiting for her to come after him. She watched for about three minutes, then returned to the bedroom. She flipped off the overhead light, turned off the bedside lamp, and settled down to a teardrenched, sleepless night.

Sometime later she heard the car trunk slam. Headlights shone through the lace curtains in the living room, making delicate designs on the opposite bedroom wall. The designs got dimmer, then faded altogether as the car pulled out and sped away down the quiet street.

In the end, it was Allen who gave in.

For the first time since he'd met Katherine, he didn't get his way. Not yet as big as a tiny toy soldier, his progeny had bested him.

At the end of the week he called and asked her to forgive him and take him back. He promised he'd marry her soon. For sure before the baby arrived.

Katherine hung up the phone and rested her hand on her expanding belly.

"How did I manage to make such a mess of my life?"

She'd quit her job in shame four months ago when her coworkers began noticing her weight gain. The pay in Houston wasn't much better than it had been in San Antonio, and the cost of living was higher. So there was no rainy-day fund to fall back on.

She moved to a smaller apartment because money was so tight. She'd just as soon her neighbors not know her too well, anyway. The fewer questions she had to answer, the better.

Next she sold her little car. That crushed her. It was the first car she'd ever owned and she loved it. Even after selling her car, money was still scarce. Luckily the tiny garage apartment she rented was within walking distance of a grocery store. She pored over magazines, looking for unexpired coupons. Her biggest concern was that she eat right for the baby.

She dare not let Del know of her dire circumstances. Besides getting even angrier with Allen, her mother would send money. Even if it meant doing without, herself.

Allen gave her money, but it was never enough to cover all the bills. He called her collect, saying he'd given up his phone to save for the baby. She wondered how he could do his job with no phone, but she didn't press the matter. Every month her phone bill ate up a big portion of her cash. The telephone was her lifeline to him, so the phone bill was the first thing she paid every month. Then rent . . . then food.

Her utilities stayed a month behind.

By the end of July, the baby was overdue and the doctor was going to induce labor Monday morning. Allen knew the plan and had promised to be there for her. He was supposed to have been home two nights ago, but called to say he had been delayed in Dallas. Big business meeting.

With only one day to go, she was getting nervous that he wouldn't make it. She couldn't locate him anywhere.

"Don't worry about me if I don't call," he'd told her. "I'll be out of pocket for a while. The place is wall-to-wall bosses. We're having daily meetings and I'm required to go out with them in the evenings. You know I don't want to, but I have no choice. I'll be there for you on Monday morning. You can count on me."

You can count on me.

The words reverberated in her brain.

Allen said that a lot. But in truth, he couldn't be counted on for much of anything.

She'd figured out long ago her mother was right about him. But she couldn't make herself leave him. She tried to not think about the times she'd caught him in lies. It was easier to pretend he was faithful than to face the awful truth.

Trying to get her mind on something other than the phone that refused to ring, Katherine looked down at the rings on her third finger, left hand. There was the plain white gold band Allen had bought for her. But there was no piece of paper or ceremony to back it up.

He'd bought it to save her embarrassment over her condition.

Apparently the modest solitaire engagement ring he'd given her two Christmases ago had no real meaning either.

The phone rang. She snatched it up, sure it was Allen.

But it was Del calling to check on her.

"Will Allen be there?" The smile in her voice didn't fool Katherine.

"He's at a business meeting in Dallas, Mom. I can't get through to him. I'm sure he'll make it, though." Trying to sound cheerful and confident, she felt anything but.

"Well, I thought I'd head out tomorrow and get there sometime in the evening. That way I'll be there Monday morning, just in case. If that's okay with you."

Relief flooded Katherine's heart. She could always count on Mom. "What about your job?"

"It'll still be here when I get back. If it's not . . . I'll get another. Don't fret."

At that moment, Katherine wished she were still connected to her, be it by apron strings or umbilical cord.

It was a long labor. Fourteen hours.

Katherine hadn't heard from Allen.

But she refused any drugs because she wanted to be alert when he got there. At the last moment, at Del's insistence, she accepted some relief from pain. All she remembered was endless pushing—then blessed, peaceful sleep. She didn't get to hear her baby's first cry when he finally arrived at 11:20 that night.

She learned later her baby boy didn't utter a sound when he was born. And the doctors and nurses in the delivery room were scrambling to help him breathe as she slept.

Much to Katherine's anguish, her baby was not brought to her at feeding time the next morning. After many frantic calls to the nurse's station, her doctor came to see her. He seemed reluctant to come into the room. He stood in the doorway and solemnly told her that her infant son couldn't be taken from his incubator.

"How bad is it?" Katherine gripped her mom's hand so hard Del winced.

"He has about a fifty-fifty chance of making it. I wish I could be more optimistic."

Katherine loved her son with a passion. She had not yet laid eyes on him, but she'd been talking and singing to him since long before his existence became obvious to the world. She'd lie on her back with her hand on her tummy, waiting for the tiny being to move. When he did, it felt like a butterfly fluttering just beneath her skin.

She couldn't bear the thought that he may not live.

Thirty-six hours after the baby's birth, Katherine and Del went back to the little garage apartment, leaving Baby Barrett at the hospital still in the incubator. But, blessedly, still alive.

Allen was a no-show.

Every morning for eight days, Katherine awoke before dawn after a fitful night's sleep and waited for the stroke of seven. Each morning she steeled herself to hear the words that Barrett had not made it through the night. Mercifully, the news was acceptable morning after morning. Marginally better each day. But no one on staff dared to extend a great deal of optimism.

He was the skinniest and ruddiest baby in the nursery. One side of his head was shaved, and there were tubes taped all over his little body for monitors and oxygen and intravenous feeding and medications. His tiny hands were tied down so he couldn't tangle them in the tubes and pull them out. What hair remained on his head was long, red, and unruly.

He was the most beautiful baby in the world.

On Barrett's fourth day of struggling, the doctor approached Katherine as she gazed through the nursery window. He put his hand on her arm. "You need to be prepared. Even if he makes it there is a distinct possibility of brain damage."

Katherine collapsed into her mom's arms. Del led her weeping daughter to the hospital chapel, where Katherine asked to be left alone for a while. She'd never done much praying and she didn't know where to begin.

"I'll accept whatever You mete out to me. *But please let him live.*"

Allen came to look at Barrett only once.

He hadn't wanted the child, but the tiny creature with the wild red hair pulled at his heartstrings. He couldn't give the child his surname, though. He was doing the best any man could under the circumstances. And Katherine's whining about it made it that much tougher on everybody.

She said if he didn't love her, she'd have preferred he leave her.

But he *did* love her and refused to be the one to make the break.

On the long drive home to San Antonio, Allen made several stops for coffee. He was trying to kill time, because he dreaded going back to his apartment.

He didn't have any business calls to make until next Monday. So he really had no choice but to go home. If things had gone differently he would've liked to spend these next few days with Katherine and the baby. But that was out of the question.

He'd missed the birth of his son, as well as the first few days of his life. And the poor little fellow was having a tough time hanging on. How terrible this had to be for Katherine. She wanted this child so badly. This last week must have been almost more than she could bear. He'd let her down badly and there was no way he could ever make it up to her. None. He could only make it worse.

He pulled into the entrance of the apartment complex and parked at the curb. Oh, how he dreaded going home. If he could only put it off for just a few more minutes. He looked down at his hands and realized they were shaking. That hadn't happened in a long time. Life had gotten so complicated.

"Too much coffee, I guess." He reached into the glove compartment and took out a bottle of prescription drugs. He popped a pill into his mouth and washed it down with a slug of cold coffee.

He pulled back out into the driving lane. One left and one right and he was home. Apartment 256.

When he opened the front door, he was greeted by an immaculate apartment, a pleasant fragrance—and silence. Too much silence.

"Anybody home?"

"I'm in the kitchen."

"Is this all the welcome home I get?"

Drying her hands on a dish towel, Stephanie dashed around the corner. "Oh, you big bear, you. I was trying to have everything perfect before you got home."

She was pregnant and looked about ready to deliver. Sporting a big diamond and a wide gold wedding band, she threw the towel down and waddled into his arms.

"I'm so glad you're home."

He reached down and caressed her belly. "How much longer before our little one gets here?"

"The doctor said it could happen any day. I was so worried you wouldn't be here. I couldn't believe you'd leave, even for a couple of days. What would I have done if I'd gone into labor without you here?"

Allen met Stephanie at a party. She was one of the many girls he dated, off and on. It wasn't that he didn't love Kat, but he wasn't ready to make a commitment and she kept waiting—so, why not?

There was something different about Steph. She wasn't like the other girls. She'd had a rough childhood and she looked up to Allen with such adoration. It was flattering. And touching. Before he knew what hit him, they had a serious relationship going on.

He was a little self-conscious about their age difference. Fifteen years. It didn't help that she gave him the pet name of Daddy. The more he was with her, the more protective he became of her.

"Don't worry, darling. You won't have to do it alone. Daddy's home." He pulled her against his chest and stroked her lustrous blonde tresses. Staring past her, he battled to keep the tears back.

He hadn't meant for it to work out this way. When he found out both Kat and Steph were pregnant, he almost went crazy. Kat had stood by him for so long. She deserved better. But Steph had been hurt by everyone she'd ever loved. He couldn't throw her to the wolves.

So, he'd married her.

The day finally came when Barrett was strong enough to go home. Del stayed on to help. She and Katherine lavished love on the precious being and he grew handsome, vigorous, and sound, with a lusty set of lungs. Miraculously, he came through his ordeal normal in every way.

But nothing changed between Katherine and Allen. He continued to come and go as he pleased while she waited for him to make a commitment to her and the baby.

When Barrett was five months old Katherine went back to work. She found a good day care center, and she and Barrett settled into a workable routine. Only then did Del move back to San Antonio.

Katherine continued to welcome Allen with open arms. But he was spending much less time with her. He would come to her only a couple of times a month, stay just a day or two, and then be on his way. For all practical purposes, Katherine was a single parent. Her need to give Barrett a proper home and family became stronger with each passing day. Finally, when Barrett was almost a year old, she came to the difficult decision she could wait no longer.

When Allen next showed up on her doorstep, she presented him with an ultimatum.

"You and I are getting married this week." Her smile was forced.

"Baby, that's not possible."

She abandoned her attempt to smile.

"Why is it not possible, Allen? Why? You don't want to talk about it and I don't know what you're thinking. I don't know anything except what you choose to tell me and I doubt much of that is true. But this *is* true. We *will* be married this week or you won't be coming back here."

"Kat, you don't mean that. I promise, I'm working on getting us married in the very near future. Don't ruin everything by giving me an ultimatum now."

"Unless the very near future is this week, the wait is over. Don't even bring your bags in, because you'll only have to carry them back out."

"Baby, please give me a little reprieve. A few more months and I can get things straightened out."

"I don't know what it is you have to straighten out, Allen. How difficult is it to say 'I do'? No! No more reprieves. It's taken me years to make this decision and I don't have the strength to make it again . . . and again. I'm not being vindictive. Barrett needs a real family. You can't—or won't—provide that."

He tried to put his arms around her.

She pushed him away. "You can't fix it with a kiss this time. That's not going to work anymore. I have someone besides myself to worry about now."

Her voice broke and she dabbed under her eye with one finger. "I don't want any child support. I think it's best we make a clean break of it." Katherine knew she'd never be completely free of Allen if he continued to make contact with her.

Inside the apartment, the baby whimpered. "Barrett just woke up from his nap. Would you like to say good-bye to him?"

He dropped the teddy bear he'd brought for Barrett. "Right now?"

"Yes, right now, Allen. What point in prolonging it? I'm not going to change my mind."

It was the first time Katherine had ever seen Allen cry. He held Barrett too tight and cried like a baby himself. Barrett started screaming.

Allen handed his baby boy over to Katherine and turned to leave without another word.

Watching him drive away for the last time, she breathed a prayer that she'd made the right decision. All she wanted for Barrett was a loving family and now he had no father at all.

4

Katherine—who was now going by her nickname, Casey—had two men in her life now. Jesus was her Lord and Savior. Barrett was her sunshine.

Four years after serving Allen his walking papers, she decided she and Barrett should move to the country. She was raised in the hill country north of San Antonio, but Mom was gone now, so she decided instead on the Ouachita Mountains. Her folks used to take her there on vacation and she'd always dreamed of someday living in the gentle mountain country of Arkansas. Being a Houstonian since birth, Barrett had only seen pictures of mountains, but Casey was sure he'd love it. What little boy didn't like big rocks, meandering creeks, and wildlife?

When Casey walked into the little church in Mena, Arkansas, one Sunday morning—Bible in one hand and Barrett clinging to the other—she liked it immediately. The pastor appeared to be in his early thirties. He seemed humble enough, yet he had a pleasant speaking style and delivered an interesting message. The congregation was friendly and they obviously adored their pastor. And the music ministry might be able to use her. There was no one to play piano. She was a pianist. Perhaps not the classical artist her dad had hoped for when he invested in her weekly piano lessons. But definitely accomplished enough to serve in the music ministry of a small country church.

She became a regular. Sunday mornings and Wednesday evenings. It was her practice to leave immediately after service to pick Barrett up from children's church. Several times Pastor Edward tried to catch up to her. But she always managed to duck into the ladies' room or latch onto one of the other women in time to avoid speaking to the attractive pastor face-to-face.

Several weeks after she joined the congregation she learned he was a widower. Even after she found out, she continued to make her exit as quickly as possible after service. She'd stand in line to shake his hand briefly, only if there were folks in back of her waiting to greet him, because she felt he wouldn't get too personal with others close by. Occasionally during service he'd look at her in a way that bordered on flirtatious. She'd quickly look down at her Bible.

Although she was friendly to all and certainly open to being used in the music ministry, she wasn't ready to trust her heart to any man. Especially a good-looking one who had a way with words. She'd had her fill of that.

Edward McAlester, though still a young man, had no plans to remarry—or for that matter to date anyone. His young wife and high school sweetheart had died in 1969, leaving him inconsolable. But for love of his church he'd have become a recluse. But they brought him through it. Now he looked on them as his family. He needed no wife. No children. He had the church.

But on the Sunday morning Casey and Barrett visited, he thought perhaps he'd been too hasty. He was sitting behind the podium, reading his Bible, waiting for the service to start. He glanced up as they entered the sanctuary. Unable to take his eyes off her, he watched as the lovely young lady with the auburn hair and her small son took a seat in the fifth row. Pleased to note she wasn't wearing a wedding ring, he hoped he could keep his eyes off her during the service. He didn't succeed very well. In fact, he lost his place in his notes . . . more than once.

She disappeared quickly after service that day. And it frustrated him that although she became a regular, he was never was able to catch her alone. She seemed to be deliberately avoiding him.

Then one morning before church, he heard music coming from an empty Sunday school classroom. He quietly opened the door and there she was, softly playing "Amazing Grace" on an ancient upright. Her back was to the door, so he was able to stand there for several minutes, basking in the echo of the sweet strains she coaxed from the old, stiff keyboard with her delicate touch.

When she stopped playing and gently closed the cover over the keys, she turned. Edward smiled at her.

She picked up her Bible and held it with both hands beneath her chin, hiding what small part of her neckline was revealed. "I'm sorry. I shouldn't have taken that liberty. I hope I didn't disturb your study time."

"It's I who should apologize for eavesdropping on a personal communication between you and the Lord. He surely found pleasure in your worship. It was beautiful."

Casey lowered her eyes and turned away from him.

He put his hand on her shoulder. "Please don't be embarrassed. I'm glad to have this chance to talk to you. I've been trying to have a word with you for several weeks."

She stepped far enough away that he had to take his hand from her shoulder, but she didn't turn to face him. "I'm sorry. I have to pick up my son right after children's church. I don't want him to worry. He's new at this."

The little guy wasn't the only one who was new at this. Professionally Edward was good with words. On a personal level he didn't have much practice in social graces. Especially talking to ladies. He wasn't even sure she was single.

"Ms. Morgan, is there a Mr. Morgan?"

She turned to look at him, her face void of expression. "No, there is no Mr. Morgan. Morgan is my maiden name." Her tone was as flat as her expression.

Suddenly he was hot. He wished he'd worn a cooler suit. Great. He finally gets the chance to be alone with her and what does he do? He offends her by being too personal.

He knew he might not get another chance after that faux pas, so he threw caution to the wind. "In that case, may I call you Casey? And since there's no Mr. Morgan, perhaps you'll allow me to take you to lunch after church. You and your little one, of course."

Casey turned him down. Flat.

Edward stuck his lower lip out. Way out.

Casey shook her head and laughed.

"Do I get a second chance?"

She smiled. "Yes."

"May I take you to lunch after church?"

"Yes."

They both laughed.

Sitting at a sidewalk café in downtown Mena, Edward was talking to Casey across the table. Barrett was a few feet away, trying to strike up a conversation with the resident parrot.

Edward thought he saw a dark figure out of the corner of his eye. He turned his head to look but no one was there.

As though on cue, Casey put her elbows on the table and rested her chin on her hands. "Pastor Edward, do you ever get the feeling you're being watched?"

"Do you think you could call me Edward? Drop the title? I won't tell anyone."

Casey grinned. "Okay, Edward. Well, do you?"

"Yes, from time to time. Not very often. Why do you ask?"

"I just had the strangest feeling."

"You too, huh? You were telling me the truth, weren't you?" He gripped the edge of the table with both hands in mock fright and looked from side to side. "There is no Mr. Morgan . . . right?"

Casey laughed. "You're funny."

Edward spread his elbows on the edge of the table and leaned forward against his hands. "And you're beautiful."

The spark lit that day grew into a beautiful flame and it soon became common knowledge around the church that the pastor was in love. He loved not only Casey but young Barrett as well. He was an obedient and winsome child. His wild red hair from birth had given way to blond curls. With his coloring, he could have been Edward's own progeny.

Four months later, Edward, Casey, and Barrett became family.

It was his first meeting, and the demon of inferiority knew he wouldn't be missed. So he hid in the dark on a high ledge—listening, watching, and learning how it was done in this district.

"Does anyone have anything to report this week?" The leader stood on his hind legs, meerkat fashion.

The underlings called him Meerkat behind his back.

But this was no small wildlife creature. He stood seven feet tall, with extremities so long that his twelve-inch claws touched the ground. No big innocent eyes, either. No eyes at all. Just deep, black holes. And where a meerkat would have fur, he was covered with slime that glistened in the flickering firelight that lit the interior of Black Mountain Cave, near the Oklahoma border.

From the back a grisly voice rasped, "I do."

"Step out here and let me see who you are."

The others tripped over each other trying to get out of the way of the weightless creature that resembled a four-hundred-pound slug and reeked of rotten meat, as it floated out from the shadows. Its out-stretched feelers left decaying gouges in everything it touched.

"Dave from Dave and Norma's Gift shop was out of town this week and Norma had sleepover company for two nights. A man."

"Who was he?"

"Not from around here, master."

"Did I ask you if he was from around here? Did I? Find out who he is. Stay on top of this. If he has a wife, I'll notify the team captain in that district. Next?"

The slug growled and coughed up nasty slobber, spewing some on Meerkat.

"Take that outside." Meerkat hooked a claw through the slug's soft underbelly and flung him toward the cave entrance, putrid fluids spraying the walls. "Next?"

"All due respect, sir, I think I may have something to report." A minute splotch of blackness shuddered with every air current.

"You think you may have something to report. How very special. Get up here. To the front, runt."

The black smear darted front and center.

"Is that all there is to you?" The tiny demon shivered as Meerkat brought his head down close and scanned it, first with one hollowed-out eye and then the other. "Great Purple Honk, have our ranks gotten so desperate that we need the likes of you? Who are you, anyway?

"Name's Doubt, sir."

"Doubt? *Doubt?* The same Doubt that once sucked the light from an entire town? What happened to you? You're just a shadow of your former self. A shadow of a doubt, get it?" Meerkat pointed a foreclaw at his audience and sneered.

He began laughing. His hyena cackle drowned out the pitiful, faked merriment of the underlings. He laughed so hard he lost his balance and fell. The crowd went wild.

He snapped his head around and directed the black holes at them. Fire shot out, singeing delicate palpi and antennas of the creatures in the front row. Everyone fell silent.

"And how did this—uh—thing happen to you, pinhead?" Meerkat was no longer amused.

"Deflated in battle with an angel, sir."

"Ah, you're a loser, in other words. So, speak up, driveling fool. What did you see?"

"Edward McAlester, pastor of a small local church, had a lunch date with one of the ladies in the congregation."

"And this concerns me how?" The hollow eyes aimed at the cringing ghoul. "Edward McAlester is toast, worm. Been worthless since his wife died. Don't waste our time on him."

"I think he's falling in love, sir. I thought it might merit our attention."

"With that kind of thinking, no wonder you're so small. You have to achieve some measure of success to grow. Throw a monkey wrench in some Christian machinery or win some souls for our kingdom. McAlester will be ours one day anyway. From here on out, unless you have something more important to report than humans falling in love, don't waste my time."

Meerkat pierced the flimsy demon and swept him to the side. A small piece of Doubt tore from his side and hit the floor squirming. Head ducked, the smudge of darkness scurried back and grabbed the writhing particle. He clutched it close to himself and shot into the corner, where he disappeared in the natural darkness.

Meerkat's wrath surfaced and bubbled over. "Now hear this, you imbeciles. Next week I expect to hear something from every one of you. No insipid stories of luncheon dates that have no impact on our mission. I want stuff we can sink our teeth into." He skinned his lips back from his fangs for added effect. "We have to keep accurate records of everything done in darkness. We never know when the big kahuna may drop in to check on us. Have I made myself clear?" A sweep of his claws drew gore from each entity on the front row.

Inferiority found a small opening to the outside in the back of the cave and slipped out before dismissal. If he was going to amount to anything in this district he had to get busy.

5

AUGUST 1990
ST. MICHAEL, ARKANSAS

"Just pick one out, Pastor Edward. Can't be that hard."

Edward heaved his gaze away from the gleaming array of vehicles on the car lot.

"No, Brother Mike, this is too much. I appreciate you for wanting to help, but I can't let you do it."

"Pastor, look at me. You know I got more money than I'll ever be able to spend. No kids to leave it to. Me and Sue had saved a bundle already and then we was paid a fortune for the farm. Didn't know that stinkin' corporation was gonna tear down the old homestead or I might not-a sold it. That like to have broke Sue's heart. And now she's gone. I think knowing the old place was torn down is what killed her." Mike rubbed a bleary eye with the back of his hand. "But ain't nothin' to be done about it now. So what am I gonna do with all that money? Sure ain't gonna leave it to my good-fer-nothin' nephew. He'd blow it all on drugs and booze. What the heck, if an old man can't do a little favor fer his pastor, what good is he anyway?" He pulled his hand down his chin, preening his short, scraggly beard.

"Buying me a thirty-thousand-dollar automobile isn't exactly a little favor, my brother. I don't think the board will approve. And I really don't think the Lord would either." Edward wanted to nip this crazy idea in the bud.

Why had he even let Brother Mike drag him out here?

"I've done run it by the board and they thought it was a grand idea. Budget won't allow fer a raise fer you this year on account of the new building. They thought this would kinda make it up to you. And as fer as the Lord is concerned, why dang it anyway, Pastor, you need a reliable machine. Who do you think put this idear in my head?"

His argument made sense, but something about it didn't feel right.

"Oh, Brother Mike. I just don't know."

"C'mon, Pastor. Let's start by lookin' at the little ones and we'll work our way up to them bigger ones."

The church was growing by leaps and bounds. The way things were looking, in a year or so, Edward could buy a nice car to replace the beater he and Casey were driving. Yet he couldn't help but entertain the thought of how great it would be to have one right now. No more hounding church members for a ride at the last minute because their old car wouldn't start. He could certainly do without that.

A Cadillac, no less. Brother Mike wouldn't settle for anything else.

And what about his little redheaded sweetheart, as Brother Mike called Casey? She'd been by his side every step of the way. For seventeen years she'd been putting in as many hours as he did—or more—making herself available anywhere there was a need. She'd followed him from church to church, never complaining when he invariably took a cut in pay to serve where the need was the greatest. She deserved so much more than he'd provided for her.

If he let Brother Mike buy him a car, then he could get her a nice little recent-model used car as soon as finances permitted. As much running around as she did for him, she needed her own dependable vehicle. Maybe he shouldn't dismiss Mike's offer out of hand.

More than seventeen years ago, the demon known as Meerkat dismissed Edward McAlester as being toast. Harmless to their cause. But recently, Edward accepted a call from the Church of the Good Shepherd—a church Satan had already declared dead—and the pastor's ministry was burgeoning.

Suddenly, his knowledge of the Scriptures and willingness to serve were casting some serious shadows on the Devil's foothold in that church. And it had happened right under his nose. Thanks to Meerkat's stupidity.

Satan was on a tear. Heads would roll.

He assigned a slew of demons to watch McAlester's every move, and bring him down. There was real trouble brewing for them in hell if they didn't stem the tide of souls being won for Jesus in that fly-by-night organization.

Meerkat had already felt Satan's fury. His impressive size had been cut to two feet, and he now served with the underlings, whose contempt for him was palpable.

Night and day, they watched McAlester's every move, looking for a chink in his armor. Until today, it seemed impenetrable. Bathed in the constant prayers of his congregation and blessed with a generous portion of humility, Edward seemed truly a man of God.

Their frustration boiled and bubbled and enveloped them in the stench of evil each time they met.

Now, with any luck, the tide may be turning.

The demon of pride called an emergency meeting in a ramshackle building on the back of Brother Mike's place. It seemed only appropriate since Mike was playing such a big part in the plan. All the ghouls assigned to McAlester's case were there. Pride—the man of the hour—Greed, Lies, Alcoholism, Confusion, and last, though certainly not least . . . Violence. Many others were sitting in as well, including a contrite Meerkat.

The demon of pride banged his gavel on every available surface, including a few heads, like a carpenter on a drunken binge. "Look alive, scumbags! I've come up with an idea. The best idea yet. You're gonna love it."

Every slimy creature in attendance looked with contempt at the demon of pride. He always thought his ideas were the best.

Pride's acrid voice rose over the crowd's rumble. "The good pastor is so piously humble he surely wouldn't dream of praying for his own finances," the odious creature declared to his cohorts. "I think this is the chink we've been looking for."

Talons extended, he slashed at the air. "Attack his finances. Begin with his car. Bring him to his knees. That puny so-called church is already overextended. They won't be able to come to his rescue. Not soon enough to save him. It's doubtful he would even *ask* for their help."

He smirked, satisfied with his presentation thus far. His stomping and kicking had stirred up a stifling cloud of dust from the dirt floor. Slimy entities were hacking and coughing. Wretched eyes glowered back at him. Hatred hung like a thick black cloud over the gathering. The old shack shuddered under the weight of their malevolence.

"Think, you imbeciles!" He paced back and forth, thrusting insults into the crowd.

The more they sizzled in their hatred for him, the more effective they would be.

"Are you brain-dead? There are dozens of ways to squash him with money problems. Hello? Come up with a good enough idea and I'll let you in on the kill, you putrid morons. Look at you. What a collection of hairballs you are."

Pride had always been on the receiving end of the insults. What fun it was to stir up their rancor and watch them stew in their own animosity. His speech was followed by a tumultuous clamor as the vultures of the spirit world cursed and sputtered. He was sure they liked his idea. Just as sure as he was that they loathed him for thinking of it.

But the demon of pride didn't tell all. He didn't reveal to the others his pièce de résistance. The event that would leave Edward McAlester wounded and bleeding—not financially—but *spiritu-*

ally. The happening through which he, and he alone, would pierce McAlester's tough armor with one sharp talon.

Ripping and tearing, he would gain ingress into McAlester's very soul.

He allowed the others to put their all into bringing the pastor down financially and saved his personal, reeling blow for last.

It looked like today was going to be the day.

Yes, it looked like Pride was going to be the winner of this ghoulish contest. And so it should be. Hadn't he put the thought of giving the pastor a Cadillac into old man Hendricks's head? And the senile fool gave God all the credit.

He'd seen the old coot on his knees, praying out loud to God about how to spend his money. All the demon of pride had to do was plant the idea. It was so easy. A few whispered suggestions and the geezer was hooked.

Yes. Pride was going to be the first in. The one to open the door to the others. The *boss!* Well, second in command, anyway.

"Pastor Edward, I shore hope I ain't embarrassin' you. When the good Lord gave me all this money, I jest know He wanted me to share it with those in need."

"No, Brother Mike. That's not a problem."

"Well, you got so quiet there fer a minute. I thought maybe I'd gone and done something wrong."

"I was just thinking, Brother Mike. Wondering how we got in such bad shape in the first place. With Barrett out on his own, we should really be in great shape financially. It just seems like everything fell apart at once. The old car—the one before this one—started giving us trouble. We thought the best thing to do was to trade it in on something newer. But turns out that was a mistake. Then the house fire—it's still a mystery how that got started. Next the washer and dryer. Now, who'd imagine they'd both go out in the same week? And of all things, the lawn mower threw a rod just yesterday. The list goes on."

Edward looked heavenward for a moment. "I know the Lord is going to see us through all this. But it does cause a man to wonder why it happens that way sometimes. Normally my salary would be sufficient for Casey and me—with some to spare."

"That's why the good Lord gave me this idear. It's gotta be. He don't want you doin' without. Not for one minute, He don't. You're always there when anybody needs you. There ain't a soul in that church that don't know you're the reason things is goin' so well. I'm so proud to be on the board that helped put you there. Smartest thing we ever done.

"You know I done made a big down payment on that there building. Why, we wouldn't even need a bigger building if it weren't for the crowds yer drawin' in."

"Not me, Brother Mike. Jesus."

"I know it's Jesus, but it's you that's preachin' Him. So, I wanna do somethin' fer you and yer sweetheart. And I ain't takin' no for an answer."

"Brother Mike. I'm not sure I'm convinced, but if you're really sure you want to do this, I do promise to pray about it. We'll take a look at them today, since we're here . . . but we're only looking."

"Whatever you say, Pastor." Mike pounded a big old farmer's fist on Edward's back. His fingers were so gnarled with arthritis he couldn't actually *slap* anyone's back.

There were no prices on the cars. It wasn't going to be easy to determine which ones were lower priced. They all looked pretty expensive. Not a tree in sight—the sun beat down and the temperature hovered around a hundred degrees. Edward wanted nothing more than to go home.

But Brother Mike steered him into the showroom. "We might as well be cool while we're looking, Pastor."

It was a slow day. They were the only customers in the showroom. A salesman glanced up from his desk as they entered. Then returned his attention to the paperback detective novel he was reading, his feet propped on his desk.

"Hey, forget the small ones." Brother Mike beamed at Edward, his perfect false teeth gleaming white. "Let's look at that big beauty over there. It's gotta have everything a fella could want."

40

The salesman slouched deeper into his chair. "Tire kickers." Some of the other guys snickered.

"Look at that rich deep color. What would ya call that? Auburn? Rust? It's not really red, yet it is . . . kinda. Get in, Pastor. Let's see how it fits you."

Edward was awed at the thought of owning such a piece of machinery. But he shook his head. They were only supposed to be looking. He wanted out of the dealership. Out of the city. Time to go home.

"It's too big. And I'm sure it's very expensive. Let's do this another day and look at something cheaper."

"Hogwash! Ain't no such thing as a cheap Cadillac."

"I'm not talking about a Cadillac, Brother Mike. We can go somewhere else. Maybe a Chevy dealership. Or better yet—a used car lot."

"Boy howdy! You're gonna turn some heads in this doozy. I've done made up my mind. This car's made for you and the Lord knows you deserve it. Your little redheaded sweetheart's gonna look like a queen in it. I'm gonna find me a salesman. Let's get this show on the road."

Has he gone deaf? Didn't he hear what I just said? "Brother Mike, stop!"

Mike looked like he'd been slapped. He eyed Edward guardedly.

Edward's patience was wearing thin and his frustration with the old man was becoming evident in his voice. "I've never made such a big decision without a great deal of prayer. I simply cannot drive off in this car without bringing it before the Lord. I thought you understood that before we started looking."

"Double hogwash! It ain't comin' outa yer pocket." His face red and false teeth clattering, Mike held his arms out from his sides like he was preparing for a brawl. "I'm payin' fer it, so the Lord don't care."

Every salesman looked up from his desk at the commotion. Mike backed down and lowered his voice.

"Besides, I've prayed enough about it fer the two of us." He laid a timeworn hand on Edward's arm. "You jest relax, Pastor, and check out yer new machine while I take care of the paperwork."

He turned and left abruptly, completely ignoring Edward's protests.

41

Reaching into the back pocket of his overalls for his checkbook, he limped off toward the office. He had a hitch, as he called it, in his right leg, but it didn't slow him down. Halfway across the floor a salesman in a sharp-looking silk suit approached him. The one who'd ignored them when they came in.

"Not you, Slick." Mike growled.

He pointed to a younger man in an ill-fitting suit. "I want that fella over there. He looks like he needs to make a sale today."

Edward could hear Brother Mike's loud rasping demands, but the sound seemed to be coming from far away. From another planet.

Mesmerized . . . like a lamb led to slaughter, Edward sidled closer to the luxurious vehicle. Almost afraid to touch it, he finally reached out and put his hand on the door handle. It opened, as though with an assist from an unseen hand. The fragrance that emanated from the rich leather interior beckoned him inside. He took a deep breath and slid behind the wheel. The voluminous black leather seat swallowed him. The control panel belonged in an airliner. Everything was a rich wood grain, black, or that delicious deep red color. Breathtaking red, like a rich, ripe, polished apple.

It flitted through his mind. *A rich, red apple did Eve in.* He shrugged off the thought before it could take root.

His heartbeat reverberated in his ears as he ran his hands over the soft leather steering wheel. His chest tightened and he felt intoxicated as he imagined how it would feel to own this masterpiece of elegance.

Edward had never owned anything so fine in his life. And he wanted it. Oh, how he wanted it. But things were moving too fast. And he hadn't prayed about it.

His willpower had been trampled beneath Brother Mike's big farm boots. "Maybe I don't need to pray. God knows I need dependable transportation. Brother Mike's a good man. And he's prayed about it."

Edward's spirit pled. "*You* must seek God's will in this matter."

He uttered a token prayer. And felt no satisfaction.

The pastor was feverish. He groaned. Putting both hands at the top of the steering wheel, he leaned forward, laying his forehead against the back of his hands. He was dizzy. Nauseated. He needed some time to regain his composure. Brother Mike was not giving him enough time to think this through. He was so persuasive. Persuasive and overbearing.

Edward thought, fleetingly, about sliding out of this magnificent machine—stomping up to Brother Mike and tearing up whatever papers he was signing. Tension gripped him like a huge claw crushing his chest. Pushing him back. He let his head fall back against the deep-cushioned seat and closed his eyes.

Why get out? Why fight Brother Mike? When all he had to do to *own* this car was to sit tight until Brother Mike returned. Then it would all be settled. Out of his hands.

His mouth was dry and his head was spinning. He made an effort to slow his breathing to relieve the tension. For the first time, he heard the soothing music playing in the showroom. It calmed him.

"I'm making too big of a deal out of this. I just need to stop being too proud to accept help."

Slowly, he opened his eyes and sought his reflection in the big mirrors that lined one wall of the showroom.

Edward's eyes met Edward's reflection. What he saw made his chest swell with *pride*.

"Lookin' good!" He smiled at the sight.

A grin slashed across Pride's face.

His victorious shout echoed throughout the caverns of hell.

"Gotcha!"

6

OCTOBER 7, 1993
SUGAR BLUFF, ARKANSAS

C asey stood in front of her vanity mirror, studying her freckles. When she was small her daddy used to tell her each one stood for something important in her life. Past, present, and future.

"This one is for Daddy. Here's Momma." He'd point to them one by one. "This is for your favorite teacher—what's her name, again? Oh yes, Miss Borders. Oh and here's one for the beautiful house you're going to live in one day."

On and on he would go, deliberately drawing out the process until she almost exploded with anxiety. Then jumping up and down she'd beg him to show her the one that was her Prince Charming. She knew exactly which one it was—but she wanted to hear it from Daddy. She giggled with delight each time he told her one day she'd marry a prince and live happily ever after. Daddies know these things.

She'd long since forgotten which freckle was for Miss Borders or for the beautiful house. But she'd never forgotten Daddy's or Mom's and definitely not Prince Charming's. He was a long time coming, and happily ever after had been short lived.

A tear slid down her cheek because right now her Prince Charming was pounding on the bathroom door, calling her vile names.

"If you don't come out, I'm going to bust the door down, woman. Get out here and admit what a harlot you are. I saw the smile you had for Steve Fuller last night. You must think I'm blind."

She popped a couple of aspirins and sat on the edge of the tub to wait. Surely Edward would wind down soon.

She'd never taken cover in the bathroom before. Hadn't intended to this time. She and Edward had a lovely supper. He retired to the den to watch TV and she indulged in a relaxing soak in a warm tub. She was getting out of the tub when she heard the sound of breaking glass. Before she could throw her robe on to go check, she heard his awful bellowing.

What began as a tantrum over TV scheduling escalated into a tirade about her imagined flirtations and affairs.

The pounding paused, and she could hear the scraping of dresser drawers.

She was glad that last week she'd packed her more precious mementos from the bedroom and stored them in the garage, leaving only a few cheap trinkets. Because from the sound of things, Prince Charming had tired of banging on the bathroom door and was systematically throwing each trinket to the floor.

Suddenly it got quiet. After a few minutes Casey opened the door a crack and peered out. Edward sat cross-legged in the middle of the bedroom floor, surrounded by broken glass, Casey's lingerie, dirt, and uprooted houseplants. He was whimpering and swaying back and forth.

Casey crouched down beside him. Overwhelmed with tenderness for this man who seemed to be totally undone—and perhaps repentant—she reached out to touch his shoulder.

He cringed away from her.

"Don't touch me, whore." He jerked up and stormed out of the room, slamming the door behind him.

Edward had lost count of how many times he'd hit the snooze button on the alarm.

He slapped the off button and started to sit up. The strain caused his head to pound. So he decided to lie back and close his eyes for just a moment more.

No, maybe that wasn't a good idea. He might sleep until noon.

Without opening his eyes, he flopped his hand across the bed, expecting to feel Casey next to him. Then he remembered last night had been one of those nights. She'd be as far on her side of the bed as possible. Eyes still shut, he squirmed closer to the other side of the big bed and felt for her again. Nothing. He opened his eyes and blinked a couple of times to clear the sleep. Her side of the bed was empty. Pillow fluffed and covers pulled up. He should have known she wouldn't still be in bed at this late hour. But why hadn't she awakened him? She knew he didn't like to sleep in except on Mondays.

How bad was last night? Enough for her to leave? *God, I wish I could remember. I wish I could stop doing these things.*

He always halfway expected her to leave him after they fought, though it certainly wasn't in her saintly nature.

He eased out from under the covers and sat up on the side of the bed, moving like an old man. The morning after, he always felt like he had a hangover. He wished it were a hangover. Oh that his problem were as simple as a drinking problem.

Try as he may, he couldn't stop the outbursts. He pressed his palms against his temples. Who was he kidding? They weren't outbursts. They were full-fledged tantrums. At the slightest provocation, it was as though someone else took over his thoughts and actions. He'd lose control and say unbelievably cruel things to Casey.

Edward didn't have a problem with Casey's past. Never held

it against her that she'd borne a child out of wedlock. In fact, he applauded her refusal to have an abortion and her steadfastness in raising her son on her own. She'd loved the boy's father and got caught up in a world not of her making. It wasn't his place to judge.

When he fell in love with her, he begged for the opportunity to make it up to her. He promised to show her what a truly loving relationship between a man and wife could be.

For seventeen years he'd kept that promise. It wasn't difficult. It never occurred to him to think badly of Casey or treat her like anything other than a lady. She was the perfect wife in every way.

But a couple of years ago things began to change. It was nothing Casey did. She remained the model wife. No, the change was within himself.

At first he felt a twinge of injury to his pride because she hadn't been a virgin when they met. Then he started noticing how men's heads always turned when she passed. And how she always had a smile for everyone—women *and* men.

Things escalated until now, at the drop of a hat, he lashed out at her. He called her unthinkable names and would start fights just so he had an excuse to fly into a violent rage. The rage had become habit forming . . . intoxicating.

Yet she stayed. Helped him in his ministry and never uttered a word to anyone to indicate she was unhappy.

"God," he cried, "if I lose her, it will be no one's fault but my own and it'll be the stupidest thing I've ever done."

He called out to her. No answer.

Oh, please let her be here.

Then he detected the smell of coffee that pervaded the morning air. She must be in the kitchen.

A wave of relief ran through him. Stiffly, he maneuvered his body out of bed and groped around for his house shoes with his foot. Hopping along on one foot, he struggled to slip one on. Then the other. He almost lost his balance. Shuffling toward the kitchen, this fit and virile man in his early fifties had all the energy of an octogenarian.

The coffee was on. Unfortunately it had been on for hours. The only sign of Casey was her favorite cup. Rinsed and in the sink.

He noticed the hall bathroom door was ajar. "Honey, you in there?"

He stuck his head in the door. Her little bathroom was spotless and smelled of her favorite fragrance, but no Casey. He breathed in the scent, half smiling as he did, thinking about how pretty she looked and smelled when she got all dolled up. He stepped into the bathroom and opened the cabinet door. He stood there, staring at her toothbrush, feeling somewhat stupid. But he figured she would never leave the house without brushing her teeth and she would never leave for good without taking her toothbrush. It was there, so he could assume that she had not left him . . . this time.

He felt it. It was still damp. She'd used it this morning. Immediately, he wanted to kick himself. Casey would have his hide if she knew he'd felt her toothbrush. He ran hot water over it, rinsing it thoroughly before returning it to the rack.

Fool. The voice in his head wasn't his. At least, he hoped it wasn't. The hairs on the back of his neck stood up. *Where's the whore's car?*

He stomped into the living room and ripped the blinds open. The empty driveway revealed Casey had indeed gone somewhere without telling him.

"Oh man." He ground his palm to his forehead and let it slide down his face across his morning stubble.

In the kitchen, he poured a cup of coffee, dumped in sugar, and settled down at the coffee bar. It'd take at least one cup before he could start thinking clearly. He stirred and stirred the brew and finally slurped some down—too dark, too sweet—trying to imagine what life would be like without Casey. Not a pretty picture. He got up and paced awhile, carrying his coffee with him. He migrated to the den and plopped down in front of the TV.

His Bible lay open before him on the coffee table. He thought about taking a moment to pray about his temper. He certainly knew how destructive a bad temper can be to a marriage. He and Casey used to teach a young marrieds' seminar on the subject. What in him would not let him take his own advice and institute a healing in his marriage?

He had never apologized to Casey for his fits of anger. He'd wanted to. Sometimes he felt like he wanted to get on his knees and *beg* her forgiveness. But each time he tried, something inside of him would nearly explode. He would break out in a cold sweat at the thought of humbling himself.

If he could turn back the hands of time, he would. Back to a gentler time, when God was first in his life and Casey was in line right behind the Almighty. His congregation came after his family. And possessions . . . well, they were not even on the chart.

He took a slug of old—now cold—too-sweet coffee.

"Ugh. I'd rather she didn't leave me any coffee at all."

He tried to shut out the nagging truth that the coffee had been fresh the first time his alarm went off. He'd rather blame Casey. He reached over and slammed the Bible shut, creasing the delicate pages. He saw them sticking out but made no attempt to straighten them.

"I'll pray when I'm in a better mood. Right now I need to get dressed and run down to the church . . . soon as I find out who won the game."

He pointed the remote toward the TV. It blared, the volume still too high from last night.

Twenty minutes later, grumbling because his team lost a close one, he turned the TV off and padded back to the kitchen to pour out the unsavory brew.

"I hate cold, stale coffee," he barked at no one in particular.

He tossed his cup in the sink. It broke. He grunted.

Stomping into his bathroom to shave, he slammed the door behind him. That's when he saw the note on his mirror, in Casey's impeccable handwriting.

"At the dealership. See you tonight."

Then he remembered they'd talked about the appointment last night over supper.

"Some note. Should've been in the bedroom where I would have seen it first thing." He yanked the note down, crumpled it up, and threw it in the general direction of the trash can, cursing under his breath as he missed.

With a hand on either side of the basin, he leaned forward, head bowed, trying to get a grip on his temper. He took several deep breaths and slowly raised his face.

He stared at the image before him in the mirror. Now that he knew she hadn't left him, he could stop berating himself. He wasn't such a bad guy. She could do worse. In fact, she had done worse with that loser, Allen. A lot worse. All he ever did for her was get her pregnant. Then find every excuse under the sun to not marry her—after what was probably the longest engagement in recorded history. You'd think Casey would be too smart to fall for a guy like that.

Pasting on a practiced showbiz smile, he examined his reflection. Thick sandy hair, just a little gray at the temples. Straight white teeth and a strong jaw. Tanned face with a healthy glow and only a few wrinkles. Mostly around his eyes. Laugh lines, they call them. But he'd earned those lines and the glow from hours spent in the sun the last couple of years, honing his golf game to near perfection. Had a four handicap. Not bad.

He'd managed to keep a good physique and was still as strong as a bear.

From the highest corner over the shower dozens of evil yellow eyes glowered from the spirit world. The demon of pride loved to sit back and observe his handiwork in Edward.

He alone had found the chink in Edward's armor, barely big enough to force a talon into. Yes, he had ripped and torn and widened the gap to make room to enter. Now he flitted in and out at will, but never let Edward out of his sight for long.

He'd opened the door to Violence and Greed. And more were coming. The demon of lies had his foot in the door and Confusion and Addiction weren't far behind.

Lies was the smallest of the demons, but that made entry easier. He would get bigger once established with exercise and good food. Pride, Greed, and Violence were exercising their specialty and feeding on Edward's soul, and they were increasing in strength and size daily.

Violence seemed to be growing the fastest of all in the fertile ground of Edward's yielding spirit. The others were clamoring to keep up. Together, they kept Edward in constant turmoil.

They could feel how hard the good pastor was fighting them. But he may as well give up. As their strength increased, his decreased. He was getting weaker with each passing day. And when it came to self-improvement—for all his good intentions—Pastor McAlester was a total failure.

"The poor dupe denies his only *real* escape from his wretched fate." Violence dropped down next to Pride on top of the shower. "Did you hear him say deliverance was foolishness?"

"Yeah, and ain't we glad." Pride took some of his eyes off Edward long enough to glance at the hideous hulk perched next to him. He ogled him up and down, not understanding why he was growing so fast. "He's at our mercy and we're not going to show him any."

"Mercy? What's that?" Violence guffawed, leaning so far forward he lost his grip. He grabbed the shower curtain and climbed back up. Muck oozed down the polyester fabric. "I have so much more in store for him. And very soon."

"Don't we all?" Pride turned to Violence, but he had already re-entered Edward.

Pride heard a groan and all eyes darted back to Edward.

He was doubled over at the basin, holding his stomach. He straightened up and wiped sweat from his brow.

"No wonder he's so big. Always on the job." Pride rose to his full height and looked at himself in Edward's mirror. "Not as big as Violence, but still a force to be reckoned with. It's too bad McAlester can't see me. He'd have a coronary." Both of his heads sported multiple eyes of varying sizes. He scratched the top of his left head with a long, sharp talon. "Not bad. Not bad at all."

The more ghouls who piled on Edward, the more he would be weighed down. One day the good man in him would completely collapse, never to get up again. Already, because of the combined efforts of a few demons, Edward's ministry was suffering and his marriage was teetering on the brink. A few more months, maybe even weeks, and the church would see him for what he really was. He'd be out the door.

The stink that would be stirred up when he went under would slow things to a halt at the Church of the Good Shepherd. Mission accomplished.

All of Pride's eyes brightened at the thought of his reward in hell for bringing this man of the cloth down. Without thinking, he laughed aloud.

Edward jerked around to look at the shower. "Who's there?" He wrinkled his brow and turned back to the mirror, shaking his head. "Now I'm hearing things."

Edward spent the rest of the morning at the church.

Pastoring this church was a breeze. Since he was called to the Good Shepherd the church had experienced tremendous growth. Ample finances were now available for any need, or whim, of such a successful pastor.

He had requested an associate pastor to take charge of visitation, because he didn't like hanging out at depressing hospitals and nursing homes. Of course he told the board he needed more time for study and one-on-one ministry. Within weeks they complied by putting Elder John on staff.

Now he spent most of his time in his study with the door closed. Studying. Well, kind of studying. He put in a lot of time on the computer each day surfing the web. Lucky for him, he had a terrific memory, a good knowledge of the Scriptures, and a knock-'em-dead speaking style. He could deliver a message that brought them to their feet, then knocked them to their knees, without having spent much time in preparation. So he put in a few hours, schmoozed the board from time to time, played endless rounds of golf, and everyone stayed happy.

Of course the board and the church didn't know about his little temper problem.

"How could they?" Edward mused, when he occasionally gave it a thought. "It's strictly between me and Casey and she'd never cause me any trouble about it. Not here at the church anyway. We'll get it straightened out. All in good time. Casey and me."

At one thirty he took off to play a round of golf. He'd joined a fancy club in the next county, knowing any golfers in the church belonged to the local club or played at the municipal course. It was none of their business how much time he spent on the links.

Casey wouldn't be home until late and he'd finished his work-load at church, such as it was. So he had the whole long afternoon off. The rain had kept him off the course for a couple of days. But today promised to be a beautiful, crisp fall day. Perfect for a round of golf.

He didn't need to worry about Casey. She was a self-reliant lit-tle lady. Not like some of the guys' ditzy wives. She kept things run-ning smoothly, handled the family checkbook, decorated, and kept their home clean and neat. She even did a lot of running around for him on church matters when he didn't want to use the church secre-tary. They didn't need to know all of his business. Yes, Casey's skills came in handy. Plus, she made excuses for him when he screwed things up.

He chuckled at that thought. Yes, everything was under control. He could relax.

Relax he did. It was dusk and he could hardly see the ball when he decided to call it a day. He'd be home in forty-five minutes and Casey would be there, patiently waiting, with dinner on the table and a smile on her face.

However, when he pulled in the drive it was dark and not one light was on in the house. Casey's car wasn't there, so obviously din-ner wouldn't be ready.

He forgot all about how efficiently she ran the house.

He forgot how she made excuses for him when he messed up.

Cursing, he yanked last night's leftovers out of the refrigerator.

"I hate leftovers. I said, *I hate leftovers!*" He shoved a plate of roast beef and a cup of gravy into the microwave, slammed the door, and hit a few buttons.

When the microwave beeped five minutes later, the gravy had bubbled over and burned. Edward cursed and snatched up the bottle of ketchup. It slipped from his hand and crashed to the floor. Breaking on contact, it sent ketchup and glass in all directions. His head was pounding again.

"No gravy, no ketchup. How am I expected to eat this dry garbage?"

He grabbed the mayo and a loaf of bread and stepped gingerly

54

over the mess. He took his plate of roast beef into the den and plopped down in front of the TV.

"She can clean it up herself. It wouldn't have happened if she'd been here like she was supposed to be."

7

Witt and Casey mopped coffee from the diner's table with their napkins, and Mae ran to help with a damp cloth.

Witt's world was spinning out of control. "Sorry. Did I spill any on you? I'm not usually that clumsy."

"No, you completely missed me." She spread her arms in front of her and looked down at the front of her sweater. "Not a drop."

"I guess I need to start drinking my coffee with a straw." He laughed as he ran his napkin along the table edge. "By the way, you have a very pretty name and you should never apologize for it."

She was here, across the table from him, thirty years and hundreds of miles away from the last time he'd laid eyes on her—striving to keep the skirt of her pale-yellow sundress from blowing in the wind. The picture of her waving back to her mother, windblown auburn hair mischievously framing her lovely face, was indelibly imprinted on his heart.

And she was married.

To a minister.

Bummer.

"Thanks." A glimmer of doubt veiled her eyes and she turned

briefly and looked toward the entrance. "Did someone just come in, or did I say something to upset you, Witt?"

"No, no, not at all. What can I say? Maybe I was looking too deep into those amber eyes of yours and forgot to hold onto my cup."

Or maybe you just turned my world upside down.

Casey wrinkled her brow and zeroed in on his eyes. "Are you married?"

"No." He looked down at the fresh cup of coffee Mae had brought him, then back into Casey's eyes. "Never married."

"Engaged?"

He shook his head and chuckled. "No. And not going steady, either."

Her cheeks turned pink and she sighed, relaxing back into her seat. "That's hard to imagine."

"Not really. College, vet school, clinic, etc., etc. Never seemed to have the time to do much dating, much less get married. You know, I always believed that marriage was a till-death-do-us-part kind of thing and I've never met anyone, since . . ." The reason he'd never married was sitting across the table from him. He definitely didn't want to go there.

A change of subject was in order if he was going to make it through this without spilling the beans. He'd sort his feelings out later.

"Animals. Now there's a subject we seem to have in common. Dogs, cats, and a possum, you said? Tell me more about your marvelous marsupial."

"Well, most people don't like possums. But they've never known one up close and personal. Soupy has the cutest habits. I found out, quite by accident, if I give him a mushroom, he'll snatch it up, look from side to side as though someone might take it from him, and make a mad dash for his bed with it.

"I pretend he's trained, give him a mushroom, and say, 'Take it to your bed,' and off he goes. It's quite impressive. But in truth, he's pretty much untrainable. Cute . . . lovable . . . but not overly bright."

Her facial expressions were adorable. He wanted to keep her

talking, just to watch her face—hear her voice. "So you'd say mushrooms are a possum's best friend, huh?"

"I wish I could write a children's book about him." She slid to the end of her bench and leaned against the wall, raising one knee and hugging it.

She was so beautiful.

He wanted to tell her he loved her.

Always had.

"Witt?"

He blinked and dragged his mind back to reality.

"Pardon?"

"I said, have you ever thought about writing a book about your experiences as a vet?"

"Uh, fleetingly, but that's been done. And I get a lot of pleasure out of working outside with my animals. I'm not much for sitting at a desk. So I have to be content with boring my friends and family with my little yarns."

"Are you into sports?"

"Only if you call wrestling with your nephew-in-law and getting pinned every time a sport. My niece's husband, Mark, and I wrestle for amusement. His and everyone else's, that is. I don't have all that much fun getting pinned and being laughed at, but I aim to please." He shrugged and grinned sheepishly.

"I do celebrity imitations." He was getting his momentum back.

"Oh really, let me hear one."

"You sure you're ready for this?"

"Ready."

He straightened up in the booth and lowered his voice. "And now you know . . . the rest of the story."

"Who in the world was that?" Casey held her hand against her mouth to stifle a laugh.

His shoulders sagged. "Paul Harvey. You didn't recognize him?"

"Oh, Witt, that was *awful*. You didn't sound *anything* like Paul Harvey."

"Ouch! Do you have to be so honest? Maybe it needs a little work." He tried to look deflated.

He wasn't a celebrity imitator and he'd made no attempt to sound like Paul Harvey. Wasn't even sure he'd recognize his voice. Witt just wanted to keep it light until he had a chance to sort things out.

"It needs more than a little work. It needs a *lot* of work." Casey laughed and slapped her knee repeatedly. "Don't give up your day job."

Leaning all the way back against the booth, Witt chuckled. "Too late. I already have."

Jousting back and forth like two old friends, they fell into comfortable conversation about everyday things. Books they'd read and places they had been. It was so natural being with her Witt could almost make himself believe he'd never lost her.

Casey told him she was a Christian. "I know that should be elementary, being a pastor's wife, but it never hurts to clarify."

"Praise God!" Witt raised one hand heavenward.

"Are you always that enthusiastic about someone's salvation?"

Only those I've been praying for all my life.

"I suspect you're pretty special to the Lord."

"That is the sweetest thing to say, Witt. You're pretty special yourself."

Casey recalled experiences she had when she lived in San Antonio some thirty years ago. Witt chose to not share that he lived in San Antonio during that same time period. He was glad he hadn't put his foot in his mouth earlier. She'd evidently made no connection between the girl and the jerk in his story and the girl and the jerk in hers. Later, maybe, if the occasion called for it, he could tell her . . . the rest of the story.

If there was a later.

He had some questions for God about this. Was he being tested? Surely God knew he was not prepared for this. He'd been blindsided.

The cashier came over to the table and put her hand on Witt's shoulder. "I wish you hadn't retired, Dr. G., Lancelot misses you."

"Tell Lancelot I miss him too, Georgie. You know, you could just bring him out to the ranch to see me. I have a supply of his favorite chew bones on hand." He patted the hand that rested on his shoulder. "Do you take him to Al?"

"Oh yes! And Dr. Al is a sweetheart. But it's just not the same without you there."

Witt took her hand from his shoulder and kissed the back of it.

"You're too kind, milady."

Georgie giggled and scurried back to her post, her face glowing crimson.

Moments later, Mae approached the table with two pieces of strawberry pie. Witt had given her a secret signal.

Casey looked down at the steaming slice of pie in front of her and licked her lips. "I said I didn't want anything but coffee, Witt. You know I can't resist it, now that it's in front of me. That's mean."

"I'm sorry. You only have to taste it. If you don't want it, you don't have to eat it."

"Right . . . like that's going to happen."

"Well, you have to eat something. I'll bet you didn't have any breakfast and it's past lunch. You may as well eat pie as anything."

She grinned and dug in. "Now that's sound medical advice, if I ever heard any."

Ticking softly, the old clocks advanced one hour . . . then two. Customers came and customers went—and Witt and Casey were still talking.

Yet when Witt reached over to pat her hand, she flinched.

He put his hand over hers and gave it a little squeeze before pulling away. Why was she so afraid? Did God plunk her down in his life again so he could protect her? From what?

Bong! Bong! Bong!

Casey heard the low, reverberating sound of a big antique Vienna Regulator that hung on the back wall and glanced at her watch. How could it be three o'clock already?

She'd told Witt her car was in the shop. But she was enjoying his company so much she'd forgotten all about the time. It was going to take at least thirty minutes to get to the dealership and get settled up. Then there was the two-hour drive across the mountains that surround St. Michael to get home. It was a beautiful drive, but slow and dangerous at night. The days were getting shorter and Edward didn't want her driving those roads after dark. She shuddered. She was going to be late.

Who knew what kind of greeting she'd get when she got home?

She didn't really want to go home, but she had nowhere else to go. And she needed to be on her way—quickly. Heaven forbid she do anything to fuel another episode like last night.

"I have to go, Witt. I can't tell you how much I've enjoyed myself. I feel like I've known you all my life. But I really must leave now." She hesitated. "We'll probably never meet again. But you've blessed me today." With a wistful glance up at him she turned to go.

"Hold on, little one. I'll think of you often and the friendship we've established today. And before you go, I'd like to pray for you."

He took her small hand in his and began praying aloud. Casey looked around her. Everyone was watching. She felt her face grow hot, but she clung to Witt's hand and bowed her head.

"Lord, please bless Kath . . . Casey. Surround her with Your presence and give her Your peace that surpasses all our human comprehension. Look after her on the long drive home through the mountains. I assign a couple of Your biggest, most powerful angels to go ahead of her and smooth the way. Thank You, Father, for giving us the angels. Amen."

Casey sighed and wiped a tear with her free hand. His prayer gave her a peace about returning to her home and her husband. She knew God was going to see her through this. Hadn't He provided just what she needed to make it through today? Just when she thought there was no reason to go on, He sent one of His own to remind her of His love.

"Thank you, Witt." She reluctantly pulled her hand from his strong grip. She had to go before she changed her mind and decided to stay and bask in this feeling forever. Once outside in the lengthening shadows of the downtown buildings, Casey sprinted toward the loaner car. She started the engine and looked toward Witt. He smiled as he waved good-bye to her, but his stance was that of a troubled man. How odd. He was the one who'd turned the day bright.

Casey could feel the presence of angels surrounding her as she waved back. Her heart was singing and her head was clear. Yes, everything was going to work out. God was in control and He *would* see her through.

She quickly settled her business at the dealership and was glad to be back in her own little 1990 Jetta Edward had bought her last year.

She sang and prayed as she drove. At first with great fervor. But her blissful peace began to be invaded by occasional fleeting visions of Edward's angry eyes.

She blinked them away.

They persisted.

She tried desperately to hang on to the warm feeling, but as she made the last turn onto the highway headed away from St. Michael and her new friend, she could feel it slipping away. Inevitably her thoughts settled on Edward and what she was going home to. Already she'd lost her grip on her newfound peace.

Then she got that dreadful feeling she was being watched. And there was a faint odor in the car she'd never noticed before. Like raw chicken that's been left out to spoil. She tried to ignore it, but from time to time it became stronger, until she could ignore it no longer.

"Did I leave a package of chicken in the trunk the last time I went to the market?" She pulled off the road to check the trunk. Nothing there. Under the seats. Nothing. "The mechanics must have left something in the car. I'll check closer in the morning."

The closer she got to home, the worse the smell, the stronger the dreadful feeling, and the tighter the knot in her stomach became.

"God," she prayed, "help me to hold on to Your peace and help me to fight the physical evidences of my emotional problems. I don't know how to overcome it. Please teach me.

"And Father, I'm feeling guilty for enjoying Witt's company to-day. I pray what I did this afternoon is not a sin in Your sight. I seem to have found such a good friend in Witt. I may never see him again, but it's wonderful to know You have people out there who care about me even before they know me.

"I won't lie to Edward about it. I may get in trouble, but I won't add lies to all the other problems we're having. Lord, the peace I knew this afternoon was unlike anything I've ever felt before. I covet that peace in You for myself . . . and my husband."

Casey drove the rest of the way in silence.

A dark cloud settled over her, and her connection with God seemed broken. The peace, the laughter, the joy . . . all gone. It was as though the day had been a beautiful dream.

She arrived at home well after dark. The front door was locked. She fumbled for the key, her heart racing, not knowing if she would walk in to find an angry Edward or a calm, disinterested one.

She walked toward the noisy media room where the base speaker was blaring. Edward had his feet propped on the coffee table and was surrounded by an array of dirty dishes, used paper towels, and two half-filled glasses of tea. She stood in the doorway until he glanced up from the TV.

"Hi, I was about to get worried about you. Have a good day?" He flashed her a halfhearted smile.

"Oh, yes, I had a really nice day." She picked at her nails.

She knew if she didn't discuss today's events with him, it would weigh on her mind until she felt as wanton as he sometimes accused her of being.

"I made a friend," she said haltingly. "We had coffee while I wait-ed for my car. He's a retired . . ."

Midsentence, a roaring crowd yanked Edward's attention back to the TV. He pointed the remote and increased the volume. The noise was deafening.

When she realized she'd been dismissed, Casey went to the kitchen to grab a bite before bath time.

Ketchup streaked the floor and walls like a murder scene, and bro-ken glass glistened everywhere. Resignedly, she cleaned it up. There would be no communicating with him until the game was over. She had no appetite, so she took her bath and got ready for bed. Maybe she could recapture some of the peace she felt earlier during prayer time.

W itt opened his front door to see his nearest neighbor, Pete Evans, leaning against the doorpost. Tears streamed from Pete's eyes.

"Pete, come in. What in the world is wrong?"

"Witt, I didn't know who else to turn to. Maggie's locked herself in the bedroom and she's packing to leave. Won't open the door. Won't even talk to me."

Witt put one hand on each of Pete's shoulders. "What happened?"

"It's an awful long story. I was hoping we could go to your prayer closet and you'd pray with me. Ya see, it's not Maggie's fault. She's a saint. I brought it all on. Ever since we went to my twenty-year reunion last weekend, things ain't been right."

"What happened at the reunion?" Witt opened the low door to the prayer room and ushered Pete in.

"Well, you and me didn't know each other back then, but my senior year I dated this really gorgeous gal, and we got pretty serious. I was kind of hoping she wouldn't be at the reunion. I really didn't want Maggie to see her. But she was. She's twice divorced and as pretty as ever. Ya know, Maggie was quite a looker too, but she's picked up a few pounds what with having four kids."

"She's still beautiful, Pete." Witt put his hand on Pete's shoulder.

"And Jen—that's my old girlfriend—she was all over me, like if we'd never broke up. I guess I didn't do a very good job of discouraging her. Well, I know I didn't. It was pretty flattering, ya know?" Pete ran his hand through his thinning hair.

"How'd Maggie take all this?"

"Well, all of a sudden I look around and Maggie's gone. Took the pickup and drove home without me. Witt, you know I love Maggie. But I got mad at her for leaving. So I stayed the rest of the evening and danced with Jen the whole time. She was flirting with me, big-time."

Witt loved Pete and Maggie and the kids. They were good God-fearing people. It broke his heart to think Satan was toying with their family. "How'd you get home, Pete?"

"Jen offered to take me home, but I didn't think that was a good idea, so I got one of the guys to give me a ride."

Pete plopped down on the floor, cross-legged, and put his head in his hands. "Thing is, Maggie wouldn't speak to me when I got there. I don't blame her, now—but at the time, it just made me madder. I laid on the couch all night thinking about Jen, and the next day I called her. We got together a couple nights later. And again last night."

"Where'd you tell Maggie you were going?"

"Oh, I just made up some dumb excuses. I know she could see right through 'em. Thing is, Witt, I started thinking I was still in love with Jen. Like it had never ended, ya know? But when she started talking about running off together, I realized I had to make a choice between her and Maggie and the kids. Well, it was no contest. Maggie's a good woman. Been there for me through thick and thin. I wouldn't give her up for all the riches in the world. But I've messed up so bad, I just don't know if I got a say-so in the matter, anymore. You think she'll ever forgive me?"

Witt took a deep breath and rubbed his forehead with his fingertips. The scenario was different from his and Casey's, but the truth was the same. Satan loved to break up long-standing marriages—especially Christian marriages. And he'd use anyone he could to accomplish his goals. A woman named Jen . . . a guy named Witt.

A heaviness grew in his chest.

"Pete, Satan's using you. He doesn't want you and Maggie to be witnesses for Jesus. And he doesn't want your children to grow up in the Lord. But you don't have to be his pawn. First, turn this over to the Lord and ask His forgiveness. Then go to Maggie. Sit outside that bedroom door until she opens it—if it's three days from now. Beg her forgiveness. Tell her what you just told me. That you wouldn't trade her for all the riches in the world. And, Pete, remind her of her beauty. The beauty you saw in her when you first married. It's still there. Open your eyes and see it."

"You're right, Witt. I gotta get home right away, before she leaves. I'll pray on the way. And I'll keep on praying until Maggie forgives me. And I ain't letting her leave, if I gotta tie myself to the hood of her car." He grinned through his tears. "I love ya, buddy. Thanks!"

Pete was so anxious to get home he forgot about the low doorway and hit his head on the way out of the prayer closet. And his feet touched only two of the five steps off the porch.

Witt watched as he ran to his truck. Then turned back to his prayer closet.

He remembered to stoop down to step through a five-foot door to get into this eight-by-ten-foot closet. He had been so glad to discover the room right in the middle of the floor plan of his old ranch house, built in the 1800s. He bought it, already restored, in 1984.

A very special place, this closet. Never entered casually by anyone. Only when someone came to the ranch who really needed a touch from the Lord, did he invite them into his private refuge. He'd led several dear friends to the Lord in this holy place, including Pete. Rough ranch hands. An elderly neighbor and his grandson. And Sarah, the sweet lady who came in daily to help him.

Now that was something. Sarah'd had a hard time getting her plump body through the small opening, but they had a good laugh about it afterward. Still did, from time to time. Now she told anyone who'd listen that the hardest part about getting saved was getting into the prayer room.

Witt called it God's room, because every time he went in he felt the presence of the Holy Spirit. It was his personal Holy of Holies.

He kept the room devoid of trappings, save a small rug to cushion the hard plank floor, a stool, a candle, and a bottle of anointing oil. There were days when he stayed and basked in the Lord's presence for hours on end. Yet he never had to rush through his chores after prayer time. It was as though God made time stand still for him.

He sank to his knees on the rug.

"What now, God? She has no idea who I am. Yet I've loved her all my life. Now I've seen her, sat with her, talked with her, and touched her. And I love her all the more." Witt groaned. "I'm sorry. I know . . . she's married.

"And Satan would like to use *me* to wreck her marriage, just like he's toying with Pete and Maggie. But I get the feeling there's more to this than meets the eye, Lord. It's like the Evil One has even bigger plans than destroying a marriage. She seems to be in constant fear— perhaps even for her life."

Like a caged tiger, Witt rose and paced from one wall of the tiny room to the other.

"You know I don't believe in coincidence, Father. I didn't just happen to run into her. I think it was deliberate on Your part. I've prayed for years that if she ever needed me, I'd be there for her. And I . . . oh, good glory, that's it!"

He came to such a quick stop he lost his balance and thumped to his knees, missing the rug.

"That's it," he shouted, his hands raised to heaven. "You're taking me up on it! How could I not have figured that one out?"

He shook his head to clear the cobwebs.

"But how could I possibly help her? She's married. To a pastor, no less. He's her priest. If she has spiritual problems, she should turn to him. And if she has marital problems, I would be the last person who should try to help. Talk about conflict of interest. Classic case.

"Lord, if I'm going to see her again, help me to not mess up and let it slip that I love her." He realized he was treading in forbidden terri- tory. "Forgive me. I know I shouldn't say that about a married woman. But please cut me a little slack. I just found out today and I haven't had a chance to get used to it yet. And being totally honest with You, Lord . . . if You have plans for me to see her again, I'm going to need more than a little help."

It had been a traumatic day and Witt was exhausted. He sat cross-legged in the middle of the room and closed his eyes. "Katherine, my Katherine. If only I'd tried harder thirty years ago. Maybe we . . ." He shuddered a sigh and a tear dropped to the floor.

He shot a helpless look toward heaven. "Use me in her life, please, if You need me. I'm between a rock and a hard place, but to quote You, 'Not my will, but Yours be done.'"

He tried to stand.

But was unable to move.

He felt the Spirit of the Lord restraining him. Witt had finished talking to God. But apparently, God was not finished with him.

Do not dismiss Me.

It was the nearest thing to hearing God's audible voice Witt had ever experienced. He was awestruck and suddenly more alert than he'd ever been in his life. "I'm sorry, Lord. I've been doing all the talking. Please speak to my heart. I'm listening."

Be still before Me and know that I am God.

Witt sat motionless and waited. His heart was about to leave his chest.

Something was happening to the atmosphere in that tiny room. The hair on his arms and the back of his neck stood on end. Silently, little by little, God's presence in that small space grew and intensified until it became so overwhelming Witt was compelled to lower his lean body all the way to the floor. It was as though a giant weight was pressing him from above. He was powerless to resist.

Lying on his back, he clamped his eyes shut against the intense and blinding light that suddenly filled every crevice of the room.

The door to God's room was closed and there were no windows. Yet the sweet fragrance of wild clover and honeysuckle wafted in on a gentle breeze, and settled around Witt like a gossamer veil. His body yielded as he allowed the Spirit to take control.

This time he had indeed entered the Holy of Holies.

He felt no fear. The blending of God's Spirit into his was an awesome thing. For a fleeting moment, Witt thought of Mary. She'd accepted God's will for her life without fear. Was this how she felt when she was overcome by His Spirit?

He wanted to question the Lord about these new feelings, but he was in speechless awe before the Absolute Reverence and Deity of God the Father.

He spent an eternity lying on the floor of his prayer room, while tears flowed. Waves of peace and ecstasy swept alternately over his spirit. He was both chastised and comforted.

Chastised because of his desire for a woman he knew was married, and comforted with the Lord's assurance He was in control as long as Witt followed His lead. The Lord was delving deep into Witt's spirit to cleanse every corner of his heart and prepare him for the difficult task that lay ahead.

When God had finished dealing with him, Witt felt the weight lift from him. The brilliant light vanished as though someone had flipped a switch. He slowly opened his eyes and sat up cautiously, his back against the wall and his legs sprawled out in front of him. Silently, he praised the Lord, not wanting the moment to end.

There were no words he could speak. Neither did he want to hear the sound of his own voice. God's voice was echoing in his spirit. He wiped a tear from his face with his sleeve, and the scent of wild clover and honeysuckle was still clinging to his shirt.

Witt knew he was being groomed for a job. A job involving Katherine. He had no doubt the Lord would be with him through whatever lay ahead and he was light-headed with anticipation.

9

Panic gripped Edward's heart. His mind was blank, and the notes before him bore no resemblance to the English language. He flipped through them, looking for a familiar word. Was this German? Polish? How could it be? They were his notes. He had written them yesterday, in his office right here at the church. But this morning they were unintelligible.

He looked at Casey, sitting in the front row. She nodded her head in encouragement, smiling submissively, as she so often did when he took to the pulpit. She looked so sweet.

"She's the only one with access to your notes," the voice in his head rasped.

Edward was stunned at the thought. *Why would she do this to me?*

"She's evil. Make her pay." From under the front pew.

Edward's grip tightened. He looked down at the notes in his hand, then back at Casey. She wouldn't look so sweet after . . .

But wait. They were in his handwriting. She couldn't have. His fist relaxed.

His eyes skimmed the congregation. Shadows weaved in and out among the people. Convolving around the pews. Twisting and turning through the seats. Through people's clothing. In a sleeve and out the neckline. Why did no one seem to notice?

He rubbed his eyes and tried to blot out the spectral activity long enough to remember a name—just one name was all he needed—so he could call on someone to pray. That would give him a moment to regroup . . . or run.

Nothing would surface.

The slate that was his mind had been wiped clean.

What did he usually do at this time? He had to do something—anything. He knew his flock was waiting for a word from the Lord.

But apparently the Lord had nothing to say through him this morning.

Edward was on his own. He groped through his mind for a familiar phrase.

His normally eloquent voice quavered. "Every head bowed, every eye closed. Let's go to the Lord and ask His blessing on this assembly. Will someone please begin?"

Glances were exchanged in the congregation. Some eyebrows rose.

After a long pause Mike Hendricks struggled to his feet and began praying earnestly for the Lord to show Himself mightily in the service. When he finished, another member took the torch and ran with it.

Casey knew something was desperately wrong. She opened her eyes and observed Edward rummaging through his notes. His hands were shaking and his brow dripping with sweat. Looking up intermittently, his gaze eventually met Casey's. He spread his hands helplessly.

As though it had been planned, Casey slipped out of the pew and went to the piano. She gestured to Susie, the pianist, she would take over temporarily. Susie looked puzzled but quickly relinquished the bench and moved to an empty chair in the choir loft.

The congregation was still praying, but some of the choir members were opening their eyes, peering around, and shrugging their shoulders. Several looked at Susie. She stared blankly at them, and slowly, with eyebrows raised, moved her head from side to side.

Edward was not one to follow a strict order of service, but his behavior today confused even Casey. He usually gave the choir and pianist some clue if he felt led to go a different direction.

The prayers from the congregation, some loud and enthusiastic, others mumbled, began to taper off. Casey started playing soft, worshipful music. A few people sang, hummed, or swayed with the music. Soon most of the congregation was standing. Some had their eyes closed. Others looked heavenward. Several dabbed their eyes with a tissue. A spirit of tranquility moved across the congregation.

Edward was seated in his baroque chair behind the pulpit, elbows on his knees, head in his hands. He looked, for all the world, like he was praying and crying before the Lord.

Casey motioned to Susie to return to the piano. Susie slid onto the bench and took over so smoothly there was no break in the music. No change in the celestial atmosphere that enveloped the sanctuary like a soft cloud. Her piano playing had never been more moving. Over half of the choir found their way to the altar. Folks were kneeling and praying all over the sanctuary.

Casey walked to where Edward was seated and took his hand. *Let this be an answer to my prayers. A breakthrough. Please, dear Lord, let Edward return to his normal self.*

She led him, like a child, down the two steps that elevated the podium from the altar and stood in front of the congregation, holding his hand. Tears flowed freely from his eyes and the eyes of the parishioners. Friends and families were embracing. Folks who hadn't spoken to each other in months were hugging. Peace poured over the congregation like a river from the throne of God.

Casey didn't say a word. One by one, worshippers came down to pray and to lay hands on Edward. They prayed for his ministry and thanked him for his obedience to the Holy Spirit. Edward didn't utter a sound, except for an occasional sob.

It was well past noon before everyone had returned to the pews. Casey and Edward sat down on the wide, carpeted steps. Susie brought the music to a tender end and slipped out the side door. People began to slowly file out. There was none of the usual chatter. Casey knew this had been a very special service. One like this church had never seen before. To do anything more would have been gilding the lily.

Mike Hendricks went quietly about his rounds, turning the heat down and the lights off. After what seemed like an eternity he slipped out and closed the front doors behind him, leaving only the vestibule lights on.

When they were alone, Casey whispered, "Edward, that was so beautiful."

"Beautiful, Casey? *Beautiful*? It was a nightmare."

His words impaled her hopeful spirit. Her shoulders sank. "Oh, Edward, how can you say that? The Lord moved in so many people's lives today. I think every person here was touched by Him in some way."

She put her hand on his knee.

He pushed it off. "Not me. Not by the Lord."

His vacant eyes sent a shiver down her spine. "Not you? But your tears, your humble spirit . . . I don't understand."

Suddenly he was on his feet, scowling down at her. "I couldn't remember anything. No one's name but yours. Not a single Scripture. I had no idea what my message was. It was like someone had scrubbed every memory from my brain. My notes are gibberish." He swung around, arms outstretched. "And this sanctuary stinks."

"Edward!"

"No, I mean it. Didn't you smell it?" He curled his upper lip and wrinkled his nose. "And I was crying because I was scared to death. The Lord has deserted me, Casey. That, or I'm losing my mind."

He grabbed some papers off the lectern and thrust them at her.

"Look at this. My notes are in a foreign language."

Casey began to read aloud, "Matthew 20:1, kingdom—like a landowner, denarius for a day, eleventh hour . . .

"Well, I can see where they wouldn't make a lot of sense to anyone else, but they're your notes, Edward. They aren't supposed to make sense to anyone else."

"Let me see that." He snatched the notes back.

"Hey, this isn't what they looked like before. I swear they were

76

written in a foreign language. So help me . . ." He bit his lip. His head twitched to one side. "This is . . . it's . . ."

"Perhaps the Lord confused you, so what did happen—would happen."

"No, He used it, but He didn't initiate it. It was demoralizing . . . sick! Total paralysis of the brain. Things . . . shadows . . . lurking everywhere. In and out." He made undulating gestures with his hand. "Voices. The Lord wouldn't plunge me into such chaos. It's not His style.

"If it hadn't been for you, this morning would have been a disaster. I was a basket case. Total chaos, I'm telling you." Edward flung himself to his hands and knees and stuck his head under the front pew.

Chaos? Casey pondered. It was anything but chaos. It was the epitome of heavenly peace for everyone . . . except her husband. He found it chaotic.

"Where are you?" He crawled on his stomach underneath the pew, craning his neck to peer at the underside of the seat.

Casey's stomach knotted. Edward had always been in total control. His mind was so clear. His memory off the charts. Composed under pressure—that was Edward. Losing his ability to bring a comprehensive message would be the crowning blow.

Whatever elation Casey had felt quickly evaporated. Certainly not a breakthrough; if this was a sign of things to come, the situation at home could only get worse. Now he was seeing shadowy things, hearing voices, and smelling phantom odors. She drew in a ragged breath and shuddered, suddenly remembering the odd odor in her car last Friday evening. It had been gone the next day.

Eyes closed, Casey sat on the step, praying earnestly for an end to this horror. But Edward was on his feet again at the front door. The vestibule lights were off, and a weak stream of light from the partially opened outside doors was all that illuminated the large sanctuary.

Edward breathed a loud sigh. "You coming or not? I don't want to miss kickoff."

"Worthless, stupid, runt imp!" Violence railed at the diminutive demon of confusion. "Can't even handle a little job like messing up a service. They loved it, you idiot."

He lunged, and Confusion darted inside a pew.

His muffled voice cried out. "No, no, it was working. I did a good job of jumbling his notes." He peeked out from the aisle seat. "Didn't you see the panic in his eyes? He was fried with fear. Then, that jezebel wife of his stepped in and saved his rear. Maybe she's the one we should go after. It would be so easy. She's got a juicy past."

He yanked his head back in. A flying hymnal hit the seat and bounced to the floor.

"Forget her. She'll be out of the picture soon enough," Pride screeched. "We were given a job to do, and it didn't include her. She belongs to Him, maggot. Don't you know anything about how this works? A little longer and she'll be a divorcée or a widow, anyway."

"We all did our part. Sliding in and out among those Christians. At least until He showed up and we had to hide." Greed stomped up and down, leaving deep talon-shaped holes in the carpet and globs of mucin on the velveteen seats. "Do you think we enjoyed that?" He kicked the seat the beleaguered ghoul hid in.

The end of Confusion's scaly tail was exposed between the cushions. Violence grabbed it and slung him into the choir loft. "You might as well go back to wherever you came from. The last thing we need around here is better Sunday services."

The little demon crawled out from under a chair, clutching his tail. With shoulders drooping and spiny filament wings dragging on the floor, he slinked away, leaving two trails of an evil-smelling substance where his wings touched the carpet.

"You haven't seen the last of me," he flung over his shoulder as he took to the air and flew headlong into a Sunday school classroom.

Seconds later he burst from the room, looking for a way out of the building.

Violence was the first to break into gales of side-splitting laughter. Then Pride. Then Greed. The underlings joined in after a safe period of time. Hundreds of ghouls rolled and laughed and coughed up putrid substances. Confusion finally found his way out, and the mawkish laughter subsided. The church carpet looked like the bottom of a sludge pit.

"Did I say you could laugh?" Violence seized an underling by the throat. "I'm outa here. I have an appointment at the McAlesters'. Looks like I'm the only one who can get the job done." Violence deployed his awful wings, sending smaller demons crashing in all directions.

10

I t all began so innocently. Casey was putting away groceries. She cut a corner and tripped over Edward's foot.

"Watch it, Casey. If you don't start being more careful, you're going to really hurt yourself one of these days." Edward looked up from his Bible and shook his head. "It frustrates me that you're so careless."

Her tummy did a flip. He found fault only when he was aggravated with her. She'd have to be careful to not set him off. As she passed him, she leaned down and gave him a peck on the top of his head. "Okay, baby, I will."

He laid his Bible down. "Don't brush me off! You *are* going to hurt yourself someday."

"I wasn't brushing you off, baby. But if I did fall, I wouldn't hurt myself. What is there to fall on but the floor?"

She held her breath. *Oh, that was the wrong thing to say.*

Edward pounced to his feet. Inches from her face. "Do you see that table corner sticking out? Well, do you? What if you hit your head on it? Hello? You could be knocked unconscious . . . or worse, you could split your head wide open."

Casey set a bag of canned goods on the countertop and sighed. She could think of nothing to say that wouldn't make matters worse.

If Edward was ready for a fight, there was no way she could avoid it. He had a knack for turning her words around to his advantage.

She tried to go about the business of putting up groceries without seeming to ignore him.

He walked up behind her, grasped her arm, and spun her toward him.

She cringed in front of him.

"You think I'm exaggerating? You think I'm stupid, when I'm only concerned about your safety."

Maybe an apology would prevent a scrimmage this one time.

"I'm sorry, Edward." She lowered her eyes to avoid his scrutinizing gaze. "I know you're very bright. It's not a big deal. I promise I'll be more careful."

He grabbed her by the hair and yanked her head back, making her look at him. "Not a big deal? *Not a big deal?* When you knock yourself unconscious and I have to rush you to the hospital, then will it be a big deal?"

He released her hair, and Casey stumbled away from him. She knew better than to provoke him, yet she'd done it again.

Tilting his head from one side to the other, Edward chanted in a singsong voice, "It's not a big deal. It's not a big deal."

He glared at her through slitted eyes. "It *is* a big deal. This is not my first day. I know exactly what you're thinking. 'It's not a big deal' is Casey-ese for 'Hey, stupid, get a life.' Am I not right?" He shoved his face up in hers. "Hello? Anybody home?"

His eyes darted around the room. He picked up his Bible and threw it against the wall.

Casey winced. "Come on, baby. Please calm down. Let's pray about this."

"I don't want to pray. I'm calm. See. How. Calm. I. Am?" He picked up his concordance and threw it. Harder. Farther. It hit the wall and the spine flew apart. Pages fluttered to the floor.

She tried to keep her voice steady. Her eyes dry. Tears were always fuel to the fire. "Let's talk about this like Christians. If we have a problem—and this doesn't seem like a very big one—it can be solved by talking about it."

He kicked a chair. It didn't go very far. With a tormented grunt, he kicked it again. This time it hit the glass storm door and bounced off. Looking disappointed with the lack of collateral damage, he picked it up and threw it to the floor. One leg splintered and left a mark on the parquet flooring.

"Please stop breaking things, Edward. You're not acting like the man of God I know you are. Please . . . please stop."

He backed her against a wall and bellowed obscenities at her. His hot breath on her face was like a blast from hell's furnace. "Why am I always the bad guy? I'm not acting like I should. Why is it never *your* fault? Oh, that's right. You're perfect. How could I forget? You remind me often enough."

He was hurting her eardrums. She wanted to put her hands over her ears, but that would be a big mistake.

"You never do anything right, yet I always get the blame." He slammed his fist on the table. Water sloshed out of Casey's floral arrangement onto his notes. "Look at that. Water all over my notes because of your stupid bouquet." He flung the arrangement from the table. Glass and water detonated when it hit the floor. "You're a contentious woman. It would be far better to live on the roof than under the roof with you."

He often backed his tantrums with Scripture.

"I'm not blaming you for anything, Edward. This is a misunderstanding that's gotten out of hand. Please, let's start over." She tried to cover all the bases. "I apologize for anything I did or said to offend you."

Casey attempted to put her arms around him. He shoved her away and she fell against the refrigerator.

A shadow of regret streaked across his face. But it was only momentary. There would be no relief until he was spent. He embraced anger like a paramour. Courted it passionately, and wooed it until he was satisfied. After which he dropped it like a spurned lover.

"If you're so innocent, why do you need to apologize? Can you tell me that? You can't have it both ways. Oh, if I give you enough time, you'll come up with some high-minded answer. Answer me. Now."

She had no idea how to appease him or answer his nonsensical question.

"What else can I say? I don't want to fight. I have no idea how it started. We have nothing to fight about, and I'm willing to apologize for whatever I've done to anger you."

"It started because you think I'm stupid. And, no, I do not accept your apology. You're not sincere. You're only apologizing to end the argument—not because you're repentant."

"Sweetheart, I don't know what I'm supposed to be repentant of. And that's the reason for an apology. To make amends, regardless of who's at fault."

"You'd like that, wouldn't you? Translated, you're right, and I'm wrong—as usual. We can quit arguing because you're so perfect, and I'm a stupid fool."

He reached for her throat, but turned abruptly and snatched the first object he saw. He slammed the jar of mayonnaise she'd just bought down on the counter. Mayo splattered everywhere.

He lifted his eyes toward the ceiling and pivoted on one heel. "All of you . . . shut up!" He clamped his hands to his ears.

All of you? Who is he talking to?

Casey dared to reach up and pull his hands from his ears.

"Please, could we talk about this in a normal tone, so the neighbors don't hear?"

Eyes on Casey's face, he shook his head and spoke in a low voice. "I don't care about the neighbors. I wish they were closer so they could hear every word." His volume increased. "Maybe they need to know what kind of woman you are." To full fortissimo. "You have them all fooled, don't you?"

With one wild swoop of his arm, he slung the broken mayonnaise jar, along with the toaster, onto the floor.

Casey started to run, but he latched onto her sweater and shoved her down into a chair. For almost twenty years Edward had led them in prayer every night at bedtime. He pastored a church and commanded the respect of a large congregation. He was filled with knowledge of the Scriptures and in love with the Lord. How could he be doing and saying these things?

He was flailing his arms, groaning and bellowing like an injured animal.

"How much more of this am I expected to endure?" He swung full circle again, as though searching for an answer from another entity.

Pulling Casey up from the chair by the shoulder with one muscular hand, he dug his fingers into her flesh. Pain shot through her arm. Wild-eyed, he shook her.

"Stop your incessant blubbering. Just answer the question."

Tiny specks of spittle hit her on the face. Eyes bristling with hate, his contorted face was just inches from hers. Distended. Ready to explode. He was making inhuman, guttural noises.

Like a grade-B movie depiction of a Mardi Gras parade, his grotesque features bore down on her. His voice swelled in volume until it came crashing into her brain. Echoing and bouncing around the inside of her skull. Pounding from the inside, looking for a way out.

Her vision blurred. When he raised his clenched fist over her, all the little black dots that swam in front of her eyes melted into one big dot, and she felt herself sliding . . .

She crumpled to the floor.

Edward lowered his fist. His face pinched in anger, he ran his other hand through his sweat-dampened hair and looked down at her. For several seconds he didn't move.

Then both his face and his fist relaxed, and he dropped to one knee at Casey's side. He lifted her small frame and carried her to the couch. A few moments later, she awoke to his gentle touch as he applied a cold cloth to her forehead.

"I'm sorry you got mad at me, baby." It was the closest he ever came to an apology. Had it been funny, it could have been called a family joke.

Casey gave Edward a wan smile and turned her face to the back of the couch.

He reached toward her. With his hand mere inches from her, he stopped.

He straightened up abruptly, his jaw clenched. "Women! Who needs the hassle?"

He walked to the den and dropped into his recliner.

Casey lay motionless, feigning sleep. She doubted she would ever sleep soundly again.

The TV was droning away in the den. The grandfather clock ticked softly in the corner of the living room. She could even hear the comforting purr of the refrigerator motor. The familiar sounds of her happy home. Her heart felt like a lump of lead in her chest.

Maybe she'd lie here awhile. But what if he came back in and found the kitchen still in a shambles?

She raised herself up on one arm. Pain shot through her shoulder, and a wave of nausea rippled in her tummy. She laid her head down momentarily. Then she gritted her teeth against the pain and forced herself to get off the sofa and return to the kitchen.

She tiptoed around, cleaning up the mess. Gingerly picking up the broken glass, mopping the mayo, and trying unsuccessfully to polish the mark out of the parquet floor. She shoved the mangled toaster down into the trash bag where it wouldn't be seen and added the broken chair to the other larger casualties of battle, hidden in the garage. It wouldn't do for anyone to see them sticking out of the trash barrel.

Edward's ministry had to be protected at all costs. There were souls at stake.

"But how far am I willing to go, Lord? And how long before his violence destroys his ministry, anyway?" Casey stood in the garage, looking at the hidden stash. Two chairs, an end table, and a treasured floor lamp given to her by her mother. Countless small items had already been disposed of.

"He's destroying everything we've built together, including our marriage." Tears found their way down her cheeks as she crept to the bathroom. "Oh, God, what am I going to do?"

Casey flipped on the bathroom lights. With her left hand, she slowly unveiled her aching right shoulder. She maneuvered the mirrors to see her back and gasped at the reflection. A large red swelling and four mean-looking round bruises, where Edward's fingertips had gouged into her flesh. The redness extended down her arm, almost to her elbow.

She turned to draw her bath. Edward was standing in the doorway between the bathroom and their bedroom. His face was ashen. His eyes devoid of expression. She didn't breathe, waiting to see what he would do. Without a word he turned and flung himself onto the bed, slamming the headboard into the wall. Within seconds, Casey could hear his soft snoring.

She abandoned her plans for a bath and backed cautiously from the room, then darted into the guest room and locked the door behind her. Casey stared at the locked door. She clamped her left hand over her mouth and whimpered. Her right arm was throbbing.

"Who can I turn to? I don't want to dump this on Barrett. But I have no one to talk to."

Witt.

It was the first time she'd thought of him in several days. Life had been too hectic since the Sunday morning fiasco.

But how?

She would take a shopping trip to St. Michael. Could she find him? She'd have to take that chance.

A tiny ray of hope crept into Casey's fragile heart at the thought of seeing Witt.

11

Leaning into the brisk autumn wind, Casey made her way directly to the antique shop where she'd bumped into Witt last week. A little bell tinkled as she opened the door. And a petite old lady smiled and waved from the far corner.

But no Witt.

She'd hoped to run into him *accidentally*, but she was prepared to go looking. She longed for a few hours of tranquility before she had to face Edward again. But her shoulder was hurting, and she knew how angry he would be when he awoke to find her gone. It was going to be hard to relax.

She shivered and pulled her sweater closer around her neck.

Down each aisle, tucked into every corner of the little shop, were hundreds of whimsical items. Perhaps she could take a few minutes to look around.

She was halfway down the first aisle when a low, rasping snarl caused her to freeze in her tracks.

Who would keep a vicious dog in a shop like this?

It came again. Close and evil. No small dog. Maybe not a dog at all. It sounded more like . . . something from one of her living nightmares with Edward.

She changed her grip on her purse, preparing to use it as a weapon, if necessary, however ineffectual. Trembling, she turned to find herself looking straight into the fiendish yellow marble eyes of a concrete statuette. The gargoyle sat on the counter among a bunch of smaller knickknacks. Its three-foot-high, gnarled body poised to attack. Its horrific face permanently fixed in a hideous grin.

Casey, you're losing it. That ugly piece of concrete artwork did not growl.

She started to turn away, but its savage stare deepened. To her horror it revealed a spark of life.

"This is some sort of trick. Right?" She glanced in the shopkeeper's direction. The old lady was preoccupied with her dusting. Besides she hardly looked the type to play pranks on her customers.

Hands close to her sides, to not touch it, Casey leaned in to examine the gargoyle more closely. No visible wiring. She stepped back and watched. The fine hairs on the back of her neck bristled. No more signs of life. Convinced it had been her imagination, Casey began once more to turn away. The fulsome yellow eyes flickered. A whiff of that awful odor.

I've been waiting for you. The threat echoed from the caverns of hell.

A shudder of terror ran through her body when she realized she could not break eye contact. She tried desperately to extricate herself from the beast's compelling grip, but an unseen source of evil energy held her fast. Eye to eye, she was bound to the hypnotizing whirlpools of yellow.

It growled again. Low and vile. A small drop of saliva formed and began to seep slowly down the side of its ghoulish mouth. In vain, Casey battled against an illusional enemy. Struggling, all the while knowing this couldn't be happening.

Helplessly, she clamped her eyes shut, hoping when she opened them again, this hellish ogre would have lost its control over her. But the vision behind closed eyelids was even more terrifying in its familiarity. The same putrid yellow eyes were staring at her. But now they were glaring at her from Edward's face, only inches from hers. Blood vessels bulging, shrieking obscenities, he clamped his strong hands on either side of her head and wouldn't let her look away. His penetrating scrutiny was filled with loathing.

How had he found her in this little shop so far from home? She'd tried to put miles between them, but somehow he knew. Why was he mad at her today? Did he know the real reason she'd come to St. Michael? How could he? She'd come with only a glimmer of a hope in her heart that Witt would know what to do. *If she could find him.*

She forced her eyes open to blot out the image of Edward. The slimy gargoyle was still there—still in control. Its grin broadened to reveal a repulsive mouth full of jagged yellow teeth.

"This is not happening. I'll simply turn my head and start walking." But she couldn't wrest her eyes from the heinous face, and her feet refused to move.

"Let me go." A pitiful whimper escaped Casey's lips.

Smoldering eyes and sardonic grin, the ghoul bid her come closer.

"Please, *please*, Edward, don't do this."

Unable to withstand the forces that were pulling her like invisible tentacles, Casey was being sucked into its evil environment. The monster glowered contemptuously at her. Then like a horribly bloated dead frog, its features began to distend. It was going to envelop her . . .

"Oh, my Jesus," she moaned.

A tortured wail.

And blackness.

12

Witt was having coffee in the coffee shop not fifty feet down the street from the antique shop where he'd first met Casey. He'd skipped the strawberry pie today. And every day this week. He'd been so subdued, the girls nagged him to see a doctor.

They meant well. But he couldn't tell them all that had happened since last Friday. His life was turned upside down. And he hadn't stopped thinking about Casey all week. He was waiting for the Lord to bring them together again so he could help her begin sorting things out.

He'd thought about driving over the mountain Sunday morning to attend services at the Good Shepherd. But that could hardly be called waiting on the Lord. God would act soon. Witt had no choice but to wait.

He ground his teeth together and ordered a second cup of coffee. Before he could take his first sip, an overwhelming need for fresh air caused him to bolt from his booth and race to the front door of the café.

A dark blue Jetta was parked just a few spaces from Mrs. Anderson's antique shop.

"I wonder what Casey drives." He rubbed his hands together briskly and looked up and down Arkansas Avenue. He'd only seen the loaner she drove last week. And for all their talking, they hadn't gotten around to discussing vehicles.

A horn honked. He turned to see Pete and Maggie waving, evidently in town for their weekly grocery shopping. Maggie was sitting in the middle, close to Pete. And Pete was grinning from ear to ear.

Witt waved back and gave Pete a thumbs-up. *Thank You, Jesus.*

Breathing easier, but still vaguely agitated, Witt reluctantly turned to go back into the coffee shop. He needed to run to the clinic to go over some things with Al. But he was stalling, hoping Casey would walk in the door any minute.

Georgie held the phone over her head. "Dr. G., phone. It's Mrs. Anderson. She sounds pretty upset."

She'd never called him before. It must be urgent, or she'd have locked her shop and strolled over.

His brow knit as he took the receiver. "Yes, Mrs. A. What's up?"

"Witt, you need to come to my shop right away." The shopkeeper rushed through her words. "There's a lady here. She's fainted."

"Sure. Sure. Be right over." Fainting women weren't exactly a veterinary specialty, but if the woman truly needed medical intervention, he'd do in a pinch while the EMTs were on their way. "Georgie, I'll settle up later. A lady has fainted in Mrs. A.'s shop. If Casey comes in, please ask her to wait."

He hurried down the street to the antique shop, where he found Sadie Anderson wringing her frail hands over Casey's prone form.

"She stood there for a long time, looking at that ugly little statue. I thought at last someone was going to buy it and get it out of my store. But suddenly the pretty little thing just keeled over in a dead faint. What do you think is wrong with her, Dr. G.?"

He should've known she would go to the antique shop first. That's where she was headed when they collided last week. Had he been here, Casey wouldn't be lying on the floor with a possible head injury.

He knelt and lifted her wrist. Her breathing and pulse were normal. But she should've regained consciousness by now. He was surprised Mrs. A. didn't have smelling salts. Didn't all little old ladies have smelling salts in their medicine chests?

Deciding a neck or spinal injury was doubtful after a simple fainting spell, he carefully gathered her in his arms, carried her to the back room, and laid her on an antique daybed. He'd give it one more minute before they headed for the emergency room.

A sliver of sunshine found its way through the leaded glass window on the opposite wall and splashed fresh intensity on a timeworn quilt hanging on a rack behind Casey. One vibrant slice of color danced across her pale cheeks.

Casey stirred, then opened her eyes—wide and filled with dread. Witt dropped to her side on one knee and took her hand.

"You had us worried, little lady. What happened?"

Relief washed over Casey's face. "Oh, Witt, I'm so glad to see you. I—I'm not sure I know what happened."

She surveyed her surroundings. A Tiffany lamp on a nearby sideboard projected a Technicolor waterfall on the whitewashed brick wall.

"Where am I? Whose house is this?"

"We're in the back room of the little shop where we bumped into each other last week. You fainted. Do you remember?"

"Thank goodness. I thought I was caught in a time warp."

Witt smiled. Whatever was wrong, he was glad it hadn't dampened her sense of humor.

Mrs. Anderson slipped into a tiny adjoining kitchen.

"Mrs. A. has gone to make you a cup of black cherry tea. According to her, it'll cure anything."

"Oh, I hope I didn't offend her with the time warp remark. Does she live here?" She fingered the crocheted blanket that covered her. "I don't want to be a bother."

"Believe me, she took no offense. She has a great sense of humor. Yes, she lives here behind the store, and she would be offended if you didn't accept her hospitality. So we have all the time you need."

Witt squeezed her hand. "What are you doing in St. Michael, Casey? Is everything okay?"

He knew this was the moment the Lord was preparing him for. God had decided the timing, not Witt. God had initiated this meeting, not Witt.

"I drove in this morning to do some shopping. Need to go to

Walmart and run a few errands. And I . . . uh. I want . . . oh dear. Who am I trying to fool? I needed to see my friend again. And I was hoping I would run into you. Not literally, like the last time."

She lowered her eyelids. "Did you just happen to be in the shop when I . . . uh . . . passed out?"

Witt coaxed an errant curl from in front of her eye. "No, but I'm usually at the coffee shop about this time. Mrs. A. phoned over and said she had a lady lying in one of her aisles who needed help. So here I am."

"And so . . ." Her cheeks glowed bright red. "You carried me in here?"

"Sure did. I'm a lot stronger than Mrs. A." Witt flexed his bicep. His heart smiled. *She's even lovelier with cherry cheeks.*

"Tell me, what do you think caused you to faint? Are you sick? Should I get you to a doctor?"

"Oh, no. I'm okay. I've been fainting on a regular basis lately. But I don't think it's anything to worry about." She shook her head.

"Okay." He drawled out his words. "You're going to have to tell me more. I'll be the judge as to whether you need a doctor."

"Witt, I only faint when I get scared. I mean really scared. Not just surprised. And I always feel okay afterward. I'm sure it's nothing."

"Brought on by an emotionally charged situation?" Witt was getting more and more concerned.

"Uh-huh."

"Sounds like vasovagal syncope. Not usually serious, but I think you should have a checkup, anyway. And soon."

"I'm glad to hear it has a name. I'm sure that's what it is. And you said it's not serious, so that settles it." Casey started to sit up.

Witt gently laid his hand on her shoulder to prevent her from sitting up. "Forgive me for asking, but what in the world's happening that you're frightened on a regular basis? And what would put you in an emotional state here at Mrs. A.'s shop?"

She fidgeted with the blanket and avoided his gaze.

"I'm waiting. Come on . . . out with it."

Casey sighed.

Witt bided his time. He had all day.

96

"There's . . . there's a gargoyle in the shop." She bit her lip and looked up at Witt through damp lashes. "It growled at me. I mean . . . I thought it did."

Obviously, she was dead serious. He felt the hair on his arms galvanize. He pressed her hand between both of his as she spoke.

"I couldn't take my eyes off of it, Witt. This is going to sound weird, but it wouldn't let me look away. I tried. I really did. I felt foolish, but I said, 'Let me go.' It just grinned and . . . oh, heaven help me, it drooled. I know that sounds bizarre. I must be going crazy. But I saw it drool, and grin, and then . . ."

She stopped, staring into space. Her body stiffened.

"And then, what?" He stroked her hand.

Casey cleared her throat. "I felt like I was going to be sucked into its evil aura. It started getting bigger . . . and more grotesque. Oh Witt, please don't call the funny farm."

He didn't think she was crazy. There had to be some logical explanation for her horrific vision. The gargoyle certainly hadn't done anything but sit there and be ugly. Who was playing these tricks on Casey's mind?

"What happened next?"

"I knew I was going to faint. I moaned, 'Oh, my Jesus.' I heard a shriek, like an animal in pain. And the next thing I knew I was in this room, with you and Mrs. Anderson standing over me." She turned her head from him and looked at the ceiling. "I know you think I'm a nutcase. But it was alive, Witt. And it was really, really scaring me," she added, looking back at him. Tears brimmed in her eyes. "Is there such a thing as a demon? Is the gargoyle possessed? Or do you think I've lost it?"

"Whoa. Slow down. First, I don't think you're a nutcase. I've told Mrs. A. about that gargoyle. It's been here a long time, scaring the socks off of her wimpier customers."

She sat up and swung her legs around, making a mock bully face. "Like me?"

"Yes, like you."

He ducked, thinking she might bop him, and her mean look dissolved into a grin.

Witt flipped through the cash in his wallet. "You don't have to prove how brave you are. Least of all to me. I'm going to buy that ugly thing just to get it out of the shop. I'll take it to the rock quarry and have it crushed into a thousand pieces. And, little lady, you'd better believe there's such a thing as demons. But they can't inhabit an inanimate object."

Suddenly, Witt realized he was holding her hand again. He didn't want to give it up—but knew he must. He stood up, released her gently, and walked over to the little window. Pushed it open a crack.

"It's stuffy in here. Let's let some of that brisk October air in."

A picture-book grandma, complete with ruffled apron, Mrs. A. appeared in the doorway carrying a tray with Casey's tea.

"Please call me Sadie," she said to Casey as she laid the tray on the sideboard. "Dr. G. insists on calling me Mrs. Anderson or Mrs. A., but I'd like you to call me Sadie, seein' as how that's my given name."

"Sadie it is. I'm Casey. I'm very glad to meet you. And I'm sorry I've put you to so much trouble. Thank you for the tea." Casey reached for the cup and took a sip. "Ooh, that's good."

Witt whispered—a stage whisper—in the old gal's ear. "I'll start calling you Sadie when you call me Witt." He planted a kiss on the top of Sadie's shining white hair, in front of her bun.

"Oh dear, I couldn't do that." Sadie tilted her head way back to peer at his face through her bifocals. "You're a doctor. Now, I am going to leave you alone with your patient. You must find out why she fainted, and do something about it." She patted his wrist. "It could happen when there is no one around who cares, you know."

Running her hand over the folds in her apron, she glided through the curtained doorway without another word.

Witt plunked down in a rocking chair, one leg over the arm. "Drink up, Casey. When you're ready, we can walk over to the park or take a little ride, if you'd like."

Her empty teacup rattled in its saucer. "Do we have to go through the store?"

Witt was concerned that the gargoyle filled her with such anxiety. A grown woman being frightened by a piece of vile concrete artwork was hard to comprehend, unless she actually was the target of demonic activity. If he could get her to talk about it, he might uncover her real problem. The problem God had turned over to him to fix.

"We have to go through the store, but we won't come within twenty feet of the little ghoul. And I'll be with you." He took the tea-cup and saucer from her and set it on the tray.

"Hold my hand. Don't look to your right and you won't make eye contact. It'll be okay. Come on, let's get some fresh air." Witt glanced toward the gargoyle as he led her out. It was surrounded by an eerie darkness. The hair on the back of his neck stood up, and he pulled Casey closer to his side.

She gripped his hand like a little child, following him through the store, taking small, cautious steps. She kept her head turned all the way to the left.

The little bell tinkled and Witt called out, "We're leaving now, Mrs. A., I'll stop in later today. I'm buying that monstrosity."

"Oh, how wonderful. But what will you do with it, Dr. G.?"

"Don't ask." He smiled and closed the door behind them.

When they stepped out into the chilly, bright day, Casey breathed a sigh of relief.

"Walk or ride?" Witt asked. "It's your call."

"I think ride . . . I still feel a little woozy. I'll be glad when that thing is gone, Witt. I really like Sadie and I'd like to go back into her shop, but I can't as long as that little sucker is there."

"I know it's surrounded by an aura of evil, Ka . . . Casey."

He'd been calling this woman Katherine in his prayers and dreams most of his life. He would have to be more careful. But she didn't seem to notice his slip of the tongue.

"I hope you'll tell me what you were feeling in there so we can get to the bottom of this. When you're up to it, that is."

They headed in the opposite direction of the coffee shop, Casey guided by Witt's ever-so-light touch to her waist.

"Casey, you said you needed to see me. Be honest with me. What's the matter? I'm flattered. But you didn't say you *wanted* to see me. You said you *needed* to see me. Well, here I am. Talk to me."

"Oh, Witt, I was going to pour my heart out to you and tell you all my troubles. But I'm afraid if I dump all that on you, you won't think as much of me. New friendships are delicate. I don't want to lose ours because I blab too much."

His heart ached for her. She seemed so vulnerable.

"*Real* friendships are never delicate, Casey. You can tell me anything. I think God had us meet for a purpose. Perhaps because you need a friend, and I want to be one. But whatever His reason, you can be sure I won't quench the Spirit." He tried to think of a way to put her more at ease. "You know, I may not be as together as you think. What if I share a few of my problems with you too? Think you could handle that?" He grinned.

"Sure. Everyone needs a best friend. One problem—I don't think my husband could handle my having a *guy* for a best friend."

"Well, you *are* an attractive lady." Witt stopped to look in a store window. He dare not look into her eyes while he was asking his next question. "Is he the jealous type?"

"All of a sudden, yes. Didn't used to be."

"Well, you and I both know how unique it was . . . the way we met and hit it off. But I don't want to keep secrets from your husband. You'll have to make that call. Tell him if you think it's wise. Whatever you decide, we won't abuse his trust. But let's see what God has up His sleeve."

He knew no other way to handle it. God hadn't given him a clue how he was going to spend time with another man's wife. But neither did He tell him how long it was going to take. Witt's part in this mission might be completed today.

For a fleeting moment he wondered if Edward deserved their consideration. But *that* was the kind of thought Witt had promised he wouldn't harbor. And the Lord said He'd be there for him when those thoughts surfaced.

Casey wrinkled her nose and shook her head.

"Actually, I tried to tell Edward how we became good friends in record time, but he turned me off because I was interrupting a game he was watching. So I'm not feeling guilty."

Witt stopped beside an old model Jeep. "Here's our ride, Casey."

100

She raised her eyebrows. "Do you have a step ladder for me to get into this thing?"

Before he could respond, Casey climbed gingerly into the vehicle. She winced and blinked away tears.

He saw the pain in her eyes and longed to hold her and comfort her. Could the fall in Mrs. A.'s store have hurt her more than she would admit? Or was it something else—something so horrific she didn't want to talk about it?

"I'd better put the top on. You'll freeze to death."

"Not on your life. If you can take it, I can. I'm not as big a wimp as you think." Casey peered into the backseat. "I can pull one of these horse blankets around me if I need to."

Witt grinned and pulled out into traffic. "Okay, here we go. Yell 'uncle' if you get cold."

A few miles out of town Casey reached into the backseat to get a blanket. Witt noticed her awkward movement and attributed it to pain. He had to stuff the impulse to pull over, draw her close, and kiss away the hurt.

He gestured that he'd stop and put the top on. She shook her head. She was smiling and the wind was whipping through her lovely cinnamon- and-sugar hair. There was too much road noise for conversation. But Witt didn't need words. The love of his life was by his side.

The mountain view was breathtaking this time of year. Gold and red autumn hues with an occasional splash of deep green where the pine trees huddled, all rising to meet the azure sky.

Casey laid her head back against the seat and gazed at the sky. She spoke against the wind to Witt.

He cocked his head and wrinkled his brow. He couldn't hear a word she was saying.

"This is the way God created us to feel," she shouted.

"You bet. Except I think He'd want us to feel this way on a full stomach."

Casey laughed and nodded.

He was off the road, pulling into a country café, before the echo of her laugher had faded.

"You must know every coffee shop and café in this area." She was tugging at her tangled locks with a hairbrush.

His voice was thick with emotion. "Don't brush it too much. It looks great all mussed like that."

That was too familiar. I've got to be more careful.

Casey apparently didn't notice. She grinned and chucked her brush back into her purse.

Thank God she remained unaware of his feelings, despite his clumsiness.

"It's one of the perks of being a small-town vet. My clients dotted this countryside. Not only did I learn where all the good cafés were, I got some wonderful home-cooked meals, too—in addition to the ones Sarah left in the fridge. Sometimes I'd take Sarah's meal to Mrs. A. She doesn't cook much for herself anymore. Since I retired I take her out to supper once in a while. I hear we're a hot item in town."

"I bet you are. Oh, I know she enjoys that, Witt. That's so sweet of you."

"Oh, pshaw." He executed a deep bow. "And now you know . . ."

Casey giggled and put her fingers in her ears. "Oh, please, spare me."

". . . the rest of the story."

"You just had to say it, didn't you?"

Witt did a silly little double step and they both laughed.

Very soon, he knew, they'd have to get down to brass tacks. But until then, she needed every laugh he could drum up.

The café was deserted. They were too late for breakfast and too early for lunch. Witt chose a booth in the farthest corner.

As soon as they were seated, he took both of Casey's hands in his. "Little lady, what happened to you today sounds mighty like demon activity."

"So, I'm not crazy—it *was* a demon?" Casey looked relieved. "That's good news, right?"

"I don't know how good it is. But you're definitely not crazy. Demons often hang around something evil-appearing, like the gargoyle, looking for a habitat. Actually, they can hang around anywhere they want. But they prefer ungodly surroundings. Guess it makes them feel at home."

Witt leaned forward. "Sometimes Christians can sense their presence. I felt it as we were leaving the shop. But seldom do demons attack one of God's people. Except in all-out warfare where they can use a Christian to their advantage."

Casey looked down at the table and began trembling.

Witt lifted her chin. "Little friend, is there something you're not telling me?"

13

Casey shifted in her seat. "I . . . I . . . don't know where to begin. I hate to admit some of the things I've done. I'm depending on you . . . that true friendships are not fragile."

Witt reached over and squeezed her hand. "God loves you and so do I."

There. He'd said it. Not in the way he'd like to. But the words were out there and it felt good.

She started with Allen. Giving Witt only the necessary facts about the affair, her pregnancy, the years of deception, and Allen's choice after she gave him an ultimatum.

If only I'd known.

All the questions he'd pondered about Allen over the years were answered. Allen was a fool. Plain and simple.

When she told him she'd thrown her wedding rings down the street as far as she could, he said, "Atta girl!"

"I know someone found them." She smiled through her tears. "And for them it must've been like Christmas."

Witt could tell she was embarrassed, but she didn't have to be. He felt only sadness that she hadn't known the joy of sharing a new little life with a loving husband.

Casey told him how she met and married Edward. At Witt's urging she covered the high points of seventeen happy years of serving the Lord and raising Barrett together.

Their marriage sounded great. Had Allen reentered her life to cause problems?

Casey dug in her purse. She popped two pills and took a deep breath. He couldn't see what they were, but hoped they were only aspirins.

Then she brought Witt to the present.

Dumbfounded, he listened as she recounted temper tantrums. Name calling. Forgotten sermons. Odd odors. Spectral shadows and voices. She wound it up with terrible things Edward had said to her last night. Then she stopped abruptly, leaving Witt waiting for the end of the story.

The gravity of her situation made him want to take her in his arms even more. But as bad as it sounded, he had the ominous feeling she was still holding something back.

"I know I'm not the perfect wife, Witt, but I don't know what I'm doing to bring on his fits of temper."

"It's not you, Casey. I know what kind of person you are. And I think I know from what you've told me what kind of person Edward is. And he's *not* the person he's become. If that makes any sense."

She nodded.

He clenched his napkin in his lap so he wouldn't be tempted to reach out and touch her.

"Did he have a problem with Barrett being born out of wedlock?"

A waitress appeared at their booth with a menu.

Witt didn't want to lose their momentum. Casey was finally talking. "Just a couple of burgers, please. Hold the onions. And coffee."

He looked back at Casey. "That good with you?"

She nodded.

Casey waited until the waitress was out of earshot. "Not in the beginning. He was wonderful. He gave Barrett his name and his devotion. Until recently you'd have thought I was as pure as the driven snow when we married." She paused and covered her brightening cheeks with her hands. "But now there's a negative force in our home that's destroying it from within. He won't acknowledge it and I can't stop it."

Casey made little circles on the tablecloth with one fingernail. "I'm sorry for putting this burden on you. But obviously I can't share it with my pastor."

She looked up, her amber eyes searching his face. "Witt, I guess I'm asking you to be my spiritual leader. My priest. That's a lot to ask, isn't it?"

No, it's not a lot to ask. Say the word and I'd die for you.

He patted her hand. "I believe we met by divine appointment, little one, so you'd have a shoulder to lean on. And someone to pray with."

All the pieces of the puzzle were falling into place. Edward was in deep trouble. And so was Casey. Along with them, their church. A church that'd been on fire for the Lord and selflessly doing His work for several years. Seeing conversion after conversion as a reward for their efforts. The Lord must be pleased with this body of believers. Now He'd placed their future in Witt's hands. All he had to do was ignore the longings of his heart.

The café door opened and two men walked in. One short and plump. The other taller and well built. The latter had sandy hair, graying at the temples, and a deep tan.

Casey turned her back to the door, slinked down in the booth, and started trembling.

Witt looked around but saw nothing unusual. "You all right?"

In a ragged voice, she asked, "Can we leave now, Witt?"

"Of course, if that's what you want." He lowered his head, trying to see into her eyes. But she avoided his gaze. "Should I get the burgers to go?"

The sandy-haired man approached their booth, and Casey turned her face to the wall. He touched her shoulder. She squealed and put both hands over her head. Witt was on his feet and between the two of them in an instant.

The stranger backed away, his hands in front of him, palms out. "I'm sorry. I didn't mean to startle the lady. But her sweater is on the floor under the table."

Witt extended his hand to the man. "Our apologies. And thank you." He reached down and picked up Casey's sweater.

She was sobbing.

Holding her close to his heart, like a mother hen covers her chicks with her wings, Witt walked Casey to the door.

He lifted her into the Jeep and belted her in. Without taking his eyes off her, he took a few minutes to put the top on. The backseat compartment had never seemed dingy and smelly before, but it did today.

"I'll be right back, Casey. I've got to run in and pay."

Witt stood in the doorway of the café, watching over Casey. Moments later he trotted out with a bag of burgers and coffee.

"I thought the guy with the sandy hair was a nice touch. Don't you?"

"What does it matter? We're wasting our time with them. They're both Christians."

"Who says we can't have a little fun on the side? I've never ridden in a Jeep before."

"I can fly backward faster."

"Watch this." The hairy ghoul lunged at Casey's head.

She winced, but kept staring out the window.

"Ha! Big scary ghoul."

"Okay, try this on for size." He slipped out the crack between the windows and disappeared. A nanosecond later he came plunging from outer space and dived into the window right in front of Casey's eyes.

His guts slid down the window. Talons grated against the glass.

Casey winced and wrinkled her nose. And continued staring.

Much thinner, he reappeared in the backseat. "Did you see her that time?"

"Big deal. She shuddered. Was it worth the pain?"

"It doesn't get any better than to creep out a Christian, if only for a second. That's what it's all about."

"No, *here's* what it's all about." Floating up to Witt's ear, the blistered, bloated demon whispered, "Take her in your arms. You know that's what you want. And why shouldn't you? Her husband's a scumbag."

A couple of miles down the road, Witt tried again. "Do you want to talk about it, Casey?"

"I thought it was Edward." She was staring straight ahead. She wrinkled her nose again and shuddered.

"Casey, you put your hands over your head. Does Edward hit you?"

"No."

Witt was pulling off the road into a roadside park. "Then why are you so frightened?"

He released his seat belt and reached over to unlatch hers. "Casey? Talk to me."

She turned to him and the urge to take her in his arms was overwhelming. Witt reached out with his left hand to draw her closer.

She yelped at his touch.

"What? Did I hurt you?"

"It's nothing, Witt. Edward grabbed me kind of hard last night and bruised my shoulder."

Witt could feel the heat of anger rising in his face. It wasn't an emotion he had embraced very often.

"He didn't mean to hurt me, Witt."

He clenched his jaws. "That's . . . not acceptable, Casey. You've got to get out of there before he hurts you badly. You say he's strong. You're a small woman. A well-placed blow from his fist could kill you."

He reached for the ignition. "We need to get you to a doctor for that shoulder."

She laid her hand on his arm. "No. I'm okay. Just a little bruised. I shouldn't have told you. And I can't leave Edward. There's got to be another way."

Witt leaned back in his seat, hands gripping the steering wheel. How could he make her see?

Casey took one of his hands off the steering wheel and held it in both of hers. "I can't believe I've unloaded all this on you the second time we've met. I wouldn't blame you if you ran for your life. Who needs this drama? You say you don't have it all together, but I think you do."

Tightening his grip with his other hand, Witt tried to conceal his frustration. It was so hard to not return her gentle touch. "Well, I've settled into a pretty comfortable rut. But if I can't be here for you and"—he could hardly speak the name—"Edward, I'm not much good to God, am I?"

He didn't want to acknowledge Edward's needs. He was fighting a battle to not hate the man. But if he could've laid hands on him at that moment, God would've been very disappointed.

Oh, Lord God, what kind of man would physically attack this precious woman?

His answer came before he finished thinking the question.

One that is demon possessed.

A wave of shame rippled through him. How could he have allowed Satan the smallest of victories by entertaining the thought of smashing the pastor into the ground? The realization that Edward had injured the woman he loved had knocked him off his pins.

Please, dear God, I'm too close to this. I can't do it. Please find another. Someone who doesn't love Katherine so dearly.

Surely an almighty God could understand He was asking too much of this mortal.

It's because of your great love I have chosen you.

The words resounded in his heart as clearly as if God were in the Jeep with them. And only a fool argues with God.

Witt Gregory was no fool.

He stepped out of the Jeep and hurried around to Casey's side. "The sun's still pretty warm, little one. Let's check out this nature trail and have a talk."

Casey blotted her eyes and smiled weakly. "Yes, I need to move around and try to shake this little black cloud that's hanging over me."

He took her hand to help her out of the Jeep and his heart leaped in his chest. Guiding her down the stone steps leading to the woods, he realized this trail walk was a bad idea.

"Wait here, Casey. I'm going to grab my Bible." He returned to the Jeep and walked back, clutching his Bible over his errant heart. *Thank You, Jesus.*

"Casey, God's given us a lot of weapons to fight Satan, but the one I want you to remember when Edward is raging is the name of Jesus. Remember the groan you heard when you whispered the name of Jesus to the gargoyle? That wasn't your imagination. Demons can't stand against the name of Jesus."

"Okay. You've got my promise. But I don't expect to be encountering any more demons anytime soon."

Witt held up a branch to keep it from catching in her hair. "Maybe sooner than you think."

She stopped in her tracks.

He touched her arm. "Casey, I don't know any easy way to say this. I believe Edward may be demon possessed."

She spun around. "Edward's not a demon, Witt. He might be acting pretty awful, but he's saved and he loves the Lord."

"Sweet lady, by his actions, your Edward seems to be harboring one or more demons. And I don't mean to scare you, but we can't know the state of his salvation. I don't think it's safe for you to live with him. I know Mrs. A. would be glad to take you in for a while, until he gets right. She has an extra room. Please let me talk to her about it."

He had to make her understand things could get worse . . . and soon. Satan was on the fast track with Edward.

She lowered her eyes. "I'm sorry. I know you're trying to help. But that's out of the question. If I didn't live with Edward, it'd get around the church, and his ministry would be ruined in no time."

"It's going to be ruined anyway. Don't you see? Without deliverance he has nowhere to go but down. The weaker he gets, the more of Satan's demons will pile on him."

"Witt, I know I asked for your help. But I've been married to Edward for almost twenty years. I know he wouldn't, for one moment, consider deliverance. He's very much opposed to the idea demons can live in people. I . . . I . . . don't know how I'd even begin to talk to him about it. It would probably bring on World War III. And I can't move out. I don't know what to do. But I can't do *that*."

She wasn't ready to face the truth and he couldn't force her.

"We can pray, Casey. Around the clock. And you've got to be ready to call on the name of Jesus at the first hint Edward is losing his temper. From what you've told me, I think the demon of violence is firmly established in him. There may be others. But none of them can stand up to the name of Jesus."

"You really think *I* can subdue demons by calling on the name of Jesus?"

"Yes, I do."

"I don't know if I can be convincing."

"Casey, you *whispered* the name of Jesus to the gargoyle and the demon left with a shriek. *You* don't have to be convincing. Jesus is convincing."

"I'm confused. You told me an inanimate object couldn't be demon possessed. And now you're talking about the demon in the gargoyle. How can that be if . . ."

"Not the demon *in* the gargoyle. You heard a shriek coming from the gargoyle. But you saw it drool, grin, and grow larger. Casey, we both know it wasn't real. A demon was playing back terrifying scenes from Edward's tantrums to frighten you. But it wasn't in the gargoyle. It could be anywhere, waiting for you. I'm convinced it can't possess you, because you're a child of God."

If I'm right, then Edward is not a child of God. Oh, my Lord, please protect her.

"Then why are these things happening to me?"

"Casey, demons will try to attach themselves to you, so the next time Edward gets violent, you'll fall apart . . . and faint. But you can ward them off with Jesus's name."

Casey looked bewildered.

"I know this must sound weird to you. I hope you don't think I'm some sort of nutcase. You've been looking at me kind of funny. I'm probably going too fast. But, little one, I've seen this before. I fear for your safety."

"Witt, I'm the one who saw the gargoyle grin, drool, and grow. If someone had said something like that to me as recently as yesterday, I'd have thought they'd gone bonkers. I don't think you're a nutcase.

It's a little much, that's all. But it is, in fact, the first thing that's made any sense since Edward changed."

She turned on the path and gazed back toward the Jeep. Determination steeled her voice. "At least I can see this is all a part of a plan, and I can see where Satan's going with it. I agree with you that God arranged our meeting." Her voice softened. "But forgive me, Witt, I simply can't go along with deliverance. It's too far out. Edward would freak."

"I won't try to force it." He shook his head in disappointment. "It's just that . . . oh, never mind. I'll drop it for now. To be continued."

"No, tell me what's on your mind."

"I won't nag you after this, but I know this couple, Ron and Indi. They have a ministry of deliverance. They're the most spiritual two people you'll ever meet. And if you'd allow them into your life, they'd handle it from there. Just make friends with Indi and the four of you can get together for dinner or something. Edward would never know you had anything to do with it. If I know Ron, he'd have Edward delivered and safe before he knew what hit him."

"Witt, you're so much more knowledgeable than I about all things spiritual . . ."

"I'm a mere babe compared to Ron and Indi. Oops. Sorry."

"I can't accept that Edward isn't saved. You've never seen him in action. When he speaks the Holy Spirit is so evident. Until lately. And he's led hundreds of people to the Lord."

"Casey, it's not for me to say whether he's saved or not. But he seems far too vulnerable to the wiles of the Devil. I could be wrong. I hope I am.

"Plenty of dynamic preachers have gotten saved under someone else's ministry. They suddenly realize although they loved the Lord and knew all the right things to say—and He seemed to be blessing their ministry—they'd never taken that big step of turning their all over to Jesus. In fact, they got so caught up in the success of their ministry they didn't realize the irony of the situation."

Casey was nibbling at a fingernail. "I never knew."

"Kind of like it being tougher for a rich man to come to the Lord than a poor one. The poor fellow turns to the Lord daily for his needs.

The rich guy gets by very well without groveling. Sometimes the Lord has to hit the rich man over the head with something to get his attention. Understand?"

"I guess I do. But it's scary to think he may not be saved."

"Prayer, Casey, prayer. That's our answer. I've no doubt the Lord has His hand in this situation and if we're obedient, the end result will be to His glory."

He watched her as she knelt down to tighten a shoelace. Even with her eyes a little puffy from crying, she was as beautiful as the first day he saw her. Like a fresh summer breeze wafting across a fragrant pond. Yes, she still made him think in poetry. Overwhelmed with tenderness for this gentle lady, he wanted nothing more than to whisk her away from everything ugly. He could get her to leave Edward—for him—if he really tried. Then, he'd devote the rest of his life to making her happy. Surely God wouldn't hold that against him.

Wait. And Satan said to Eve in the garden, Surely you will not die. But Satan's a liar and he'll say whatever we want to hear, to turn us from God.

He closed his eyes. *Father God, please help me to get my thoughts, and my heart, right. Remind me of why You've put me here with her.* Over and over, he repeated the words to himself, *not my will, not my will,* until the Holy Spirit cleared his head and gave him a vision.

He saw a large crowd of people. Himself, Casey, Edward, the hundreds Edward had led to the Lord, as well as hundreds more that would come to a saving knowledge of Christ as a result of Edward's continuing ministry . . . if Witt were to remain true.

A dark cloud appeared over them and cast an ominous shadow over more than half of the people. They faded from sight. Witt cried out. "No! Satan, get behind me." The cloud passed over and the people reappeared. They all began praising the Lord and celebrating Witt's victory over Satan.

The vision faded. He opened his eyes.

Casey was sitting on a big rock with her head in her hands. He saw in her a sister in Christ, in need of a touch from the Lord. He saw a good woman grieving for her husband, lost in the clutches of

Satan. And he saw a dear friend whom he could only hurt by his declaring his love.

He sat down beside her. "Casey, do you recall the exact time Edward began to change?"

She straightened up and looked at him. "It was the Cadillac. Three years ago. He was always so sweet and humble before he got that car. But the day Brother Mike bought him the Cadillac, he came home with a different attitude."

Yes. As Witt suspected, there were other demons at work besides Violence.

"He left home that morning in our old rattletrap and came home that evening in a brand-new paid-for luxury vehicle, compliments of Brother Mike. He's so proud of it. It doesn't even bother him that he didn't earn it. It was given to him by a foolish old man. Does the pride in him make him violent?"

"No, I think the demon of violence has a good grip on him. But perhaps Pride was the first in and he's opened the door to others." The more Witt heard, the more he feared for Casey if she stayed with Edward.

Casey brightened. She stood up, then crouched down in front of Witt, her hands on his knees. "Could I cast the demons out of him myself? You know, not involve others." Her eyes searched his face. "Maybe I could do it while he's raging and he'll never know what happened."

He wanted to jump up to get her hands off him. How much could he take?

"I'm afraid the casting out of demons is not that easy. Satan's crafty, Casey. You'd be outnumbered and on unfamiliar ground. Promise me you'll forget that idea. And while you're promising . . . promise you'll think about Indi and Ron. I said I wouldn't nag you, but just pray about it, okay? Now, we'd better head back to town. We don't want to give Edward reason to be angry.

"Besides, this rock is getting hard." He pushed up, his muscles stiff from sitting on the cold stone.

Casey shot him a quick grin. "Yes. The Jeep seats are comfy by comparison."

While Casey was buckling up, Witt scribbled his phone number on an old receipt and handed it to her. "Memorize this, then throw it away. You can call me anytime. And if you change your mind about getting out of the house, call me. Please . . ."

She glanced at the paper, folded it into a tiny square, and tucked it into her purse. He knew she wasn't going to call. All he could do was pray this, too, was part of His plan and Casey would be safe.

Witt offered Casey the bag of burgers off the backseat. "Sorry, I guess they're cold by now."

Casey shook her head. "No thanks. Not hungry, anyway. You want one?"

"Nah. Too worried about you to eat."

They rode the rest of the way to town in silence. The gaiety they usually enjoyed had been dampened by the naked truth about Edward.

Back in St. Michael, the sun was hiding behind the city buildings, casting long shadows just like it had last week when they parted.

Casey looked up at him. "Witt, I don't know how I'd make it through this without you." She put her hand on his arm. "Remember how you put your arms around me the first time we met? Has it been only a week? You knew exactly what I needed. And you had the boldness to do it. It was like throwing a life preserver to a drowning woman. Would you do that for me again?"

He hesitated, uncertain of the wisdom in holding her. But how could he refuse? He hoped he could hold her without crushing her to his heart. And putting his lips to hers . . .

He put his arms lightly around her shoulders. This time she wrapped her arms firmly around his waist and rested her cheek on his chest. He recalled the innocence with which he'd held her the first time. He'd surprised himself by being so forward. Something in him made him want to comfort a lady in distress. Now he knew that *something* was the Holy Spirit. Had he not followed the lead, they may have made their apologies and gone their separate ways. Never to know God's plan for him in her life.

The nearness and the light, sweet scent of her was wreaking havoc with his heart. No matter how many times he turned it over to the

Lord, Satan continued to tempt him with desire for the girl he had loved so long.

Calling on his tremendous willpower, borne of his faith, Witt pulled away. With a catch in his throat, he said, "Drive carefully, precious . . . friend."

He helped her into her car and made sure her seat belt was on and her doors were locked. Then he turned quickly, hoping she hadn't seen the raw emotion in his eyes.

Only after he was in his Jeep, his face partially obscured, did he turn and wave.

14

Edward awoke before Casey did. He rolled over, propped his head up on one arm, and watched her breathe. The dim morning light that seeped through the slats of the Venetian blinds nestled on her face. Without makeup, her freckled face looked like that of a guileless child. So peaceful.

But he knew Casey had no peace in her life. And he was the reason. His bouts of temper and his incessant badgering kept her in constant upheaval. He was surprised she was able to sleep at all.

But he was in turmoil too. He had no idea why. Didn't he have everything a man could want? An adoring wife, a successful ministry, financial security, and a devoted congregation. It was certainly much more than he'd expected out of life. He'd have been content with a lot less, as long as he could minister God's Word.

But somewhere along the way possessions had become more important than people. He cajoled and manipulated those who trusted him, until they gave him what he wanted. And he tortured the one person in the world who loved him the most. He chewed at his lower lip and reached out to touch her hair.

Casey stirred.

He laid his head back on the pillow and closed his eyes. But she didn't awaken, so he resumed his position of scrutiny and began listing her virtues. He felt a compulsion, a need to punish himself for what he was doing to her by reminding himself what he inevitably would lose.

She was compassionate. The lowliest of creatures found favor in her eyes. Even an opossum in need was welcome in her home.

She was patient. She put up with him. His tantrums and insults. And never complained.

She was loyal. She never threatened to leave and she never shared her misery with anyone, because it could cause a problem for *him* in his ministry.

But how long before she couldn't take any more and left him?

Or worse, what if she didn't leave? What if the day came when his fists took on a life of their own the way his tongue already had?

He'd already hurt her once. He hadn't meant to.

I lost control. Oh God, what if I kill her?

That seemed pretty far-fetched. But once it had been far-fetched to think he would throw his Bible across the room and curse God.

When these rages of anger came upon him, he wasn't in control.

But who was?

"I've got to get help before I destroy everything God has given me."

To whom could he turn—the respected pastor of a fast-growing church?

The only person in the congregation he'd feel comfortable confiding in was Brother Mike. He'd have to go looking for him, though. That old man didn't let any grass grow under his feet. *Maybe if I get an early start I can still catch him at home.*

He slipped out of bed and gathered his clothes, shaving gear, comb, and toothbrush. He dressed in Casey's bathroom to avoid waking her. She deserved a few more moments of innocence and rest.

Twenty minutes later, with the sun just peeping over the horizon, Edward pulled out of the drive. He'd left a note for Casey that he was going in early to study and didn't want to be disturbed. It was a lie. But the end result would justify *one little white lie.* This was a good plan. Yes, very good.

"Hey, Mothball, I see you finally got one toe in the door. Not much of a lie, though." Pride exposed his gnarled teeth in a fulsome grin. "I don't see it clinching the deal on his soul."

The tiny white demon's lips creased in an oily smile. "When you consider he's never told her even the smallest of untruths, it's not that bad. You know, getting clergy to lie isn't always easy. It's not like politics. But the lies will get bigger."

"You'd better hope so. One good wind and you're gonna blow away."

"I'll be bigger than you by next week. I've got every detail planned right up to the day he croaks."

"Yeah, right." Pride's wingspan had gotten bigger. He preened. "Where'd you get those wings? Off a dead mosquito?" He slapped his knee and slime flew in all directions.

With a mighty whoosh he took to the air. He had to get to Mike's house. There was work to be done before Edward arrived. And he didn't want to let Edward out of his sight for long.

The demon of lies, aka Mothball, beat his little wings as fast as he could to keep up. "I gotta get busy on McAlester. I hate being small. Wish I really did have a plan."

Edward didn't feel like his usual dapper self this morning. His choice of clothes in the predawn light hadn't been the greatest. But he tried not to care. And old Mike Hendricks certainly wouldn't. This was going to be a great day.

Brother Mike's pickup was still in his driveway. Edward stood poised with his hand ready to knock on the kitchen door.

What if he wants to call all the elders together for prayer?

Edward shook his head to shut out the voice.

And knocked.

How do you know you can trust him?

121

"Shut up." He looked around to be sure no one had heard him.

He knocked again. No answer. He tried the door. Locked.

Edward walked around the back. Mike wasn't in his shop. It looked like he'd recently hoed his winter garden; but he wasn't in it, and all the tools were neatly hung on the side of the storage building. Mike's four-wheeler and tractor were parked in the shed.

He's avoiding you. Face it, no one cares about your problems. But we do.

Edward's head started throbbing. He turned full circle, looking for a sign of the old man. He was nowhere to be seen. Someone must have picked him up this morning.

Deflated, he climbed into his car and started the engine.

"Guess I'll go by the church. He could be there."

Meerkat was stretched out on a rafter, catching a few rays through a hole in the roof. The warmth of the sun caused his hide to weep a resinous substance. Below him, Mike Hendricks picked up boards that had fallen out of the ceiling of the old shack.

"I need to tear this old place down. It's a fire hazard and an eyesore. And it stinks to the high heavens."

There was an inch of dust on everything. And cigarette butts and empty beer cans. The place had a lived-in-by-demons look.

"Looks like someone's been having parties back here. That good-fer-nothin' kid and his druggie friends, mos' likely. They better not let me catch 'em."

Meerkat scowled at Pharm-Boy. "He's hacked. I knew you shouldn't have told his nephew about this place. Now the old codger is going to tear down our digs."

"He's not gonna tear anything down. He's too busy. I'll get him outa here." Pharm-Boy, the demon of drugs, blew a toxic cloud of dust into Mike's face.

Coughing and gagging, Mike exploded from the shack. "Enough of that for one day. I got stuff to do in town."

One hinge held the door on. He pushed it shut as far as he could and limped down the path through the woods toward his house.

"Pride wanted the old geezer out of his house for a while." Pharm-Boy looked down at a drop of resin on his foot. "You're dripping on me, slug."

He took flight and plowed into Meerkat, knocking him from his perch. "As I was saying, Pride couldn't let old Mikey-boy and McAlester get together and spoil everything. So he put a bug in the old man's ear that this place was an eyesore and needed checking on *right away*." He snorted. "Well, I got clients to call on. Have a good rest, Beeping Sleauty."

Pharm-Boy whirred his wings furiously to stir up a ton of dust and made a new hole in the roof with his exit.

Edward paced his office floor.

Brother Mike wasn't around. He wasn't in the mood to study, and he looked like a clown in his mismatched clothes.

He strode down the hall and ducked into the men's restroom. It was empty. Leaning against the marble basin, he stared at his image. His face hadn't changed. A little older, more tired, maybe. But he was still Edward McAlester, Christian . . . pastor . . . husband. Still a presentable human being. Not sporting horns or canine fangs. He wet his hands at the sink and smoothed his hair back.

No one knew he and Casey had problems. Everyone thought they had the perfect marriage. Why should he ruin it by admitting that in his private life he abused his wife? Once those words were spoken there was no taking them back. And they *would* come back to haunt him.

Maybe it was better if he didn't talk to Mike. Or anyone.

But if he didn't get help, how was he ever going to change? All his good intentions didn't amount to a hill of beans.

Tears of desperation burned his eyes. "Flow, tears. Wash me clean." Tears streamed down his face. He cried until his throat was raw and there were no more tears.

But he didn't hear any words from God. No miraculous transformation. He was just as wretched.

He splashed his face with cold water. Snatching a couple of paper towels, he rubbed it vigorously.

If only I could rub away my shame.

He heard the hall door open and slipped into a stall.

Several boys from the youth department came in. It was teacher's work day and some of the kids had gathered in the gym to shoot hoops.

As he listened to them chatter, the irony of it hit him. The pastor of the fastest growing church in the county, he was hiding from the youth in a stall in the men's rest room. A wave of nausea hit him and he thought he was going to lose it right there.

The boys laughed as they went back into the hallway.

Did they see my shoes and know I was hiding in here?

Cautiously, he opened the booth door and peered out. They were gone.

He waited a moment. Then slipped into the hall and hurried toward the rear exit. He'd walk around the building to his car. He didn't want to run into anyone looking the way he did.

He made his way to the parking lot, taking a shortcut through the hedge. The same shortcut he forbade others to take because it would, in time, cause a hole in the hedge. He was almost to his car when he heard footsteps.

"Yo, Pastor."

Drat! It was Elder John, running up behind him. From his heavy breathing it was obvious John didn't do much running. He didn't watch his weight either. Younger than Edward by at least fifteen years, his lack of pride in his appearance was appalling.

Pasting on a pleasant expression, Edward stopped and turned to let John catch up.

"Been looking all over for you," John panted. "Heard you were here and I thought you might have a cup of coffee with me in my office."

A cup of coffee . . . in private? Has he heard something?

Suddenly the shadows appeared. In and out of John's suit coat. Edward's eyes darted to keep up with them. Then a rancid smell wafted by him. He puckered his nose and stooped down to look under cars. There was a dead animal somewhere.

"Are you okay, Pastor?" John's brow wrinkled.

"No, I mean yes, I'm . . . I'm fine. Don't want to take up your time today. I'll get with you tomorrow or the next day." Edward wanted to run.

"No, Pastor. My time is yours. Why don't you come back to my office? I'll put on that pot of coffee. You're always game for a cup of fresh coffee."

There was a white spot floating in Edward's peripheral vision. He blinked. Then rubbed his eye. Or was the spot on the parking lot? He jerked his head to see it, but it always stayed just out of view. Now it was on his shoulder, no bigger than a speck of dandruff. He brushed it off vigorously.

"Sorry. Not today. I just came by to glance at the progress on the nursery building. Talked to a lady yesterday who plans to visit, and I bragged a little on our facilities. Just checking to be sure I wasn't exaggerating."

The elusive white spot fluttered by. *Inflated.*

How quickly and convincingly he'd contrived *that* lie. Popped into his head without a moment's hesitation.

"And to be perfectly honest, I forgot I'm supposed to be at someone's house in about fifteen minutes for personal ministering. I hope you'll forgive me and let me take a rain check."

You're getting good!

"Sure thing, Pastor. You need any help ministering? You know I'm at your disposal."

John was so accommodating. To the point of being tiresome.

"Thanks, John, but this is apparently something of a very personal nature. The fellow specifically asked me to come alone."

"Understood. Let's get together for coffee tomorrow, okay?"

John looked at him, a tentative grin on his full face. He reminded Edward of a big, chubby puppy, panting and wagging its tail, craving its owner's approval. But that was part of his charm. He seemed totally without guile and completely trustworthy.

Edward hesitated.

He opened his mouth to say, "*Let's go to your office right now, John. I need to talk to a friend.*"

But the words stuck in his throat.

"It's a date!"

He opened his car door and slid in, effectively dismissing John.

John looked at him questioningly before giving him a small wave and turning to go.

Edward thought he looked a little suspicious.

"Now I'm getting paranoid." He jammed his key into the ignition.

15

Casey was on her hands and knees in front of the couch, trying to coax Soupy from under it, when the front door opened behind her.

"Your car's in my way again." Edward slammed the door. "Why can't you stay on your side of the drive?"

"I'm sorry, baby. I thought you were going to be at the church all morning and I'm leaving again in a few minutes." She jumped up and grabbed her keys from the end table. "I'll move it right now."

"Never mind. I parked on the street." He dropped the morning newspaper onto the coffee table. "Where're you going?"

They saw movement at the same time.

Edward jerked his head around. "What is that stinking possum doing in the living room?"

"It's time for his rabies shot. I just put his bed in the car to take him to the vet."

"Shots . . . *shots* for a possum. What are we running here, a zoo?" He reached down and scooped the trusting animal up by his tail.

Disoriented, Soupy splayed out his back feet, and his front paws grasped in all directions.

"Edward, put him down. You're scaring him. What on earth are you doing?" Casey frantically reached for the frightened creature. Soupy latched onto her sleeve.

"I'm taking him out back and putting him out of his misery. Whack him against a tree. That's what I'm doing. I've had it with your animal kingdom."

Soupy's claws dug into Casey's sleeve. She grabbed him around his furry middle to take the pressure off his legs. Wild-eyed, Edward was pulling on his muscular tail and spewing obscenities. They were having a tug-of-war with Casey's precious pet.

Lord, help me. He's going to kill Soupy.

Witt's voice echoed in her mind. "Call on Him, little lady. Say the words."

Casey stomped her foot. "Stop. *In the name of Jesus*, release God's creature."

Edward quit yelling and let go of Soupy's tail. He reached for a lamp. Threw it at her. It skimmed by Casey's head and smashed into the wall.

His eyes went blank and he slouched onto the couch. A robot with a dead battery.

Clutching the terrified possum to her body, Casey raced to her car before Edward's rage could come back to life.

About two miles off the main highway, down a winding blacktop road, Witt's two-story stone ranch house sat back from the road about a hundred yards.

Several well-mannered dogs of mixed heritage greeted Casey as she parked her car behind Witt's Jeep. The other vehicle, a late model Chevrolet, probably belonged to Sarah.

Next to her on the front seat, Soupy had burrowed deep into his covers. Only his tail poked out. She lowered the windows and opened the sunroof. He'd sleep most of the day, so he'd be fine.

She sat in her car for a minute, wishing she'd called ahead. Afraid to take the time, she'd driven too fast and made no stops, having no idea if Edward was following her. But he was nowhere in sight, so navigating through a sea of wagging tails, she made her way up the porch steps to the screen door.

The greeting she got when she rang the doorbell erased any doubts about dropping in unannounced.

Sarah threw the screen door open wide. "Good morning, pretty lady. You've got to be Miss Casey. Dr. G. has told me all about you. Please come in." She wrapped her arms around Casey, folding her into her generous bosom.

"Dr. G., come quick, you've got some special company."

Casey felt her face grow hot at such a royal welcome. "And you're Sarah. I'm so glad to meet you."

Sarah beamed as she took in the sight of Casey, from head to toe. "Well, ain't you a pretty thing."

Witt burst into the front hall, dishtowel in hand. The undisguised delight in his eyes when he saw her made Casey feel very special.

"Casey, what a pleasant surprise. Come in and sit down. I see you and Sarah have already met. How did you find the place?"

"You didn't know? Everybody in St. Michael knows where Dr. G. lives. And, Witt, I don't want to keep you from anything. Looks like Sarah might have you helping out in the kitchen."

"Miss Casey," Sarah bubbled over with laughter. "Dr. G. decided he wanted to help me this morning so I put him to work making cookies. Not a wise move. You should see my kitchen counter."

"I hope you can stay." Witt glanced at Sarah, who nodded in agreement. "We're having a celebration this evening. The kids will be here, and Ron and Indi, and a few other folks I'd love for you to meet."

"I'm afraid I can't. Not today . . ."

Sarah spoke before Casey could finish. "I'm going to leave you two alone to talk. I appreciate your help, Dr. G., but I think I can handle the cookies all by myself."

She winked at Casey as she turned to leave. "Wish you were staying, Miss Casey."

"Thanks, Sarah. Maybe another time."

"Witt, does Sarah know about . . . you know?"

"Oh, mercy no." He led her onto the porch. "Let's talk out here, Case."

It was the first time he'd shortened her name to Case and it had a familiar, comfortable sound, like they'd known each other forever. No one had ever called her that before. She liked it.

Witt leaned over and stroked a big yellow cat as they passed the porch swing. Sleepily, it reached out, claws retracted, and batted at his hand. With a slow, toothy yawn it dozed off again.

They settled down in two big rocking chairs.

"I've only told her I met a very sweet lady, and we became fast friends in record time. I may have told her a little about how you look and that got her all excited, thinking I was romantically involved. I brought her back to earth by telling her you were a pastor's wife."

Casey looked down at her folded hands. *For now.*

"What are you celebrating, Witt?"

"My sister's graduation day. I told you about Faith's automobile accident when the Lord called her home? Well, that was a year ago today."

"Bittersweet day, huh?"

"Well, we like to celebrate spiritual birthdays. The day you're saved. But this is a first. We got together and decided to celebrate Faith's graduation day instead. The day a Christian goes home is by far the most important day of his life."

Casey nodded.

Witt clasped his hands between his legs and looked down at them. "My niece and nephew had a pretty rough time with their dad's death. He died five years before Faith did. When she was killed, they became orphans. But she'd spent a lot of time helping them understand the blessings of death for the deceased Christian, even though it's tough on those left behind."

"Faith sounds pretty special."

"Oh, she was. By the time she died, they had a pretty good handle on things. But it's never easy for kids when their folks die. Even grown kids. I'm glad Sis and I were close. Now they turn to their old uncle when they need a friend."

"And their kids will be like your grandkids."

"Right. I guess I told you Megan is working on her first."

"Uh-huh. Does she know yet what she's going to have?"

"No, they're old-fashioned. They don't want to know until it arrives."

"I kind of like the old-fashioned way, myself." Casey realized she was picking at loose threads in the chair pillow and locked her hands together in her lap.

"Got good news. The gargoyle is history."

"Oh, Witt, thanks. Have any trouble?"

"Well, one of the guys at the quarry wanted to take it home with him, but I told him I'd promised my friend to crush it into a thousand pieces. He said as long as he didn't have to count the pieces—and went about making mincemeat out of it."

"That's a load off my mind." Casey couldn't think of anything witty to say.

Witt leaned forward in his rocking chair. "Well, little one, you didn't drive all this way just to hear me talk. Are you having problems?" He put his hand on her arm. "He hasn't hurt you again, has he?"

He couldn't know it, but she would drive just about any distance to hear him talk. As much as Jesus was her spiritual rock, Witt had become her rock here on earth.

"Witt, I left Edward sitting on the couch, in sort of a trance."

"A trance?"

"He was going to kill Soupy." A sob escaped her lips. "He had him by the tail and was going to bash his head against a tree. I remembered what you told me and called on Jesus's name. He let go of Soupy and threw a lamp at me."

"Dear Jesus, are you all right?" Witt ran his hands up and down her arms.

"I'm okay. After he threw the lamp, he slouched down on the couch and sort of turned off like a robot with an automatic shutoff."

"Where's Soupy?"

"In my car. He's fine. I was planning to take him to Dr. Al for his rabies shot today."

"You're at a vet's house, little one. I've got vaccine here." He stood. Casey followed him to the kitchen to get the vaccine out of the refrigerator and they walked to her car together.

"He's a beauty, Case." Witt held the squirming marsupial up.

"But you might want to hold back a little on the grub. He's got a bit of a paunch here." Witt smiled and gently squeezed Soupy's tummy.

The shot took only a few seconds. Soupy burrowed back into his self-made cave.

"I'll get with Al and you can pick Soupy's tag up at the clinic next time you're in town."

"Shall I pay you or Al?"

"On the house, Case. It was worth it just to see the little fellow."

They walked up the porch steps. Casey sat back in her rocking chair. Witt went inside and disposed of the needle, came back out and stood at the rail.

He looked out over the landscape for a long time before speaking. "I can't let you go back to that house with Edward." His jaw was set when he turned to face her. "I'm calling Mrs. A."

Casey grabbed his hand. "Wait, Witt. I have to. Me and Soupy. I have an outdoor pen with a padlock where he can live for a while until I decide what to do."

He knelt in front of her chair and took her hands. "I love your little pet, Case, but I'm worried about *you*. I wish you weren't so hardheaded. Can't you stay and meet Ron and Indi this evening? You'd see that they're not weird people. They are perfectly normal, good Christian folks who just happen to hate Satan with all their might."

"I may not need them, Witt. I'm not sure my marriage is salvageable, but I have to go back to keep from tearing the church apart. I must stay with Edward for now. But I'll be much more careful not to upset him."

Witt stood up. "Case, please. *You* don't upset him. The demons do. And you can't control them." He turned his back to her and gripped the railing.

He had to stop her from going back. Hadn't he done everything in his power to help Edward? Could he have misinterpreted God's instruction? Maybe the Lord had been testing his obedience before granting him the desires of his heart. He could give Sarah the rest of the day off and be alone with Casey. Surely she was ready to accept his embrace and his pledge of love. She was starving for love. If he didn't do it, someone else might come along and sweep her off her

132

feet. Wouldn't that be ironic, finding her after thirty years, only to lose her to some Johnny-come-lately?

What a family they'd make. He and Casey would be like parents to Megan and Zach. Grandparents to their kids. It'd be as though he'd never lost her.

His knees nearly buckled at the thought of being alone with her at the ranch.

This was a pivotal point in his life. Satan was hot on Edward's trail and there was little doubt that Edward was within his grasp. Without Casey by his side, lifting him up to the Lord daily, he'd succumb to Satan's evil powers in no time.

Witt was in a position to win Casey's love.

But in doing so, he'd destroy Edward.

I can't let my heart betray me, God. Please help me think straight.

"Witt?" Casey stood and put her hand on his arm, interrupting his thoughts. "I'd like to go to your prayer closet with you."

I can't go in there with her. Too intimate. I'll defile the temple. I need to send her away.

He turned and strode into the house, leaving Casey on the porch with a puzzled look on her face. The screen door slammed behind him.

On his knees in the prayer closet, Witt lifted his hands toward heaven. "Father, she's going to figure out where I am and poke her head in here any minute. I need Your strength to make it through this. I need to know . . ."

The scent of wild clover and honeysuckle permeated the room.

Your will or Mine, son?

Witt breathed in the fragrance and felt a new strength coursing through his veins.

"Yours, Father. Always Yours."

He opened his eyes to see Casey standing just inside the door gaping at him. "Come in, Case. He's waiting."

She sat on the floor beside him.

"Case, I'm sorry you're contemplating giving up. There's so much at stake. Your vows. Your family, and the years you've had together." God was feeding him the words to speak.

"Witt, there may be too much water under the bridge to turn things around."

Witt knew he had to turn the tide and convince Casey her marriage was worth preserving. For her sake as well as his own, he needed to do it before his willpower was tested to its limits one too many times.

He began to pray for Edward. But felt a check in his spirit. Something was wrong. His prayers were not getting past the ceiling.

"Forgive me for asking, but I must . . . Case, do you have aught against God? Because if you do, it may get in the way of our prayers."

"Oh no. How could I? That would be blasphemy, wouldn't it? My Savior, my Creator, the Maker of the universe. Me, mad at Him?"

"Not blasphemy, Case . . . human nature. Christians deny being mad at God, because it's scary to be mad at the only One who can save us from an eternity in hell. But humans get mad. Even at God. And He knows it whether we admit it or not. We think He could have done things differently—maybe saved us some heartache with just the blink of His eye."

Casey squirmed. "I know He wants us to have the desires of our heart, Witt, so why is life so difficult for Christians?"

"Case, it's hard to understand with our finite minds, but everything the Almighty does is for a purpose, and in the right timing for His ultimate plan. And everything that tests your faith makes you stronger for the next task. He's not going to put more on you than you can handle. But He is molding you into a stronger Christian."

Is that what He's doing to me? How much He must love me, to put up with my inconstancy.

"I don't feel very strong, Witt. I've got guilt feelings from years ago I can't seem to work through. Now this mess with Edward. It's as though God has given up on me."

"He never gives up on us, Case. None of us. But we do need to settle all accounts and be sure we're not holding anything against Him. So, out with it, little lady. What has the King of kings, Lord of lords done that has disappointed you in Him? You may as well speak out. He already knows."

Casey was slow to answer. "Witt, I've lost three loved ones. My entire family. I wasn't there for them. And I didn't get the chance to say good-bye to any of them. I've felt so guilty about it. Maybe I *have* placed the blame on the Lord."

"Talk to me about it, Case."

"Mother got terribly ill one weekend. She assured me she'd be okay because she was under a doctor's care. I should've rushed to her side. But I didn't. I put it off for a day—just one day—and she died with no one there for her. She was my only friend when I had Barrett. Back then it was a pretty shameful thing to have a child out of wedlock. She gave up her job and her apartment to be there for me when I needed her. And had to start all over when I finally got my act together. She was the best mother in the world and I'm surely the worst daughter."

Witt had wondered about his friend Del. She'd gone on vacation one year and never come back.

"I'm sorry, Case. I know you loved her. And believe me, she loved you . . . very much."

He had to say it, for Del. He hoped Casey wouldn't connect the dots.

"Who else did you lose?"

He was anxious to move on from Del. She was a strong common bond they shared. Too precious to both of them to linger on her memory together without the truth coming out.

"My brother died in Europe. He was married and happy and then, suddenly, he was gone. His wife didn't speak English. She never answered any of my letters, so I had no closure. I don't even know where he was buried." Her shoulders quivered. "He was so bright and compassionate. My hero. Why, if it weren't for him, I wouldn't have passed freshman algebra. After I was an adult he'd send little gifts for no occasion, but he could never remember birthdays or holidays. Mother and I called him the absentminded professor. It's been over fourteen years and I still miss him every day."

Witt just nodded. Speaking it out seemed to be doing her good.

"And many years ago my daddy was hospitalized and on the brink of death. On a Friday morning I was told he was doing well and I should take a few hours off."

She blinked back the approaching tears.

"I decided to catch up on a few things I'd gotten behind on. He died that morning while I was busy. I should've been right there by his side. Seems I was never there when someone I loved needed me."

Casey broke into sobs.

"Case, they'd want you to be happy. Not guilt ridden. Can you forgive yourself? Because you can't do your best for God if you've burdened yourself with guilt. He's already forgiven you. If you insist on carrying guilt, you're literally taking it back from Him."

Casey reached for the tissue box. "Since you put it that way, I guess I'm going to have to release it—with God's help. I've been living with guilt so long, it's become a crutch. I need your prayers, Witt."

"Always, Case." *It was the only place she was all his.* "You'll always be in my prayers."

"On the bright side." Her mouth shaped a fragile smile. "I'm pretty sure each of them accepted Jesus and I'll see them again."

"Thank you, Lord." Witt had prayed many times for Del.

"But how can I pray He'll not let that happen to me again? I never got to say good-bye. That would have meant so much to me. Is it selfish to pray I don't lose any more loved ones without the chance to say good-bye?"

"No. You know He'll do all things according to His plan, but I think you should tell Him that you're hurting and ask Him, if possible, to not let it happen to you again. He *really* does want you to have the desires of your heart. Let's pray right now."

He broke into prayer. And heaven came down into that little room.

As Witt was about to wind up his prayer with an amen, Casey broke in. "Father, I plead Your mercy and at the same time, I accept Your decision—whatever it may be—because, after all, You have a universe to run. Amen."

His eyes were moist, but he laughed aloud.

"Yes, Case, He has a universe to run." Witt chuckled. "But I bet He'd turn it upside down to make you happy. You've got to be one of the most precious souls in His kingdom."

"Thank you, Witt." Casey flashed a weary smile and looked

around at the four walls of the tiny room. "Coming in here is everything you said it would be."

"Well, it's time we get down to business for Edward, Case. God loves him and He's called us to his rescue. We can't let him perish." He knew he was pushing her, but it couldn't be accomplished without her.

"I'm tired of laboring for Edward, Witt." Her shoulders sagged and she looked exhausted. She dragged herself up to a kneeling position. "But even if I decide to leave, I guess it's still my duty to lift him up to God."

Witt nodded. "Your place in his life is secondary to his walk with the Lord."

"Forgive me for being weak and wanting to give up on him. We'll pray. But you have to send me home by two. I don't dare stay any later."

Send her home. To him. Oh Jesus, how am I going to do that?

He would be sending an innocent child to do battle with Satan himself. She carried only one weapon. The name of Jesus.

16

Enjoyed the vittles, Pastor. Thanks for the treat."

Mike Hendricks had a little chunk of mashed potato hanging on the corner of his mouth. Edward didn't know whether to mention it or just let nature take its course.

"Why don't we take a little spin while we're in town, Brother Mike?" Edward looked Mike straight in the eye, trying to avoid the piece of potato that drew his gaze like a magnet. "There are a couple of things I'd like to buy for the church. And I'd like to see if you can feel that tremor in the engine."

Brother Mike blinked.

"Remember, I told you about it over lunch. The Cadillac. I feel a tremor at about fifty miles an hour." Edward tried to keep the impatience out of his voice. *Dense old bird.*

Mike wiped his mouth on his sleeve, transferring the mashed potato to his checkered flannel shirt. "Oh yes. Grand idea. We can leave my car here and pick it up when we head home. But I wouldn't worry too much about that there tremor. Let the next guy worry about it."

"I beg your pardon?" The old coot was playing right into his hands.

"I been a-thinkin', Pastor, it's about time we got you a new car.

This one's a-startin' to give you some trouble, and I'd like to have a look-see at what's out there."

"No, no, Brother Mike, I couldn't justify another new car to Casey."

Mike scratched a spot behind his right ear with his forefinger. "Pastor, you let me worry about yer little redheaded sweetheart. You know as well as me if yer going to be successful, you gotta look successful."

What a laugh. He's the biggest hayseed to ever come down the pike, and he's loaded. Edward was getting used to the voices. Oftentimes his spirit blended with them. Almost like he'd been the one to say it. "You and I both know that, my friend. But for some reason, Casey doesn't think it applies to clergy."

Edward pulled deftly out onto the loop around St. Michael and they rode in silence for several minutes. His breath was getting short. Just like when Mike bought him his Cadillac. Only this time he was thinking about Jaguars while trying to look pious, as though he may be mulling over the Scriptures.

Edward cleared his throat to speak, knowing Mike would jump right in and start talking. He always did. He liked to get in the last word—and the first.

"Ya know, Pastor, this didn't just now occur to me. I've been a-thinkin' now fer the past couple of weeks it was 'bout time to turn this here old gal in and get you a new one. Unless you think Miss Casey would like to keep the old one fer herself. Nicer than that German jitney she drives."

"Oh, no sir, she'd never give up her Jetta. She loves that thing. Says it's easier to handle and more economical than the Cadillac."

"Well then, why don't we get her a new Jetter, too?"

Edward's chin dropped. *This is too good.* "You're way too generous, brother. But she wouldn't go for it."

It was working out better than he'd dared to hope. All he had to do was channel that generosity toward the Jaguar he'd been drooling over. Cadillac plus Jetta equals high-end Jaguar.

It was time to step up from the Cadillac. They're nice, but they scream establishment. Anyone with halfway decent credit can get one. Now a Jag. That's a different story. It's the only way to go if you want to really impress.

They were getting close to the Jaguar dealership. Edward had mapped their route carefully. And choreographed their conversation the best he could. But this new development concerning a new Jetta for Casey called for a last-minute script change.

Just a couple of minutes of pensive silence and . . . now. Time to throw out the bait.

"Besides, Brother Mike, that's way too much for you to do for us." Edward gestured toward the Jaguar dealership. "Why, a fellow could get one of those Jaguars for what he'd pay for a Cadillac *and* a Jetta."

Brother Mike spit out the bait. "Jaguar? Why would anyone want one of them sissy cars, anyway?"

Edward gritted his teeth and felt his face get hot. Not the reaction he'd hoped for. *Suck it up, it's not going to be as easy as you thought.*

He forced a smile. "You got that right, Brother Mike. Gotta wonder why a sissy car like that is considered such a status symbol. Guess it's the money. Not many folks can afford one."

A gentle prod to the old guy's ego. Edward hoped he wasn't laying it on too thick.

"Well, I sure could, if'n I wanted to. Jest don't want to. *You* like them things?"

"Well, personally, I lean toward something a little more patrician." He was pretty sure old Mike had no idea what *patrician* meant. All the better. It was one thing to talk his lingo to butter him up, but Edward didn't want the old geezer to lose sight of the fact his pastor was better educated than he.

Edward shrugged his shoulders. "It's a mystery to me, but if a fellow wants to just ooze success, a Jag trumps a Cadillac. But hey, I don't need to look *that* successful. And it's too much money . . . even for you. They cost a big wad of dough."

"All due respect, Pastor, don't be a-tellin' me what I can or can't afford."

"I don't know why we're even talking about it, Brother Mike. It's out of the question." Edward looked at Mike and shook his head indulgently. "Why do I let you get me into these conversations? First you want to buy another Cadillac and now you're talking Jaguars. I can't even accept the Cadillac, much less a Jag. You've done too much already. End of discussion."

Mike folded his arms over his chest and glared at Edward. "If I wanna buy a sissy Jag, I'll buy one."

Sissy Jag. Edward looked away. He could feel his pulse pounding in his temples.

"And I jest might wanna. 'Course you'd have to trade in the old Caddy. I'll make up the difference. Now turn around and go back to the dealership we just passed. I wanna take a closer look. Maybe I could get used to seein' my pastor in one-a them sissy cars."

If you're lucky, the old goat won't be seeing much of you anyway. Come on, Eddie, humor him. He's dying to spend his dough on you.

Edward hated being called Eddie. He stomped on the gas and passed a break in the median, expecting Brother Mike to put up a fuss.

He did.

"Hey, ain't you gonna turn around? You missed a turnin'-around place back there."

"No." Edward faked calm, but his heart was beating like a trip-hammer. "No, it's just too ludicrous. I'm telling you, you can't afford one of those babies."

Mike's face turned fire red and his eyes blazed. Edward sucked air between his teeth. *Bad move. I've overplayed my hand.*

Leaning forward, Mike squinted and aimed his steely gaze across the seat at Edward. His bushy eyebrows almost obscured his eyes. "You know, *son*, I've always been pretty respectful of the fact that yer my pastor, even though you ain't nothin' but a snot-nosed kid. But I'm old and I'm rich. And I'm used to gittin' my way. Don't plan on changin' anytime soon. So either turn this wreck around and take me to that dealership or drop me off at the next service station and I'll git a cab back to my car."

Edward felt the blood rush to his face, and his grip on the steering wheel became a stranglehold. He thought about calling the old man's bluff, stopping the car right there, and kicking the stupid old codger out. But that little act of defiance would cost him a Jaguar at the least, and probably a lot more in the long run.

He could swallow his pride—just this once—for a new Jag.

Gritting his teeth and exuding remorse, Edward said, "Gosh, Brother Mike, I didn't mean to upset you. I guess I haven't learned to accept your generosity. I mean, how can I let you buy me any kind of car, much less a Jaguar?"

"I done said you'd have to trade in your Caddy, so it ain't no big deal." Mike leaned back and wiped his brow with a bandana. "And by George, I've done made up my mind to buy you a car. You might as well quit a-kickin' against the gourds. Now let's git back there and have a look-see."

Looking properly repentant, Edward flipped his left directional signal and prepared to make a U-turn at the next break in the median. Back to the Jaguar dealership.

"It's not every day we sell to cash customers, gentlemen." The general manager held a bottle of champagne in one hand and extended his other hand to Edward. "Would you like to come to my office for a drink?"

"No thank you." Edward was sure Mike was a teetotaler. This was no time to experiment with alcohol.

"Of course, how thoughtless. Not before you drive. Here . . . take the bottle with you."

"Back off, mister." Mike stepped up. "This here's my pastor. He don't want no alkeehol."

Edward looked away. He'd wanted that bottle.

It was the most expensive Jaguar on the lot. "Stand up there by it, Pastor, and jest let me see how you look. Boy howdy, you picked a good one. If a fella's gotta drive a pantywaist car, black is lots better than one of them there girly colors."

Let him call it sissy and pantywaist. Your name's on the title. His name's on the check.

Edward grinned.

He opened the passenger door and gestured. "Hop in, Brother Mike."

"No. You go on and take yer new machine for a spin. I'm gonna get our salesman to take me back to my car. I need to get back across the mountain a-fore dark. My old eyes don't do too good a-drivin' at night."

"I can't leave you standing here while I drive off in a car you just bought me. Let me take you back to your car."

"Nonsense. It'll do my old heart good to see my pastor a-drivin' off in his new Jag." He banged his old knobby hand on Edward's back. "Besides, I don't know if I could curl my bad leg up enough to get in." Mike gave Edward an exaggerated wink.

One last jab at your new car, Eddie.

"Stop calling me Eddie," he muttered, then cringed, hoping Mike hadn't heard him.

Mike was already on his way up the steps.

The service crew had given the vehicle a quick detail and it sat, sparkling like a black diamond, in front of the building. The top was down at Edward's request, in spite of the ever-increasing chill in the air. And the engine was purring like a smug panther, waiting for Edward to tame it.

He could feel his heart pounding in his head as he climbed in. It was so different from the Cadillac. The pedals were very small. He hoped he could shift the gears smoothly and not make a fool of himself driving off.

Turning to wave, Edward was suddenly engulfed in guilt. At the top of the steps, his gullible old benefactor bared his false teeth in a big grin and attempted a pitiful thumbs-up.

Easy now, don't go getting mushy. Edward grappled with his emotions.

He's just an old fool. And you know what they say about fools and their money. He has no better place to spend it and you put up with his screwball country ways in return. No harm done.

But he didn't turn to look again. He wanted to get the haunting picture of Mike out of his mind. It struck some old, obsolete nerve of sentimentality that had no place in his life anymore.

Besides, it reminded him he was still dependent on others to get what he wanted. He longed for the day he could get it all on his own. But he was going to have to start his own TV ministry before that could happen.

TV. His next step. That's where the money was. But it would take a lot more backing than a pastor's salary could provide. He'd have

144

to keep working old Mike long enough to get things off the ground. And the new retired couple that just joined. Their gifts to the church were almost as obscene as Mike's. Given a little time, he'd get some of their loot headed his direction. *But I must be careful to not make Mike jealous. Don't want to kill the golden goose.*

He felt an almost imperceptible prick to his conscience but shook it off.

Once his TV ministry was up and flying, Edward wouldn't need anyone.

He drove to downtown St. Michael. There were two things he wanted today. One was to try the Jag out on the open road. The other: to be seen. And downtown was the place to be seen. He could put it through its paces later out on the highway after dark.

He hadn't been downtown long before he questioned the wisdom of driving his fine new vehicle in this traffic. Country bumpkins pulled out in front of him and stopped short to make last-minute turns. No signals. Where'd they learn to drive, in the hayfields?

"Deliver me from these clodhoppers." He whipped around the corner of Arkansas Avenue and Fifth Street. "I don't know where this goes, but it's got to be better than being in the center of this hick town."

It was then that he saw Casey's Jetta parked in the middle of the next block. On Arkansas, the street he'd just exited. "That's right, it's Friday. She comes to town to shop. God forbid she should stay home and scrub a floor or something."

He didn't really want to see her. He was sure she'd have something negative to say about the Jag. But curiosity bid him turn around to see if it really was her car.

He turned another corner, thinking he would take two more turns and be back on Arkansas. But at the next corner traffic was one-way—the wrong way. So he went another block out of his way. When he made it back to Arkansas Avenue, the little blue car was pulling out of the parking space. He could see Casey's red hair glinting in the dipping rays of the sun. There were about six cars between them, and both lanes were bumper-to-bumper. He would have to wait until traffic thinned to catch her.

"Stupid city engineers. The lights are set all wrong. I should be able to sail right through."

To make matters worse, a simple-minded Good Samaritan in front of him stopped to let every car out that wanted out.

"Who needs this? Just when everyone's clearing out of town I have to have Mrs. Sunshine in front of me."

Soon he was ten cars behind the Jetta.

Wonder what she's been up to? Too bad you're not man enough to find out. The voice was not in his head. It was in the backseat. He yanked his head around but saw no one.

The hair prickled on the back of his neck. He gunned the engine and tailgated the car in front of him. He couldn't let her get away.

Witt turned from waving Casey off and was heading for his Jeep when the sleek black Jaguar caught his eye. Actually the driver caught his eye. A nice-looking gentleman—well dressed and neat, except having the top down in this chilly, windy weather had made a mess of his hair. He seemed very agitated. Gunning the engine and slamming the brakes with every slight movement of traffic. And there was a darkness surrounding him that wasn't physical. Witt felt a shudder of oppression run through his body.

"Please bless that fellow, Jesus. He has problems a flashy Jaguar can't solve. At the very least, he's going to catch his death of cold. Doesn't he know the temperature has dipped fifteen degrees in the last hour?"

Witt strode to his Jeep. He opened the door and hopped in, in one deft movement, glad he'd left the top on this morning. He took a moment to pray for Casey's safety. He'd urged her to go straight home, because severe weather was headed their way and she didn't need to be crossing the mountains in it.

He reached down to start the Jeep but stopped with his hand on the key and looked down the street at the Jaguar. It'd moved only two or three car lengths. Something about that fellow was pulling at his heart and he didn't know why.

He might only be late for an appointment. Don't let your imagination run away with you.

He started the engine and turned to check the approaching traffic. It was several minutes before there was a break big enough to back onto Arkansas Avenue. He could still see the Jaguar about a block ahead of him, hugging the right as though hoping for a space in the parked cars big enough to pass the car in front of him. Brake lights flashing, he hastily pulled forward every two feet only to slam the brake again, the consummate picture of impatience. Witt couldn't dismiss him from his mind.

"Well, Father, I don't know why You've put this man on my heart to pray for, but since You have . . . please, bless the Jaguar man. I pray he has a loved one who cares enough to see him through whatever situation is hanging over him, like a black cloud with its own entity. Father, watch over him and get him safely to his destination. If he's not Your child, Lord, I pray the Holy Spirit will speak to his heart and draw him to You. I pray Your richest spiritual blessings on the Jaguar man. Amen."

A couple of blocks up, Witt could see Casey's car take a right. He knew at the next block she'd take another right and would be headed home. If he turned right immediately, he'd be at the next intersection when she got there. He could stop her, pull her out of her car, carry her over his shoulder to the Jeep, take her to the ranch, and never let her go.

And that's what he longed to do.

Instead he turned on his left blinker and changed lanes. The next left was his. Sarah would have a good meal waiting for him in the refrigerator. After a shower and supper, he'd spend a few hours in the Word and in prayer. Maybe catch a good action movie. Anything to take his mind off Casey.

Driving down Arkansas Avenue, Casey was immersed in a frightening thought.

It was getting harder and harder to leave the peace of being with

Witt to go home to the turmoil of living with Edward. Tranquility multiplied when she was with Witt, just as rage begat more rage in Edward's presence. Praying for Edward was a lot more pleasant than living with him. The latter had become nearly impossible. *Lord, something's got to give.*

She lived for Fridays, when she could come to St. Michael. To her amazement, Edward never questioned her. He assumed she was shopping. Witt, on the other hand, assumed she had come only to pray. Only she—and God—knew her time with Witt was all that gave her a firm grip on her sanity.

"Sometimes I wish I could curl up in his arms and stay forever." In the lonely interior of her car, she felt her face grow hot. This wasn't some love triangle, and she couldn't afford to let herself imagine it was. Her place was with Edward. Divorce was not an option and there was no choosing to be done. The choice was made nearly twenty years ago. She'd taken a vow before God. If only she had known then . . .

She took a right at the second light as always. One block and another right. She was headed in the opposite direction of the ranch, Witt, and tranquility.

Witt had never given her any reason to believe he wanted to be with her in *that* way. In fact he'd made it very clear, in word and deed, she must do all she could to mend her relationship with her husband.

"Why does my mind even concoct such daydreams? Witt's a wonderful friend, and *only* a friend. There's no doubt if I ever mentioned these thoughts to him, he'd run like a scared rabbit. And I'd lose a very good friend. He only wants what God wants. And God wants my marriage to be healed."

A chill ran down her spine. She reached down to adjust the car heater.

Miles passed. The traffic and buildings thinned. Finally she was coming into the last small settlement before she must cross the deserted mountain pass.

"Wish I had a cup of coffee." She spoke aloud. It made the lonely drive a little less ominous to hear a voice, even if it was her own. "I think I'll stop for one before I hit the pass."

She signaled and pulled off the highway into a little gas station.

"Might as well fill up while I'm stopped for coffee."

Shivering, she leaned against the car as she was pumping the gas. She began praying.

"Father, I pray . . . well, what do I pray, Lord? That things with Edward don't get out of control? Hmmm. They already have. But deliverance? I could never get him to agree to that. Please show me Your way out of this, Lord. I'm in over my head."

The temperature had dropped considerably and the wind was picking up. The early evening sky looked strangely threatening as Casey sprinted into the store to pay for the gas and pour a steaming hot cup of coffee. With quick steps, she made her way back to the car. Once inside the warm interior, she pulled her favorite pale-blue sweater around her shoulders and leaned back for a moment.

The sweater was soft against her bare arms. And the coffee cup was warm in her hands. She took a long sip of the aromatic hot liquid and concentrated on the peace of God. It felt good, for as long as the moment lasted.

Too soon, a car pulled up behind her and honked. She was blocking the gas pump. She had to be on her way to Sugar Bluff and . . . Edward.

Her thoughts of God were banished, and that pungent odor began gathering in her car again. Why did she smell it only when this spiritual darkness came upon her?

17

I t was eight o'clock and Edward was freezing.

He'd given up on catching Casey. She'd be home by now, wondering where he was. Pulling into a parking lot, he stopped to put the top on the Jag and turn on the heater.

He'd thought it would be more fun. But the newness had already worn off his latest toy. He pulled his coat around him and pointed the heater vent at his face. The heat made him sleepy. He didn't feel like going home but couldn't think of anywhere else to go.

A car pulled up next to him and two couples hopped out, laughing. They stopped talking long enough to admire his Jag and both guys gave him the high sign. Then they turned and went into the store, the girls running ahead, giggling. For the first time, Edward realized he was in a liquor store parking lot.

He'd never tasted liquor. Until recently he hadn't been curious about it. But lately he'd been tempted to try—to better understand its lure.

"Looks like today's the day."

He wrapped his muffler around his neck and stepped out into the brisk wind.

The choices, once inside the store, were overwhelming. Did he want wine, bourbon, scotch, gin? The fellows before him bought bourbon. They were masculine-looking guys, so that was probably a safe choice.

The half-pint looked pretty small. Not enough to whet your whistle. And a fifth was too big for his coat pocket, so he settled on a pint bottle of the most expensive bourbon he could find on display.

He paid for it, crumpled the receipt and the paper bag, and shoved them back at the clerk. Slipping the bottle into the deep pocket of his cashmere overcoat, he strode out the door, head high. Now he was a real man.

Less than a half mile down the highway it caught his eye. "Fine Dining! Margaritas! Live Music!" Red, blue, and yellow, throbbing against the dark sky, the neon sign issued him a personal invitation he couldn't refuse.

He deserved to relax before hitting the torturous road across the mountains. And he'd always wanted to try this place. A margarita and a steak might restore the euphoric feeling he had when he still had the world on a string. Before the string started unraveling. He tromped on the brake pedal and skidded into the gravel lot.

It was nicer inside than he'd anticipated. Tablecloths and napkins. The works. The hostess led him across the deep pile carpet and seated him with the promise someone would be with him shortly.

Moments later a skimpily clad young lady sidled up to the table and asked if he'd like a house margarita.

He accepted, hoping he'd enjoy whatever sort of alcohol was in a margarita.

"Frozen or on the rocks?"

"On the rocks." That sounded more sophisticated.

Glad he'd stopped at the bank, he slipped a ten-dollar bill into her hand.

Edward's attention strayed to the live entertainment. A sensual woman with a low voice—and neckline—was singing. Her lips were caressing the mike. The words ran together into one suggestive slur.

Her eyes seemed to linger on him. Or was it wishful thinking? No, it was real. She was definitely coming on to him. He'd seen that look before, though it had always been carefully veiled in the pretense of innocence. Because of his calling. And he'd always pretended not to notice.

Until a couple of years ago, he *hadn't* noticed. Casey had to tell him if a lady was flirting with him. It made him feel so dumb that he didn't realize it. Casey thought it was cute.

The girl in the skimpy outfit was back with his drink.

He took a tentative sip—he'd been told liquor tasted nasty. But this tasted like lemonade. What a pleasant surprise.

He put his hand on the cocktail waitress's arm and inspected her name tag. People love to be called by name. Remember their name and they'll go the extra mile for you.

He slid another ten along the table. "Mandy, please bring me another."

The entrance door swung open wide and a well-dressed, striking gentleman strolled in, oozing confidence. His black hair was combed straight back and his piercing black eyes roamed the large dining room.

"Meeting a friend." He dismissed the hostess and headed directly to Edward's table.

"That your Jag out there?"

Edward looked up, grinning. "Sure is. Got it today. Like it?"

"That is some magnificent piece of machinery. Mind if I sit down?" The stranger had already pulled a chair out.

"By all means, join me." Edward was glad to have some sophisticated company. "Mandy. Over here. A drink for the gentleman, please."

"What'll you have, uh . . . ?"

"Sam. Just call me Sam. I'll have what you're having."

Edward extended his hand. "Edward McAlester, Sam. Good to meet you."

Sam's hand was clammy.

Edward withdrew his hand quickly and discreetly wiped it

on his pant leg. "Seems like I know you from somewhere. Have we met before?"

"I don't think so. Not in this world." Sam peered across the table and smiled. A crooked, abstruse smile.

Brow wrinkled, Edward was trying to remember where he'd met Sam before.

Sam snapped his fingers. "My friend, why so serious? You've got some celebrating to do. It's not every day a man gets a Jaguar. What'd you trade?"

"A Cadillac."

Sam looked impressed. Edward felt his chest swell. But his heart was troubled. There was something familiar about this guy.

Mandy returned with Sam's margarita and Edward's second one. "Drink up, friend." Sam held his glass high.

An unquenchable dryness had suddenly jumped on Edward. He grabbed his second drink and took a big slug.

Sam toyed with his drink but never raised it to his lips. He nodded toward the singer.

"I think that gal has a thing for you."

"Yeah, she's been coming on strong. But she's wasting her time on me. I've got a pretty wife at home."

"Oh yes. Have to honor those vows, no matter how cold the little woman gets." Sam nodded knowingly. "Makes me wonder, when they get like that, if they've been . . . you know." His lip curled.

Edward gritted his teeth. *Not Casey. She's true blue.* But how'd this guy know things weren't going well at home?

Sam reached over and shoved Edward's drink into his hand. "You're slowing down, Edward. Drink up. And while you're at it, give that poor girl a break. She's up there trying to sing but can't keep her eyes off you. A little smile from you would make her day."

A waiter carrying two menus approached the table, but Sam waved him off. "Later."

Trying to bolster his courage, Edward took another long drink, nearly emptying the glass. He had no previous experience with blatant sexuality. He was afraid to return her furtive glances. His inexperience would be glaringly obvious.

But he didn't want Sam to think he was henpecked.

I'll give her something to think about . . . just give me a minute to get in the mood.

The bridge of Edward's nose started tingling. Like when he'd worn his reading glasses too long. He jiggled it between his thumb and forefinger . . . that usually helped.

But instead the tingling feeling proceeded down his nose. He pressed on the end of his nose. It felt funny. Almost like it was on someone else's face.

Sam folded his arms on the table. With an amused expression he watched Edward play with his face.

Edward pressed on his cheekbones with his forefingers.

"Something wrong, friend?" Sam smiled indulgently.

"My face feels funny. Kinda numb." Edward pinched the flesh between his nose and mouth. "There, too."

"Should we be concerned? Take you to a doctor, perhaps?"

"Nah. It'll either get better or it'll fall off." Edward giggled.

"You're a fun guy, Edward. We should do this more often."

"You're not so bad yourself, Sammy-Boy." Sam's face was fuzzy, but Edward could see he was smiling.

"We could have even more fun if that gal would come sit with us. Why don't you do your magic? I'd like to see you in action."

Yeah, why so prudish, Edward? What harm can come from a little innocent flirtation?

Edward looked toward the sexy songstress and winked.

She returned his wink with a big smile and held up five fingers.

He looked at Sam. "What's with the five fingers?" Edward's tongue was the size of his fist.

"Five minutes until break time." Sam leaned back in his chair with a smug grin. "There, wasn't that easy? Her name's Dolores, and I bet she'd like a ride in your Jag."

A fleeting picture of himself and this sensual singer, cruising in his Jag, flashed through his mind. He dare not entertain that thought. Casey was at home waiting for him. No matter how much he enjoyed the game, he couldn't step over the line and break his marriage vows. But the more suggestive nods Sam made in Dolores's direction, the more the illicit illusion persisted. He needed to wrap up this adventure and go home.

"No, that's not gonna happen, Sham." Edward's head drooped. He forced it up to look at Sam. "Actually, I'd better be going. I'm not feeling very well."

He stood up to look out the window, grabbing the back of his chair to steady himself. An icy drizzle was beating against the pane.

Sam pulled him back to a sitting position. Edward didn't resist.

"No, you can't leave now. Look at that weather." Sam slid his own drink over to Edward. "Why so tense? Relax, my man." He patted Edward's hand. "Alcohol is your friend. Drink."

Edward's face felt warm under Sam's scrutinizing gaze. He didn't really want any more to drink. But Sam was so insistent.

Can't have Sam thinking I'm a hick who can't handle his liquor.

He put the glass to his lips and sipped.

"Drink like a man." Sam's eyes blazed.

Edward took a couple gulps and slammed the glass to the table. "No more," he slurred.

Sam walked around the table behind him and rested his hands on Edward's shoulders. "You need a fresh drink." His voice a soft satin pillow. "This one's mostly melted ice."

Edward tried to stand, but Sam kept firm, gentle pressure on his shoulders.

He called the waitress over close. "Mandy, the man needs another one. There's an extra ten in it for you if you make it a double, top shelf." He reached into Edward's pocket, took out a roll of bills, and handed Mandy a twenty.

Mandy turned away from Sam and waved her hand in front of her nose. She looked questioningly at Edward. He tried to speak, but words wouldn't come.

"It's all right, sweetheart. I'll see that he gets home okay." Sam was stroking Edward shoulders. "My friend's had a hard day, Mandy. Show him a little compassion." His black eyes raked over her body and he flashed his crooked smile.

He walked back to his chair, sat down, and started twirling his half-empty glass between his palms. His fingers seemed too long for his hands. Edward tilted his head and blinked his eyes repeatedly, trying to focus on Sam's fingers.

He giggled.

"What's funny, my friend? Sam held him in his hypnotic stare.

"I feel weird and I'm leaning. Can't seem to sit up straight." Edward's torpid tongue wouldn't cooperate. "And your fingers are too long." He chuckled. "Way too long."

"What you need is another drink." Sam glared at his own fingers. "Long fingers run in my family, my funny friend. Now let's have that drink. You need some R and R before you fly apart."

"I don't want a drink. I wanna go home. It stinks in here." Edward curled his nose.

"One more drink and we'll go home." Sam slowly pushed the double in front of Edward.

Edward picked it up with both hands and drank from it for a long time. With the glass still raised, he wrinkled his brow and looked over the rim. "You going home with me?"

"I promised Mandy I'd take care of you."

"Oh good, 'cause I'm not sure I can drive." He was rocking back and forth.

"Oh, look, Edward, Dolores is taking a break. Why don't you call her over?"

Edward slung his head in her direction and, mouth gaping, he beckoned her with one hand to come sit beside him.

She shot him a disgusted look and sat down with another patron.

Sam's black eyes smoldered. "Oh, that's cold, Edward. She led you on and now she's dumping you for another guy. Let's leave before I lose my temper. I don't like to see my friends treated that way." He put his hand on Edward's arm. "Let's go."

Edward smiled wanly at his new friend and scratched his head. He wanted to like him. But he hardly knew him. Yet Sam was willing to drive clear across the mountain to see him safely home. That's real love for your fellow man. If only he could shake the nagging feeling they'd met before, *and they weren't friends.*

When he stood up, the room did a three-hundred-and-sixty-degree flip and Edward fell back into his chair. His hand came down on a glass. It broke, ripping a nasty gash in his palm.

He looked down at his hand, dumbfounded. Coolly, Sam picked up a clean white napkin, wrapped it around the cut, and rushed Edward out the door. The makeshift bandage dangled from Edward's hand, leaving a trail of spattered blood. Sam half-dragged Edward to the Jag, hustled him to the driver's side, and pushed him in.

"You drive." Sam jumped in the passenger side. "I'll hold the bourbon."

Edward stared unsteadily at the dashboard. His hand hurt and he felt sick. "I don't know if I can."

"Drive." The blazing eyes again.

The hostess was standing in the club entrance, dialing a cordless phone. Straining to see the license plates. Edward fumbled with the key. Spinning his wheels, he pelted the gathering crowd with gravel.

They threw up their arms to protect their eyes and Sam guffawed. "Pitiful creatures."

Edward pulled onto the highway, barely missing the iron post that marked the right side of the drive. Headed for the mountain pass, he didn't lift his foot from the accelerator until he was going well over a hundred miles per hour.

"Why don't we break out the bourbon?" Sam urged. "I'm afraid you'll lose your buzz."

Edward could feel his hot stare on the side of his head. "What bourbon?"

"The bourbon in your overcoat pocket, friend."

Edward had forgotten about the bourbon. "How'd you know?"

"Not important. Just hand it to me. I'll be your server tonight."

Sam opened the bottle and ran it under Edward's nose. "Better than margaritas, friend."

"Whoa." The fumes stung clear into Edward's lungs.

Taking the bottle from Sam, he closed his eyes, threw his head back, and took a long swig. It burned so badly going down, he declared between gasps that he'd never drink again.

"It gets easier, Pastor."

"How did you . . . who are you, anyway?"

158

"I told you . . . Sam. Your new best friend. Have some more." Sam poked the bottle into Edward's chest.

Edward decided to give it another try . . . and another. Each time the kick became a little more bearable.

And Sam became a little more likeable. *After all, he's just a guy . . . like me.*

The turnoff to the mountain pass loomed ahead. Edward navigated it on two wheels. The first quarter mile was almost straight uphill. At the top of the hill was a sharp right, as it began winding into the mountains. Edward knew he had to slow down to make the curves. He eased up on the pedal. Sam kept the bourbon coming.

The freezing rain began to slacken up, but the unyielding cold prevailed. Every surface was becoming as slick as glass. Edward had made it almost halfway across the deserted mountain pass before Sam spoke again.

"We're about there."

"Nah, we're not even halfway across the mount'n. There's a long stretch ahead and then a curve to the left . . . or is it right?"

"Left."

"You know this pass? You from around here?" Edward looked over at Sam, trying to place him. The car started drifting off the road.

Aha! He's from around here. I knew I'd met him before.

Sam reached over and wrapped his long fingers around the steering wheel. "Yes. And here's the stretch."

"How long've you lived here? What's your last name?"

Sam put his foot over Edward's on the accelerator and pushed. "Name's Pride. Sam Pride. Been around for a few thousand years."

Edward tried to raise his foot. Sam was too strong. "Quit clownin' around, Sham."

"I'm not clowning, preacher man." He pushed harder.

The speedometer registered one-twenty, then one-forty . . . one-fifty . . .

The wheels touched black ice. Edward had the sensation of leaving the road's surface—floating—like a small plane that had just lifted off. For several hundred yards the Jag slid smoothly and soundlessly across the ice in a forward motion. The road took a gentle curve to the left and the Jag continued in its straight path. When the wheels hit the gravel on the right side of the road the car went into a horizontal spin.

Mute with terror Edward gripped the steering wheel so tightly pain shot through his injured hand and up his arm. A gush of fresh blood spewed through the napkin onto the leather steering wheel.

Like a giant Frisbee, the Jaguar sailed over the edge of the steep embankment.

Yellow eyes glared at him from every corner of the vehicle. Edward looked helplessly at Sam, who'd lifted his foot and was sitting calmly in the passenger seat, waiting for the crash.

Gesturing around the interior, Sam gloated, "I brought a few friends along for the ride."

The brilliant headlights illuminated the grove of pines ahead, then the road, then pines. Time stood still. All was silent, save the quiet purr of the engine. Pines, road, pines, road . . . the spin increased in velocity and the trees came closer.

Edward's wide, incredulous eyes and the steely, soulless eyes of Pride met. And locked for an eternity.

There was a loud, sickening thud as the magnificent piece of machinery slammed broadside into a giant pine tree, wrapped halfway around it four feet above the ground, and hung there . . . suspended.

Edward's body careened through the air like a rag doll.

Sam was nowhere to be seen.

One wheel spun to a jerky stop. A jagged broken limb protruded through the twisted, shredded, black fabric top.

There was a soft murmur of falling pine needles as the shivering tree absorbed the brunt of the impact.

And silence.

160

18

Edward forbade Casey to call a church member with a problem. Any member. Any problem. Ever.

So when he didn't come home for dinner and hadn't shown up by 1:00 a.m., Casey was pacing the floor. He'd never stayed out past nine or ten. Where would a man in his position go that would keep him out later? An evangelistic meeting? Casey would be with him. And he wasn't in someone's home ministering. He hadn't done that in months.

The wind was howling. Freezing rain pelted the window. She pulled her robe tighter around herself and peered out. It didn't look like it was going to let up anytime soon.

Terrible pictures flooded her mind. Lately Edward liked to think he was sophisticated. But in reality, about worldly things, he was completely naive. He'd been in the pastorate since he graduated from seminary.

By 2:00 a.m., she couldn't carry the burden alone any longer. Digging through her purse, she retrieved the folded-up receipt with Witt's phone number on it. With trembling fingers, she dialed.

"Hello." His voice sounded muffled.

"Oh, Witt, I'm sorry to call you so late. I don't know what to do."

"Case, what's wrong?" The anxiety in his voice canceled out the sleepiness.

"Edward hasn't come home. He's made me promise never to call a church member in an emergency. The weather is so bad. I'm getting really worried."

"Do you know where he went today?"

"He took Brother Mike to a late lunch in St. Michael. That's all he'd planned, as far as I know. I'd call Brother Mike, but everyone would know by morning and Edward would never forgive me. I've tried calling his cellular phone, but he hates it and doesn't turn it on often."

Witt was silent for a moment. "Case, has he started drinking?"

"I don't think he'd ever touch alcohol."

"I'm coming over. How do I get to your house?"

"I don't know if that's a good idea, Witt. He could come home anytime and he probably wouldn't be very understanding if he found a man here."

"Or he could come home and cross the line. Hurt you again. If I'm right about the demons, they may try to kill you."

Goosebumps peppered her arms. "Kill *me*? Why would they . . ."

"I'm on my way, Case. I'll carry my cellular and call for directions when I get close. You have someplace to hide if he's drunk or violent?"

"I'll be okay. Witt, please be careful. We've got freezing rain here and I heard on TV the mountain roads are treacherous. If anything happened to you, I'd never forgive myself."

As soon as she replaced the receiver, Casey began pacing.

"What a fool you are. Your husband is missing and you've called your best, *and only*, friend out in this weather." *Oh, Lord, please watch over Witt. And bring Edward safely home.*

The impact had slung the hood some fifty feet away. It lay, wrinkled like a piece of used gift wrap, against the foot of another pine tree. As the wind picked up, the silence that pervaded the desolate wilderness was broken by a soft hissing sound as freezing rain began to fall again, landing on the exposed hot engine of the dismembered Jaguar.

Soon even that faded, as the cold air and driving rain cooled the twisted ruins.

The mountain roads were quickly becoming impassable. It was doubtful anyone would discover the wreckage for days. By that time the wildcats, coyotes, and buzzards would have left little in the way of flesh.

About twenty yards to the left of the wreckage something moved. A twig snapped. Out of the deep shadows, a dark figure emerged.

He pulled himself up from a big pile of hay left for the open-range cattle. Thrown from the car on impact, he'd missed the trees and miraculously been deposited on the only soft spot for hundreds of yards.

What was left of his pint of bourbon had also survived. Edward was glad Sam had put the lid on and stuck it back in his pocket. The warm liquid had been a welcome friend as he lay in the hay trying to pull together the evening's events.

"Sham? Where are you, you crazy idiot?" A hollow cry in the wilderness.

"How long have I been out here? Why hasn't Casey come to find me? My hand hurts like blue blazes."

Thrashing around in the grove, he hit his head on the fender of the Jag, which was perched partway up a tree.

"Whoa. Look at that." He slapped his knee. "Brother Mike is going to be hacked. Hope it's insured." A giggle escalated into a belly laugh.

Suddenly his laughter abated. He flailed around in the underbrush. "Sham? Are you okay? Answer me."

Sam had a lousy sense of humor. He caused the wreck. Why would anyone do that? Thousands of years old? Weird guy. But he may be badly hurt. No one should be left out here to die.

He staggered through the slush, calling Sam and stopping occasionally to take a swig. Clutching his open bottle of booze in his good hand, he tucked the other hand in his coat between buttons.

The freezing rain was coming down harder now. Edward's foot

caught in a vine and he toppled forward. Holding his bottle of bourbon high, he yanked his injured hand out of his coat to catch himself. The bloody napkin fell into the icy dirt and the wound began bleeding again. He slopped the filthy rag around it as tight as he could. Edward sat in the slush, swaying, hand throbbing, his head about to burst.

"Ought to use some bourbon to disinfect it, like in the movies. Ha. What a waste of bourbon." He raised the bottle to his lips again. It was nearly empty.

Suddenly he remembered his cellular phone Casey insisted he carry. He hadn't charged it in several days, but maybe it had enough juice. He fumbled in his pockets with a bloody hand.

"I hate this big thing. Would've had room for more booze if I wasn't carrying it."

It slipped from his hand and fell in the slush. Edward picked it up and shook the wet dirt off. His fingers felt like they were going to crack and break off.

"Here's your emergency, Casey," he hooted to the desolate surroundings. "See, I'm calling."

Somehow he remembered how to turn it on. Casey had put in the important numbers. All he had to do was to hit two digits. Just two. It took several tries, but finally he heard his home phone ringing.

Casey picked up on the first ring. "Edward, where are you?"

"How am I supposed to know? Come get me. You can't miss me. I'm the only one walking."

"Edward, please, you must give me some idea where you are."

"On the mountain pass. Better be quick. I'm gonna freeze, if I don't bleed to death first." Cursing, he threw the phone into the darkness.

Pulling himself up, he began stumbling around again, going in a big circle around his once-beautiful car. Lifting the empty bottle to his lips again, he tried to glean one last drop.

"I shoulda bought more."

He threw the bottle over his shoulder.

Casey dialed Witt.

"Hear from him, Case?"

"Yes. He's somewhere on the mountain pass, walking . . . and Witt . . . he sounded drunk." Her worst fears were being realized.

"Okay, little lady, I'm a short way from the turnoff. I'll keep my eyes open. You *do* know if I can't find him pretty quick, we've got to call the sheriff.

"Yes, I know. But I'm scared for him. He said something about bleeding to death. Witt, I can't believe this is happening. It's like a bad dream."

"I'll find him, Case. I'm about to make the turn into the pass. I'll call as soon as I see him."

The next forty-five minutes were a living hell for Casey. She didn't want to pester Witt, but she could barely control the urge to call him to be sure he was all right.

Maneuvering an easy left on the icy road, Witt squinted as his head-lights picked up something at the tree line that looked like a mangled automobile. He stopped to take a better look. Then pulled over and got his flashlight out of the glove compartment. Praying, he hopped out onto the icy roadside shoulder.

He worked his way down the embankment and across the narrow field between the road and the pine grove. As he got closer, he was relieved to see it was not a Cadillac. Too small.

He neared the wreckage. When he smelled the hot engine he knew it was a recent accident. His heart sank. It didn't look good for someone.

He shone his flashlight on the demolition that lay before him, steeling himself for the worst. But the twisted metal held no captives. There was blood on the steering wheel . . . still sticky. He swept the light in all directions in a big circle around the carnage. There was a large pile of hay and a chunk of blown-out tire that had probably been there for years. And fresh footprints. Turning his light back to the vehicle, Witt recognized the make. A brand-new black Jaguar.

A phone rang.

"What the . . ." Witt followed the sound. Ten yards away, he found a discarded cellular. He picked it up.

His throat was tight. "Hello?"

"Witt?" He heard Casey's incredulous voice. "What are you doing answering Edward's phone?"

"Found it on the ground near a recently wrecked car. There are footprints, Case, so he must be around here somewhere. I'll get back to you."

Witt followed the single set of footprints into the thick brush. Stickers were tearing at his boots and slapping his face as he struggled toward the sound of someone crying. Finally his light shone on a pitiful derelict who lay prone in an icy bed of mud. He was covered in brambles and briars that dug into his pant legs like prehensile claws and rendered him helpless.

Edward's bloodshot eyes blinked in the bright beam of light. "Praish the Lord and pash the bourbon."

Witt could scarcely believe his eyes. It was Jaguar man. Now he knew why the Lord had laid it on his heart to pray for the stranger in the Jaguar. This man had been the object of his prayers *for weeks.*

He'd seen Edward looking elegant and aloof. Now he was a bum and a derelict. And it was the bum he'd be taking home to Casey—his Katherine. Something had to be done to save Edward . . . and soon.

He struggled to get Edward in an upright position.

"Edward, what happened?"

"I shtopped for a shteak. Where'sh Sham?" His head lolled back.

"You've got to stay awake and talk to me. Who's Sam, Edward?" Witt dipped his hand into the slush and rubbed some on Edward's face.

Edward slapped at Witt's hands. "Whatcha doin'? Who're you? Where's Sham?"

"Who. Is. Sam?" Witt had dealt with drunks before, but never a drunken pastor.

"Sham Pride. You know, long-fingered Sham," Edward drawled. "He made me drink. Made me wreck. Held my foot down. I don't think I like him anymore." He slumped into Witt's arms.

Witt shone his light in another big circle. There was no sign of another human being. And only one set of footprints. But he couldn't take the chance of leaving someone out here to die.

"Edward. Wake up. Where's Sam from?" More slush on the face.

Edward raised his head and looked at Witt through slitted eyelids. "Round here. For thousands of years. Breath smelled like it, too . . ." He collapsed again.

A shudder ran down Witt's backbone.

He pulled a pocketknife from his jeans and freed Edward from his briar prison. And half-carried, half-dragged him through the frozen sludge and up the embankment. It was almost beyond his capability. Muscles quivering from exertion, Witt finally plunked Edward's dead weight onto the passenger seat and heaved a sigh. He stripped off Edward's wet coat and put his own fleece-lined jacket around him.

Edward jolted awake. "Where's my frien' Sham? You gotta find him." His head plopped to one side and he was out again.

Witt belted him in and covered him with two horse blankets. Casey's fragrance still clung to the one she'd used recently. Witt drew in a ragged breath and tucked the blankets under Edward's legs and around his shoulders.

He dare not start the Jeep and turn on the heater. Edward might awaken and drive off while he searched for Sam. Leaving them both to freeze to death. He had to move fast. Edward wasn't out of danger yet.

In his shirtsleeves, Witt ran back to the scene of the accident.

He thought he heard groaning from deep within the thicket and plunged into the overgrowth. But when he got to where the sound originated, no one was there. Making a wide sweep with his light, he searched the terrain. Nothing.

His shirt was soaked and debilitating cold gripped his body. He was shaking so hard he could barely hold his flashlight, but he couldn't leave until he found Sam.

He tried to take a step forward. His boots were entangled in briars. Leaning over to cut them away, he felt something snag his back. A thorn ripped into his shoulder as he twisted around to look. Then another on his arm. And across his face like a cat-o'-nine-tails.

An odor seemed to rise from out of the ground. It was the same smell he'd detected in the back of his Jeep just days ago.

Indistinct murmuring and laughter plagued his eardrums.

He slashed at the briars that ensnared him, but they were pouncing from trees, seizing and tenaciously clinging to him faster than he could dispatch them. Burrs penetrated his denim jeans, jabbing into his flesh as he helplessly watched vines encircle his legs. The murmuring and laughing grew louder. The stench stronger.

Was the cold playing tricks with his mind?

His flashlight dropped into the slush. His numb fingers were about to lose their grip on his pocketknife.

Barely discernible over the incessant babbling assaulting his ears, his phone rang. He was sure it was Casey, but briars were fastening upon his arms, digging in. He couldn't reach his phone. The ringing stopped, then started again. And again.

The repeated ringing was all that kept him from losing consciousness.

Katherine needs me.

Suddenly his foggy brain grasped what was happening.

Edward's friend, Sam Pride, *was thousands of years old.*

"In the name of Jesus," his voice boomed through the desolate wilderness. "Be gone."

He heard the awful whoosh of dozens of leathery wings, and a blast of odor-laden air hit him in the face, gagging him. The fetor dissipated. The murmuring and the heinous laughter ceased.

He could once again smell the fragrant pine needles and hear the sound of the fierce wind provoking the stiff pine branches.

He chopped away at the choking vines, some as thick as his forefinger. The deadening cold impeded his movements and he grappled with an overwhelming desire to close his eyes and nap, for just a moment.

I gotta stay awake. Katherine needs me.

Finally liberated, he lunged toward freedom. The short distance to the Jeep was torture. His shirt was stiff with ice. Mud sucked at his boots and the incline to the road felt like a thousand-foot cliff.

Inside the Jeep, his passenger was writhing in his seat, trying to escape the confines of his seat belt and yelling for more bourbon. Witt jumped in, started the engine, and turned the heater on high. Within moments heat was pumping into the Jeep. And Edward was snoring.

Witt removed his wet shirt. Sure that Edward was warm enough, he removed the fragrant blanket from around him. Pulling it over his own shoulders, he closed his eyes and breathed in Casey's fragrance. His heart swelled. *God, this is so painful.*

He removed the filthy napkin from Edward's hand and took a quick look, determining the wound was not life threatening. It was more important to get this man into a warm bed than to a hospital. He'd clean and dress the wound at Casey's, where he could see what he was doing. He rewrapped it with a clean bandage and dialed Casey.

She answered before the first ring had finished.

"I've got him, Case. He had an accident, but he's okay. And you're right, he's drunk. Wet, cold, and drunk. He has a cut on his hand, but I think he'll be no worse for the wear after a good night's sleep and a little doctoring. Tell me how to get to your house."

He decided to hold off on telling Casey about the demon battle he'd just fought. There was no point in frightening her needlessly.

She gave him directions and asked him to pull around back. They'd be less apt to be seen by neighbors.

After they hung up, Casey slipped into a pair of jeans and a sweater and went to the kitchen to make a pot of coffee and wait. She sat by a front window, watching for headlights. At nearly 5:00 a.m. Witt pulled in.

She ran to unlock the back door and watched as Witt, with a blanket over his shoulders, walked to the passenger side and unbuckled Edward's seat belt. Holding another blanket tightly around Edward, Witt lifted him out of the vehicle and carried him in like a baby.

So strong.

She held the door open for them.

He was hurt. "Witt, your face . . ."

"I'm fine, Case. Can't say the same for this fellow, though. He needs some doctoring."

Casey looked at Edward and shook her head. "Are you sure he's okay? He looks awful."

"He's going to have one heck of a hangover when he wakes up, Case, but I think he's okay. I want to have a look at his hand. It needs cleaning and bandaging. I brought my case, but if you have peroxide and fresh antibiotic ointment, that would be better."

She showed him to the bedroom, where she'd already turned down the bed. Then hurried off to get the medicine. When she returned, Witt was already cleansing Edward's wound. The patient was sound asleep, stripped to his underwear. The blanket had slipped from Witt's shoulders and he was bare chested too.

Casey's heart forgot to beat and she felt her face grow hot. She looked away and hurriedly excused herself.

When Witt arrived in the kitchen, she could see the exhaustion in his eyes.

I'm asking too much of him.

"Witt. You need medical attention yourself." Casey ran her fingers over the cut on his back. Her fingers tingled at the touch of his bare skin and suddenly she was short of breath. Alarmed at her own emotions, she drew back and moved to the other side of the table, too far away to touch him again, and stood there. "What happened out there?"

"It's nothing, Case. Just scratches. Lots of briars and brambles in those woods.

"I'm afraid his overcoat is ruined." He lifted the welcome mug of hot coffee to his lips. "But it probably saved him some serious injury. And I don't think the cut on his hand happened in the accident. It was wrapped in a filthy restaurant napkin. That place on the highway, right before the turnoff. You know the one I mean?"

"You mean the place with the big, flashing 'margarita' sign out front?"

He nodded. "That's the one."

"Maybe when he wakes up I can find out what happened last night." She sighed. "Won't you stay and get some sleep before you hit the road across the mountains? You don't need to be out in this weather and you look like you could use some rest."

She'd be devastated if anything happened to Witt.

You've known him less than a month. Get ahold of yourself.

"Sweet lady, it will be light soon and I don't think I need to be here if he awakens. He may be very grouchy. I don't think he'll be dangerous, because he's going to feel miserable. But it'd be best if I be on my way. Just let me enjoy one cup of coffee with you first." He patted the chair next to him. "Come on, sit down."

Casey wanted to apply salve to the scratches that covered his body. It didn't seem fair. He did so much for others and had no one to comfort him.

It was all she could do to keep from hugging him. But somehow it didn't seem right, here in her home, with her husband sleeping in the next room. *And Witt stripped to the waist.*

For the first time since they'd met, she was uneasy in his presence.

Their relationship seemed to have shifted into another gear.

She was staring at him. He was so much more muscular than he looked with his shirt on. Witt glanced down at his chest. "Oh, I'm sorry. I shouldn't be sitting here like this. I need to get that blanket back on. My shirt got all wet."

"I'm ... I ... my mind was a million miles away. Let me get you a shirt from Edward's closet."

"He might miss it. My shirt's in the Jeep. Ten minutes in the dryer and it'll be okay. You mind?"

"Of course not."

Witt jumped up and went down the hall to the bedroom.

He came through on his way to the Jeep, carrying his jacket and a blanket. The other blanket was back around his shoulders. "Edward's sleeping like a baby."

"Oh good." Casey was shaking.

She wanted him to go. She wanted him to stay.

"Case, how do you set the timer to go off in ten minutes?" Witt was standing in front of the dryer, scratching his head.

She came into the small laundry room, pressed a couple of buttons, and the dryer came to life. Smiling up at him indulgently, she shook her head. "It's not rocket science."

"It's girl stuff though, so I didn't know." He shrugged his shoulders and his blanket fell to the floor.

She leaned down to get it at the same time he did. They bumped and she lost her balance.

Witt reached out to steady her and Casey fell against him. She began trembling.

This is too much for her to face alone. There must be something I can do.

With only the thought of comforting her, he pulled her close and stroked her back. But her cheek against his bare chest sent a jolt through his body.

Her face was turned up to him, her eyes closed.

His heart was primed to explode.

A whisper. *She's yours. What are you waiting for?*

Witt reached out to touch her soft cheek. All three dogs started barking below the laundry room window. Casey squirted out of Witt's arms like a bunny out of a trap and ran to the window.

"Looks like Soupy had company. There was a wild possum looking into his pen. Isn't it something how the dogs know when it's not *their* possum?" She laughed nervously.

The dogs settled down. Eyes on the floor, Casey turned her body and slid past Witt without touching him. He could see she was frightened.

Was she frightened he'd stay, or go?

He followed her out of the laundry room, holding the blanket together over his chest. "I think I'd better leave, Case."

"No. Please stay until your shirt dries. I can't send you home shirtless."

Coffee sloshed onto the table as she poured each of them a fresh cup. "Is the Cadillac drivable?" Her voice quavered.

He put his hands around his coffee cup, lest he reach out to her. "I don't know where the Cadillac is, Case. He was driving a

Jaguar. And it's wrapped around a pine tree in the middle of the mountain pass."

"A Jaguar?"

"Yes, I saw him driving it in town yesterday. Of course, I didn't know at the time it was Edward."

"You're *sure* it was him?"

"Very sure. Even prayed for him. I wondered why the Lord laid him on my heart. I guess I know now."

"Oh, heaven forbid. He must have wheedled a Jaguar out of old Brother Mike. He's been talking about needing something better than a Cadillac, if he was to look truly successful. And he's already wrecked it. Oh, Witt, he's no longer the man I married. I don't know this man at all." Her shoulders sagged and she shook her head. "I'm so sorry I dragged you into this."

"Don't be sorry, Case. Just admit we need to take action. Only God's intervention allowed him to survive the crash. Apparently he landed in a huge pile of hay left out for range cattle. Five feet in either direction . . . and little one . . . I'd have been bringing *his body* home to you."

She clamped her eyes shut and lowered her head into her hands.

Then peered up at him over her fingertips. "Yes, Witt, I agree."

She lowered her hands and touched them to her chin in prayer fashion. "Do what you need to involve Indi and Ron. Right away, okay?"

"Praise God. Yes."

The dryer buzzed and Witt got up to get his shirt.

"Are you sure you won't stay . . . for a little while?" Her amber eyes were dark with emotion and her lips trembled.

"I can't, Case, as much as I'd like to."

If Edward awakened angry to find him there, it might be showdown time. He wasn't sure he could deny his love for Casey, were he put on the spot by the very man who was hurting her. There was no way God could get honor from that scenario.

"If he wonders how he got home, tell him a doctor from St. Michael picked him up. You won't be lying. And I doubt he'll remember enough about last night to cross-examine you."

Casey turned her back while he put his shirt on.

It's not just me. She feels it too. Oh, Lord, don't let my love bring her more pain.

"Case, call me later today. I'll get in touch with Indi in the meantime. Now I've got to go before Edward wakes up."

From her side of the table, her eyes never left him as he carried his coffee mug to the sink and rinsed it. "I really wish you didn't have to leave, Witt."

Don't, Case, please. Don't you tempt me too.

She was so sweet and trusting. And he was leaving her here with a demon-possessed man. Maybe he *should* stay. She may need protection from that fool in the next room.

Father, what should I do?

Is My strength not greater than yours?

With his back to Casey, Witt clenched his left fist and pressed it to his mouth, faking a cough. It gave him time to recoup before he faced her. He dare not touch her. He had to put some miles between them before he did something downright ungodly.

Finally he turned to her and smiled.

"Call me, Case," he said before he walked out of the house. He closed the door quietly behind him and sprinted to his Jeep. This time he didn't turn to wave good-bye.

19

"More coffee, honey?"

Indi looked up from the morning newspaper. She gazed at Ron a long time before answering. Thick black hair, close cropped with a touch of gray at the temples. She liked his hair longer, in an Afro like he used to wear it. But that was out of style and this was more befitting of a mature gentleman. Otherwise, he hadn't changed much in twenty-two years. Same muscular bronze body. Same dazzling smile. If anything, he'd improved with age.

"Well? Yes or no?" Wearing only his hot-pepper pajama bottoms, he drummed his fingers in mock impatience.

Indi could drink the whole pot herself. But she tried to hold it down to two or three cups. Stretching her arms high above her head, she intertwined her long brown fingers and drawled, "Oh, if you insist."

Mornings started early in the Williamson household. Indi and Ron sat reading the morning paper and drinking coffee. At eight o'clock sharp they headed to their bathrooms to get ready. And thirty minutes later their workday began.

Indi was an author and speaker. Her genre—the spirit world.

Ron called on his years in construction management and lifetime of lay ministry to help churches make wise decisions about the physical growth of their property.

They'd prepared for retirement and Indi's books had done well, so Ron was able to offer his services for free.

Unknown to most of their friends and neighbors, they had an underground ministry of deliverance. Their names were passed from believer to believer as the need became apparent. Witt had called on them more than once.

Their works were better known in the spirit world than in the natural.

Yes, the demons knew them well . . . and hated them.

Indi flipped her mass of long black curls away from her face, her eyes trained on Ron. "What do you think? Can we work our way into the McAlesters' lives without being obvious?"

Ron put a spoon of sugar in Indi's coffee and stirred. "I just hope the wife makes up her mind soon, 'cause it looks like he's pretty high on Satan's list of things to do."

He dropped the spoon into the sink and handed Indi her coffee as he passed her. "We won't need any help worming our way into their lives, though. I'm pretty sure I've met this guy. Well, I'm *very* sure."

"Really?" Indi put the coffee down and cocked her head to one side. "How long ago did you meet? Was it a consulting job?" Her eyes followed him to the front entry hall.

Ron opened the front door and examined the outer side. "Looks like you got it all off."

"Baby, please close the door and come talk to me." Indi sighed and took a sip of coffee.

"Okay. Just can't figure out who'd do something like that."

He refilled his cup and leaned against the kitchen countertop. "So, as I recall, he'd been a pastor all his life. Widowed and remarried while he was still pretty young. Second wife already had a son."

"Does she minister too?"

"Played church piano when her husband was a small-time pastor. I think he has a professional doing it now. Back then when he moved it was always to a smaller, needier congregation. He'd work his fingers to the bone and usually meet with great success. Most likely because he gave the Lord all the glory. I'm telling you this guy was a real prince, as Brother Hank used to say."

A crash and shattering glass in the entry hall. Ron reached the door in three strides.

Indi sank to her knees in front of her chair. *Dear Father, whoever is doing this, please speak to their hearts.*

"Another rat carcass on the front porch, baby. He's a big one, the door took a bad hit. We'll have to replace the window."

"Oh Ron. Four rats in four days. What are we going to do? I'm afraid to leave the house." Indi walked into the living room and slowly sank into an overstuffed chair next to the fireplace. "They might burn it down."

"And I'm afraid for you to stay in it alone." He knelt in front of her.

Indi shook her head. "They're not going to hurt me, baby. Someone's trying to scare us."

Ron picked up the phone. "We need to call the police."

"No, wait. They haven't been able to come up with anything from the first three. And we've lost hours of work with each one, answering questions. Let's not give the devil any more of our precious time."

Ron heaved a sigh. "You're probably right."

Indi held her hand out to him. "Whoever they are, we can't let them stop us from doing what the Lord's commissioned us to do. So, let's keep discussing Pastor McAlester. He's got problems and we have the answer."

Ron settled down onto the floor in front of her. "I think we have problems too, Indi. We can't serve the Lord if we can't leave the house. And if we leave we might come home to a pile of ashes."

"The pastor, Ron, the pastor. His soul is more important than our house. Finish your story."

"Okay . . ." Ron sighed. "The little church he was serving caught fire for the Lord and was growing like a weed. About two and a half, maybe three, years ago." Ron got up and walked over to the door. He looked out from one end of the block to the other.

"They're not going to stand out there and wave at you, Ronnie."

"Sorry." He rubbed his well-defined upper arms briskly. "How about I build a little fire. It's chilly in here."

"Not this late in the morning, baby. You might want to consider putting on more clothes, although I *am* enjoying the view." Indi grinned. "We've got plans to make." She pointed down at the floor in front of her. "Sit. Talk."

"Okay." Ron sat back down. "One of the members, Mike Somebody—gave the church a lot of money. He was old and had so much he couldn't count it. He wanted to do something good before he died, so he gave two hundred and fifty thousand dollars, I believe, for a new building."

"Hold that thought. I need more coffee." She was already headed for the kitchen.

"You're drinking way too much coffee again, honey. Need to pace yourself."

"I'll pace myself, all right. I'm counting the steps to the coffeepot as we speak." She shot him one of her extraordinary smiles.

Nothing Indi did was ordinary. Even the way she walked turned heads. She seemed to be gliding. Watching her this morning, in her silky pale-blue robe, belted at the waist, and hemmed at the knee to reveal shapely dark legs, Ron felt a catch in his throat.

She returned with her coffee, glancing at the front hall as she passed. Settling back into her chair, she lifted the huge mug to her lips with both hands. Ron didn't speak right away. He was silently thanking the Lord for the life he shared with this spiritual spitfire.

"Okay, please continue."

"Can't a fella take a minute to thank the Lord for his fabulous wife?"

"Oh, I'm sorry. Take all the time you need." She put her coffee down, walked to his chair, and leaned over to plant a kiss on his nose.

He straightened up to meet her lips with his. With his hand on the back of her head, he pulled her close and held her briefly in that awkward position. She wiggled and he released her. They both laughed.

"Back to the good pastor. I tried to talk the board into building with the money available and expand later. No mortgage. But nothing would do except to spend closer to six hundred thousand on a really beautiful worship center. Cramped their style for a while. But they knew better than I what was happening in that little church. As far as I know it's still growing. And the building was paid for in just over a year."

Settling back into her easy chair, Indi nodded. "That certainly explains why the pastor is under attack. He's been doing too much for the Lord. Satan's not at all pleased."

"Yep. Satan has a good-sized army to choose from, and I bet he has some of his best on this case, Indi."

She hopped up and began pacing. "Think about it, Ron. It's taken three years for the powers of hell to get the pastor in this shape. He must be quite a fighter. And Satan's climbing the walls to get the job done. We don't have any time to waste. How long will it take to wiggle your way in?"

"I'll call this morning and ask how the building is working out. With any kind of luck, he and I will have a golf date by Friday. And you and I will have the preliminaries out of the way and be ready for action."

"Isn't the weather kind of bad for golfing?"

"It's supposed to warm up. But I doubt it would make a difference. Word is McAlester prefers the golf course to his church office these days. Hardly spends any time studying. He depends on his knock-'em-dead speaking style. He schmoozes the board and charms the people. Boy, I hope I can stand this guy long enough to get my foot in the door. We hit it off great three years ago, but . . ."

"Ronnie, you can do anything the Lord sets your mind to."

Ron chuckled and excused himself to look for his address book.

When he returned, Indi was just hanging up the phone. "Who was that, babe?"

"It was Witt. The golf can't wait until Friday, honey. The pastor got drunk last night and totaled a brand-new Jaguar."

"Is he okay?"

"He's fine. Landed in a pile of hay. How likely is that?"

Ron took one last slug of coffee and put his cup in the sink. "Evidently there's a full-scale contract out on him. And God's put some mighty good agents on him too or he'd already be history. But we can't expect the angels to run interference for us forever."

"Ronnie, listen to this. The wife, Casey, said he's gone in to his office this morning. Hangover and all. And—hallelujah—she's ready to get started."

"That's super. I'm going to drive over to the church instead of calling."

Indi threw her hands in the air and started dancing a jig.

Ron suppressed the urge to join in her happy dance. "I'll have to go the long way to Sugar Bluff. Heard on the news the mountain road is impassible. So if I'm going, I need to hit the road."

Indi was still prancing around, snapping her fingers.

Ron increased his volume. "And I'll probably be after dark getting back. What do you think?" He caught a hold of Indi as she whirled past him. "Come on, girl, stop dancing long enough to answer me."

She bent over to catch her breath, holding her sides and panting. "Well . . . it's twice as far that way, but this . . . is pretty important."

"I'd better clean up the mess and put a board over that broken window before I go." Suddenly it hit him. "Oh, Indi, I can't leave you here alone."

"I can take care of myself. Besides, they won't be back today. If you'll dispose of Mr. Rat, I can handle the broom and the hammer. You get yourself out of here. It's important to get to him quickly. Not only is he entertaining a hangover, he's probably sore from the accident. He's not going to put in much time at his office today."

"If I can see him we'll be on the links by Monday, weather permitting."

"Maybe you ought to dust off your old bowling ball, just in case." Indi grinned.

Ron took her hands in his. "I don't feel good about leaving. Could you ask someone over to keep you company?"

"You know I can't get any work done with someone here. Besides, I'll spend most of the day in prayer. Now scoot."

Shaking his head, he gave her a peck on the cheek and turned toward his bathroom.

"Wait." Indi stood at attention and saluted. "Any instructions for me, sir?"

She looked so doggone cute Ron really wished he didn't have to leave. How could one woman be so cute and playful and yet so deeply spiritual? God does such good work.

Maintaining a serious demeanor, Ron executed a crisp salute. "Officer Indi, keep every night this week open for a last-minute date with a demon or two. Edward doesn't know it yet, but he's going to like me so much he'll invite us over in the next few days. Guaranteed. Wait and see."

She was still at attention. "I don't doubt it for one minute, sir."

"And before I forget—at ease, soldier."

Indi flopped back into the easy chair. "I'll be ready," she called to him. "But there's one thing I'm curious about. Did I have any choice about falling in love with you or was the whole thing your idea?"

He poked his head around the corner of his bathroom door. "I'll never tell."

The sky was darkening before Indi laid her Bible down, closing her eyes for a moment. She leaned back in the chair and sighed. Ron had been gone all day and she hadn't heard a word from him.

"Does everyone know his part?" Working his way back up the ranks, Meerkat had wrangled a small leadership role. "I'll take care of the husband. I've got a big pine tree with his name on it."

Violence's thundering voice and blast of atrocious breath blew Meerkat against the shack wall. Dust flew.

"I've already done my part. Recruited ten of them at no small expense." His piercing laugh splintered the dense atmosphere hanging over the gathering.

Meerkat glared at Violence and picked himself up. He made a sweeping gesture over the assembly with one talon extended. "The rest of you . . . don't get cute. You're spectral shadows. No bodies, no words, except for moaning. Take turns wrapping your pitiful murky selves around the light bulbs. Keep it gloomy."

A groan from the back. "Can we decimate the place? You know, tear things up?"

"I know what *decimate* means, slimeball. Yes, if you can invoke the power of touch, by all means, knock a few things over. But don't forget the real reason you're there."

"Which is?" A rumble from under the ground.

Meerkat looked down between his two big toes. "To crumble her tough exterior, numbskull. Do whatever you *need* to do to make her useless. She and her old man are getting involved with the McAlester case and we gotta stop them. You bumbling idiots couldn't even kill McAlester when he was drunk, and now we've got to deal with the Williamsons. I'm putting old Ronnie-Boy out of commish all by myself. Surely the whole lot of you can handle one woman."

Quivering in the front row, a small demon stood. "It's no fun coming up against her. I have before and look at me." He spread out his membranous wings. Riddled with holes. "Prayer. When she prays, He listens."

"So don't give her a chance to pray. She'll be grossly outnumbered, harebrain. And she's a human. They're weak. Every last one of them. But you have to be smart enough to know which buttons to push. I'll give you a hint . . . she's squeamish about things getting in her hair."

Meerkat pumped his fist in the little demon's face. "The sun has set. Get to work."

A thud at the front door. Indi opened it. In the fading light she saw a dead bird, already decaying, on the front steps. She closed the door.

I'll clean it up later. I might get hit in the head with one if I go out there now.
She shuddered.

Another thud. From the back entrance. A dead mouse.

Thump. Thump. Objects were hitting windows throughout the house.

Indi turned on the porch light. It provided no more brightness than if it had been wrapped in black cellophane. She hurried around the house, turning on every lamp, but they afforded very little illumination. She began to pray. The thudding ceased for a couple of minutes, then resumed. She shone a flashlight through the slats of the Venetian blinds and saw decomposing chicken parts strewn under the window.

The thermostat was on high and the heat pump was throbbing, trying to keep up. But an eerie coldness enveloped the house. Perhaps a fire would give her warmth *and* banish the unrelenting darkness that cloaked the room like a gloomy veil.

Ron, where are you?

She placed some logs and tinder in the fireplace and struck a match. It went out. A whiff of rancid air. A second match went out as well. The smell stung her nostrils.

Ron kept a lighter in the garage to light his blowtorch. Indi found it and lit it. The flame flickered from side to side and the stench of rotten flesh hit her from both sides and gagged her.

She managed to get a roaring fire going and fell exhausted onto the couch.

A vague shadow emerged in the far corner of the room. She rubbed her eyes.

Adjusting to the gloom, she saw what appeared to be filmy shrouds of black gauze. Floating into the room from the chimney. From around the window facings. Clustered in the corners and dangling from the ceiling fan.

In defiance she got up and turned on the fan. Black membranes soared in all directions. Slithered down the walls. And wafted on the air currents.

The sound of distant moaning filled the air. And an unidentifiable awful odor.

An authority on matters of the spirit and a child of God, Indi was more excited than frightened. She'd felt the presence of demons before. But she'd never seen one.

She grabbed her notepad and pen from the coffee table. Scribbling a description from time to time, she observed them as they seemed to gain energy. Diving at one another and speeding within inches of her face before boomeranging in another direction.

A flimsy black entity encircled a vase on the mantel. Indi squinted and followed its movements. Twice it seemed to go right through the vase. On the third try the vase quivered before the form slipped through.

It's trying to move the vase.

Spellbound, she put down her pen.

Another failed attempt.

Finally the vase wobbled and hung at an angle briefly before crashing to the hearth below. Indi squealed in spite of herself.

Her involuntary reaction seemed to empower the demons. A lamp hit the floor. The hands on Grandpa Williamson's antique mantel clock started spinning wildly. Everywhere around her inanimate objects began moving. And more demons kept coming in.

Indi watched, wide-eyed.

They couldn't harm her. Even Satan had to follow the rules.

The wailing and moaning swelled. Savage noises originated below the carpet. Perhaps below the ground. She cringed on one end of the couch and clutched a pillow to her chest.

Watch your body language. No cringing. No clutching. Take notes, girl.

She sat up straight, dropped the pillow, and picked up her notepad. She scribbled a few words. *No one is going to believe this.* The demons seemed to be working themselves into a frenzy. She wished Ron were here to witness this manifestation with her.

Please come home, Ron.

Her notepad fluttered to the floor and she realized she was clutching the pillow again.

So many demons.

She felt something move in her hair. It made her skin crawl. When it brushed her scalp Indi grabbed her head with both hands.

No. They're not allowed to touch me.

Her combs and hairpins flew from her hair, jettisoned into the fire.

Fear gripped her when Indi realized they had discovered her weakness.

Her long locks cascaded around her shoulders. Feeding on that weakness, the first of many demons rolled up into a serpent and slithered into her hair. Then another and another. The cachinnating shadows raked through her hair, twisting and turning.

Snakes in my hair. Get them out!

She desperately clutched at the creatures, whimpering and squealing. Slipping through her groping fingers, they squirmed in and out of her thick tresses. Panic gripped her. She grasped and snatched at her hair.

Faster and faster the frenzied demons churned through her mane, sliding across her face, nudging at her lips, until Indi—afraid to open her mouth—was gasping for air.

Her tormentors laughed all the louder. Indi's voluminous black hair was over her eyes and plastered to her cheeks. A tangled mess of writhing creatures.

She tried to call on Jesus's name but couldn't draw a breath.

She had no voice left. She mouthed His name. "Jesus."

Demon activity ceased. Total silence. Indi didn't move. She'd never know how long she sat there immobile, unseeing. Taking one shallow breath after another until her breathing was almost normal.

Finally she pushed the hair back from her eyes. Something that felt like a cobweb stuck to her hand. She shook it off. The room was in a shambles. Gauzy creatures were draped over every surface. The back of the couch. Her lap. Her shoulder. The smell was unbearable.

She made a face and held her hands away from her body, trying to figure out whether to brush them off. They were surely still in her hair too. The thought made her retch.

From the corner of her eye she saw a movement. Then another. The creatures were beginning to move, flex—regroup. His name had knocked the wind out of them. But they were recovering.

Indi had imagined she could withstand the powers of hell alone in order to study them. *It would have made a great book.* But she couldn't. She needed Jesus. Now.

"In the name of Jesus, I command you to leave this house."

Their instantaneous evacuation tore pictures from the wall and left Indi breathless. Screams of anguish echoed all the way to the caverns of hell.

The phone rang.

Trembling, Indi picked it up. "Hello?"

"Honey, I'm sorry I'm running late. You won't believe what happened on the way home. I'll explain when I get there. Praise God, I'm blessed to be alive."

"Tell me, please. What happened?"

"I slowed down to avoid hitting a possum, baby, and a huge pine tree fell across the road not three feet from my hood. If it weren't for that possum, I'd be dead."

A shudder ran through Indi's body.

"The possum's okay, too." Ron laughed weakly. "Probably won't come near that road for a while though. I had to wait while they cleared the road. You all right?"

"I'm okay. Just need you here with me. Be safe."

"Bye, baby. I love you."

"Bye." Indi dropped the receiver and cradled her head in her hands. *Thank You, Jesus.*

Thump. It came from the kitchen. Another from the bedroom. It was starting again.

20

The reality of the demon attack on Indi was evident all around her. Broken glass, furniture out of place, and a glance in the mirror revealing a disheveled woman in wrinkled and torn clothing. But the gloom and filth that had covered every surface were gone. And with every light in the house on, it shone like a lighthouse beacon.

But in spite of the brightness Indi steeled herself for another attack. The thumping had resumed. She was on the lookout for black gauzy creatures. With the name of Jesus on the tip of her tongue, she wouldn't be lulled again into believing she could keep the lid on a demon attack without His help.

A voice from outside. "Stop right where you are. Believe me, you *don't* want to cross me."

Indi peeked through the blinds into the backyard. Dark figures milled around. One large entity seemed to be herding the others into line. The smaller ones fought among themselves. Demons preparing for attack.

"Front and center, *now*." It was *Ron's* voice. Using the military terms he'd last used with their boys, now grown, like a drill sergeant disciplining recruits. She counted them. Five.

Indi slipped a sweater on, turned on the back light, and went out. "Ron, what's going on? Who are these boys?" She put her hand to her nose. "And what in the world is that awful smell?"

"Hi, baby." Ron did a double take. "Oh, Lord, what *happened* to you?" Ron ran his fingers over her hair and she shivered. He held her chin up. His eyes scanned her face. "Are you all right?"

"I'll explain later. There's no short explanation and right now you need to tell me what's going on out here."

Ron wrinkled his brow and touched her hair again, then gestured toward the house. "Well, I sensed something wrong when I called you. And when I pulled around the corner to see every light in the house on, I decided to park down the street and come the rest of the way on foot through some neighbor's yards—just in case."

One of the boys sidled away.

"Get back here. I'm not done with you."

Ron could sound so mean—for a pussycat. The young man of about thirteen stepped back into line.

"The boys here were having a wonderful time throwing something nasty smelling at the house. I caught a couple of them by the shirt collar and the others decided they'd rather surrender than have me come after them."

"What's this you're throwing, guys?" Indi looked into one of their bags. She closed the bag quickly and turned around to gasp for a breath of fresh air. "Yuck, spoiled chicken parts. Where'd you get them?"

"From the big guy," one of the boys volunteered.

"What big guy?" Ron had mellowed a little.

"The one with the tattoo on his neck."

"It wasn't on his neck, stupid, it was on his arm," another boy protested.

A third one spoke up. "You guys don't know nothin'. It was on his chest."

"Wait a minute." Ron rubbed his palms together. "Let's see if we can agree on what the tattoo was."

All five boys spoke at once. "It was a V."

"Okay, there was this big guy with a V tattoo somewhere on his body. Can you tell me anything else about him?"

"He was the biggest, meanest-looking, stinkiest guy I've ever met." The tallest of the boys became their self-appointed spokesman. "He gave me twenty dollars to throw stuff at your house."

"Yeah, me, too."

"Me too."

Each boy confirmed he'd been given a twenty-dollar bill and a huge bag of rancid chicken parts to throw at the house. But no two boys had seen the mysterious man at the same time. And there were conflicting accounts of his appearance. They all agreed on these things: he was mean looking, big and stinky, and had a V tattoo.

"Did he give you dead rats to throw too?" Ron put his hand on a boy's shoulder.

"Nah. We found them at the dump. He said we'd get a bonus for dead rats and birds. He's coming back tomorrow to pay us the rest."

Indi's heart went out to the boys. "Handling rotten flesh is so dangerous to your health, boys." She'd seen some of them riding their bikes down the street in front of the house. "And did you realize you were breaking the law when you threw that stuff at our house?"

"The guy said it was a Halloween prank and he was paying you back for what you did to him last year, and you'd think it was funny." The smallest boy was near tears.

"Don't touch your face. I'll be right back." Indi ran into the house and returned with a towel, soap, and a bucket of warm water. A couple of trash bags were shoved in her pocket. "Come on, guys. Wash your hands."

She stood by with the towel to be sure each one washed up properly.

"Let's sit on the steps." Ron put his hand on the shoulders of two of the taller boys and the others followed. "Is this all of you or are there others?"

"We started out with ten, but five of the guys got scared off a while ago. They ran when they saw all the black stuff exploding out of the house."

Ron raised his eyebrows and looked at Indi. "An explosion?"

Indi shrugged. "You'll see when we get inside. But it helps to know some of the chaos was the work of small human pranksters.

Let's finish talking to the boys so they can go home. I know they're ready." She winked at the littlest one, who was wiping his nose on the back of his hand.

Ron pulled Indi aside. "This guy sounds like he might be one of Edward's guests, don't you think? V might be for"—he lowered his voice—"violence."

"That's what I was thinking. He never looked exactly the same. Big, mean, and stinky. The timing was perfect to scare me out of my wits. Believe me, he did a great job of *that*. But where did he get the money? Twenty dollars each to ten boys. That's two hundred dollars. And dem . . ." She glanced at the boys. They were all staring at her. "His type have no access to cash money."

She turned back to the boys and held out her hand. "May I see the twenty-dollar bills he gave you?"

They exchanged glances, but no one produced his stash.

"I won't keep it. I just want to look at it. Promise."

One by one they began digging in their pockets.

"Hey! This is just a folded-up piece of newspaper."

"Mine too. But I know he gave me a twenty. I stretched it out and looked at it."

One by one the boys pulled out their hard-earned money to find each bill had become a worthless piece of newspaper.

"What a gyp. How'd he do that?"

Ron looked each of the boys in the eye. "Boys, this is a tough lesson, but I hope you've learned something from it. Evil deeds done in the dark can bring only disappointment, if not worse."

Indi nodded in agreement. "Before you go, I'd like to pray for you."

The boys groaned.

Indi and Ron stretched their arms around them. "Father, I ask You to protect these boys from the Evil One and not let V or any of his associates entice them, now or ever again. Amen."

They opened their arms and the boys scattered like mice, each running to his own house, sneakers slapping the ground.

"I doubt they appreciated my prayer, but God will honor it anyway." Indi handed Ron a trash bag. "Let's clean up this mess."

They carried both bags laden with rotting chicken parts to the curb and deposited them in the trash receptacle.

"Thank goodness tomorrow is trash day." Indi steered Ron to the laundry room to wash up. Then took him by the hand and led him to the living room.

He looked at the mess before him and pulled her close. "Oh, baby, I knew I shouldn't have left you here alone."

"They tried to suffocate me, Ron, with my own hair. And they tried to kill you by pushing a pine tree over on you."

Ron shook his head. "And they've attacked Edward with intent to kill. Witt, too. I talked to him today. They're not playing games, baby." Ron squeezed her a little tighter. "I don't want you involved anymore. It's not safe. Let me handle the deliverance."

She pulled away gently. "Did you have any luck with Edward today?"

"Tomorrow we play golf. Halloween night you and I are invited to dinner. But I'm going alone."

That's what you think, handsome.

Indi nibbled on her lower lip and squeezed Ron's hand. "Halloween. How apropos."

21

S oupy, I've got to get you outside before Edward gets home. Now come out, wherever you are." On her hands and knees, Casey was searching under the king-sized bed in the master bedroom.

"What's this?"

An old shoe box. Casey pulled it out and sat on the floor with her back against the bed, preparing to open it. Soupy waddled out from behind the easy chair.

"There you are, you bad boy." She pushed the box back under the bed, scooped him into her arms, and carried him to his pen.

Soupy wasted no time crawling into the cave Casey had built out of cement blocks. He wasn't much for daytime gallivanting. He'd be back out after the sun went down to check for bugs and scraps.

She hurried back to the bedroom to check on the mysterious box. Carefully opening it, she was bewildered to find an old pistol along with a bundle of information on how to maintain it. Also a key taped to the inside of the lid.

Casey recognized the key. It locked the cabinets over the wet bar in the living room. The bar had never been used in its intended capacity. They kept soft drinks in the small refrigerator and ice cream in the freezer. The overhead cabinets came in handy, from time to time, to store items that overflowed the pantry. But they hadn't been utilized in many months.

Then a few days ago she'd needed some extra space. The cabinets were locked. Edward said he had no idea where the key was and promised to have someone come out to open them very soon.

Casey pulled the key loose, her hands shaking in her efforts to avoid disturbing the gun.

She hurried to the living room. Edward would be home any minute because he'd invited Ron and Indi over for supper. Praise the Lord.

When she opened the first door and saw bottle after bottle of liquor, she suddenly felt light-headed. She opened the second door. Same thing. And the third. There was enough liquor to open a night-club. In her living room.

She locked the doors and ran back to the bedroom to put the key back. Edward must not learn she'd found it.

Coming back into the living room, she noticed the couch pillows were out of place. Soupy must have been burrowing. Edward wouldn't tolerate that. She fluffed the pillows, then sat in the chair nearest the window so she could see if he pulled in.

Casey dialed Witt's number. It rang six times.

Please be there. Please be there.

She was about to hang up when he answered, panting.

"Case. What's wrong?"

The sound of his voice was a refuge to her heart. *Come get me, Witt.*

"Witt, I don't know how to reach Ron and Indi, but will you tell them Edward has a gun hidden under our bed, and literature on how to use it? And he has enough liquor locked in the cabinets to get an army drunk. He'll be home any minute and I don't know what to expect."

"Case, get out of there *now*." She'd never heard him so demanding.

"I can't, Witt. Tonight could be a very important night. If I'm not here when Edward gets home, he'll come looking for me, I'm sure. He's gotten extremely possessive since the accident. Deliverance is our only hope, so we've got to be here for Ron and Indi. I can't deny I'm scared, but—"

"Case, I want you to pack an overnight bag. If Ron and Indi aren't successful you must promise me you'll leave with them."

"Yes, I will. I promise. Please call them right away. And pray. Just . . ."

The door flew open and Edward stormed in. Casey slammed the receiver down.

A glint of chrome down the street caught her eye. He'd parked two doors away.

"Who were you talking to?" Both hands balled into fists.

"I was trying to get a message to Ron and his wife." Casey cowered against the back of the chair.

"You don't even *know* Ron. They're coming at seven and *you're* going to be ready. Stay off the phone. They're my friends until I say they're your friends." He stomped down the hall to the bedroom and slammed the door.

Casey breathed a sigh of relief. She'd been pretty sure he'd react just as he had. For once, his jumping to conclusions had been a blessing.

She tiptoed to the kitchen to prepare a three-day supply of food for Soupy. If she were gone longer than that, she'd call one of the neighbor kids to throw food over the fence for him while Edward was away during the day.

When she went out to feed the possum, just the end of Soupy's little pink nose poked out of his cave.

"I'm putting out plenty of goodies, Soupy, and letting your water drip. Mamma may be gone for a couple days." She locked his pen and put the key in her pocket. Edward didn't have a key and he certainly wouldn't attempt to climb the fence. Soupy was safe from his wrath. He hardly gave the animal a thought unless it was in the house.

Next she filled the automatic feeders for the dogs and cats. They got their water from a small creek on the back of the property.

Now to pack a bag. Oh, God, please let tonight be the end of the nightmare.

Indi had never looked more beautiful.

"I can't stay home, because we're a team, Ron. The quarterback is important, but he's gotta have his running back or there's no game. Same with us. God's called us as a team. Besides, I learned a pretty valuable lesson the other night about my own limitations. We'll be fine because Jesus will never be farther away than the tip of my tongue."

They were running late. His car wouldn't start. Neither would hers.

Ron dug in his pocket for the key to their neighbor's garage. "Guess we're lucky the demons didn't know the Perkins family is on vacation and asked us to use their car some while they're gone."

Indi grabbed his arm as he aimed the key at the lock. "Wait, baby. Before we lay eyes on the car, I want to pray. Father, I pray this vehicle we're about to borrow is in good running condition. And I ask You, God, to send Your angels with us on this trip. One on the hood, one on the trunk, and one flying on either side to protect us from the wiles of the Evil One. You know what an important mission this is. We do it to Your honor and glory and thank You for the privilege. Amen. Okay, I'm ready, Ronnie."

Ron chuckled. *What a woman.*

He had to work with the door. It was stuck. It finally flew open with the help of Ron's shoulder. There sat a late-model Mercedes. "No wonder I didn't recognize the car key. The Perkinses have been holding out on us."

"Isn't Halloween supposed to be on the thirty-first of October?" Ron asked as he turned onto the road.

"Technically, I suppose. But when it falls on Sunday, everyone celebrates it on Saturday night." Indi laid her Bible in her lap.

"Well, anyway, it's ironic we're going to their house for *this* on Halloween night."

"Kinda spooky, huh? But what better time to have it out with a bunch of ghouls, honey?"

Ron looked over at her and grimaced. "I just hope no kids come to the door trick-or-treating about the time Edward gets delivered. They might see some honest-to-goodness ghouls exploding out of the doors and windows."

"There's a new rule these days, babe. For treats you go to the houses where the porch light is on. Of course, people who leave their lights off stand a good chance of getting tricked."

"Sounds like an invitation to get wrapped to me. All these years you've been leaving the light on and I thought you were being nice." Ron looked over at her and winked.

"Well, I had to leave it off tonight because we're going to be gone all evening, so we'll see. I hope you're wrong about the wrapping." Indi pulled her sweater up around her shoulders.

Ron put his hand over hers. "Witt called right before we left. Edward's stockpiling liquor. But he hasn't had a drink since the accident. It's like he's waiting—*they're* waiting—for just the right time to launch a drinking binge. To make things worse, he's got an old gun. Casey found it under their bed."

Indi bit her lip. "A gun. That poor woman. She must be so frightened."

"She promised Witt if we're not successful, she'll leave with us. Stay with us tonight and then go to Mrs. Anderson's until she can figure out what to do. Prayerfully, it won't come to that. Witt's worried sick about her. He's gotten himself pretty involved in this lady's problems." Ron was feeling around for the heater control.

My baby's chilly.

Indi steered his hand onto it. "I hope she knows how blessed she is Witt happened along. He's like a dog with a bone. He won't let go until it's settled and God's victorious."

She stared at the road in front of them. A little frown creased its way to her forehead. "Oh, Ron, we've *got* to be successful tonight. The Devil's a stone's throw from utterly destroying Edward. And though we might save Casey from physical harm, her life would never be the same. Edward's deliverance is worth whatever it takes."

The mountain pass was open again. They were passing a club with a margarita sign when they began praying aloud together. Eyes wide open, watchful for anything Satan might throw their way, they sought the Lord's protection over Edward, Casey, and themselves. They rebuked Satan and praised Jesus. They left no spiritual stone unturned.

Edward was expecting company, so why was the house dark? Ron would think he was trying to save on electricity.

"Why isn't the porch light on? You want Ron and his wife to fall and break their necks?"

Casey jumped like a neurotic cat. "I . . . I left it off so no trick-or-treaters would come. I guess I could turn it on until they get here, if you think I should."

"Good grief, yes, woman. What difference does it make if kids come to the door while they're here? They're friends, not royalty."

Casey started from across the room. Edward was standing next to the switch.

"Never mind, I'll get it." He jammed the switch up, cursing under his breath.

"What are they like, Edward?" Casey was nibbling a fingernail.

"Why are you so nervous? You're really acting stupid, you know. Like you've never met a stranger. What's with you tonight?"

He was ripe for a fight, but there was no time. Their company would be here any minute.

Casey turned and went to the kitchen.

Edward walked down the hall to her bathroom to check his appearance.

He peeked into her cabinet. No particular reason. Just a foreboding feeling he needed to stay on top of things.

Her toothbrush was gone.

He closed the bathroom door and began rifling through her makeup. It looked like some things were missing. He couldn't be sure. Then he opened the linen closet and there it was . . . her overnight bag.

He locked the bathroom door before taking the bag down. Unzipping it, he tried not to make any noise. She'd packed a few personal items. Not enough to stay anywhere for long. Her toothbrush, some makeup, a couple of changes of clothes—her black nightie.

She was planning a romantic liaison.

Casey?

Never.

The blood rushed to his head. A pounding headache seized him. Why would she do this to him?

"*You'll be the laughingstock of the religious community.*" A whisper in his ear.

"*Aren't you man enough to make her stay home?*" Another voice.

No. She wasn't going anywhere. He'd keep her home if he had to . . . what? Just how far *would* he go?

For starters, he took the lid off her bottle of foundation, removed the wand from her mascara and the top from her lipstick, and dropped them all on top of her clothes. Then he squeezed the entire contents of a bottle of hand lotion into her neatly packed bag and put an open box of talc on top. He zipped the bag shut and shook it vigorously.

He couldn't resist unzipping it to see the results. It looked like one of the dogs had been romping in it and had to regurgitate.

"Not too romantic, is it?" He zipped it back up, laughing. Picturing Casey opening her bag and getting ready to meet her lover.

Her lover . . . her lover. . . .

The words throbbed in his head.

"*That might frustrate her.*" The voice taunted him. "*But she'll still be gone . . . with him. And you'll still be the laughingstock.*"

"*Want to see your competition?*" A voice from behind the shower curtain.

Edward ripped the curtain back. There was no one there. The chrome faucet knobs gleamed. Casey kept them sparkling.

Something moved. He looked closer. A reflection on the cold water knob. A woman with red hair. He jerked around. Casey?

He was alone.

He turned back to the knob.

Feeling foolish, but too jealous to care, he spoke to the voice. "Competition? Yes, show me."

He sat on the edge of the tub and waited.

"*Look closely, my friend.*" Edward had heard that voice before. "*Embrace my power. Yield yourself to me. And I'll give you proof of her infidelity.*"

Edward stared at the knob. Mesmerized. A foggy image appeared.

The redheaded woman. It was Casey, smiling. And a tall man. Edward couldn't see his face, but they were walking down a stone step and he was holding her hand. They headed into the woods and disappeared.

"Noooo!" He grabbed the doorknob and pulled frantically. It was locked—he was locked in. He fumbled with it. Wrenching the door open, he bounded down the hallway, ready to drag the truth out of her. His fists were clenched. His stomach in knots.

Headlights flashed in the foyer mirror. Ron and Indi were here. And Edward was primed for battle.

"Where are you?" His anger undisguised. "They're here, woman."

He steeled himself for the sight of this wanton woman he'd married, as she hurried out of the kitchen. Of course she looked sweet and innocent. Didn't she always? One would never know, to look at her, what kind of woman she really was.

Casey breezed into the foyer and glanced at her reflection.

Edward's heart was pounding. His face was flushed. The sight of Casey sickened him.

Why did I invite these people over? Tonight of all nights. I'll have to handle her later, when they're gone. She'll be so sorry when I get through with her.

He pasted on his best smile, smoothed his trousers, and cleared his throat. He looked terrific. His head was splitting.

22

Edward felt exceptionally sharp this evening in a cream-colored silk turtleneck under a long-sleeved shirt with a touch of muted green that brought out the color of his eyes. A splash of Fendi Umo. Neatly pressed Ralph Lauren jeans. He could have been a male model.

Two giggling princesses, a hobo, and Spider-Man had just left, their buckets overflowing with candy. Edward and Ron sat in the den chatting while the girls cleaned up the kitchen.

Edward's oversized diamond, which had usurped his wedding band's position last year, caught a ray of light from the crackling fire and winked back. He'd tried to talk old Brother Mike out of the extravagant gift. But sometimes it was easier to give in than to fight the old guy.

He'd cooled down from his frenzy. Actually, he was looking forward to confronting Casey with her packed overnight bag . . . his proof of her infidelity. She couldn't pretend innocence this time. He had her dead to rights. He'd know the sweet taste of victory tonight. It was exhilarating to anticipate. But there'd be time enough after their guests left.

"Boy, it's great to have you two over." Edward pushed a dish of mints out of the way, then propped his feet on the coffee table.

"Good to be here." Ron was wearing jeans also—Wranglers—and a tan-and-red-checked shirt that was a little tight in the upper arms. "Super meal, Edward. Casey's a great cook. She and Indi sure have hit it off. You'd think they'd known each other all their lives instead of having met just this evening." He leaned over for a mint and popped it into his mouth.

"Good thing. They'll be seeing a lot of each other now that I've found a golfing buddy. I enjoyed our round the other day. And I'm impressed. You can hit the ball a smooth mile, Ron."

I'm going to have to spend more time on the links to keep up with him.

"I enjoyed it too, except for the six I got on—what was it—number seven? I can't believe I three-putted after taking three strokes to get on the green. Guess I'm a little rusty."

"Hey, that's a tough hole. Hardly anyone pars it. With your build, man, you're a natural. You just need to get out to the club to play more."

Ron rocked back in his chair and put his hands behind his head. It made his arms look even larger.

If I had arms like his, I could turn pro.

"Edward, your country club is spectacular. And I appreciate the comp round. But that was a onetime thing and I wouldn't want to pay the green fees there very often. I'm more of a municipal course kinda guy."

"No problem, my brother. I can get you in on my membership." Edward felt his chest expand. "Give me a day or two and I'll fix it so you can play anytime, even if I'm not with you. Use my cart. Pick up my key at the pro shop and help yourself."

Ron was shaking his head. "I couldn't do that, brother."

Edward took a deep breath and smiled inside. He had a fine golf cart with its radio, headlights, and horn. And his membership at the country club. It made him feel a little heady. "Then how about taking the little lady to the Club Bistro for lunch . . . on me." He glanced at his Rolex. "Hey, we have time to run over right now and have a drink."

It would be the first time he'd had a drink around people he knew. He understood where he'd messed up last Friday and was anxious to have another go at it to prove he could handle his liquor.

Ron crossed a leg over his knee and brought his hands from behind his head. "I'll take a rain check. I know Indi wouldn't want to go and we can't leave the ladies here while we go gallivanting."

With those big biceps tucked away, Edward was better able to concentrate. "How about we take a little spin in my new Jag then?"

Edward's story about his recent brush with death had gotten him a lot of mileage at church. "Yes, sir, I got a new car a week ago in St. Michael. A Jag. A fellow called with family problems, so my first pleasure drive in my new Jag was to go to an old friend's to minister."

Casey walked into the room. She had an incredulous look on her face. Edward hesitated but couldn't change his story now. He'd have to trust Casey wouldn't give him away. She wouldn't dare.

"Didn't mean to spend so much time there, but one thing led to another. The weather knocked the phones out, and my cellular battery went dead, so I couldn't call. It must have worried Casey sick."

She turned abruptly and ran out of the room.

Oh boy, now he's going to wonder what that was all about. Wench.

"Anyway, it was after 1:00 a.m. before I finally headed home. Had to go over the mountain. You remember how nasty the weather turned last weekend? Well there I was, on the mountain pass in the worst of it."

He paused for effect. Ron looked at him, expressionless.

A little ooh or aah would be nice.

"I was creeping along on the ice when a doe ran out of nowhere, right in front of me. Slipping and sliding. I'd have hit her for sure, if I hadn't braked. That sent me into a spin. I left the road and crashed into a tree. The car was totaled, but I walked away with only a little cut on my hand. Get this—I landed on the only pile of hay for miles in any direction."

He held out his hand for examination. A small bandage covered the wound he'd gotten during his battle with the margarita glass.

"You tell me it wasn't the Lord. Man alive. I guess He still has work for me to do."

Ron didn't comment.

His silence irritated Edward. "Anyway, insurance covered everything. So, I have in my garage"—he did a drumroll on the coffee table with his forefingers—"a brand new Jaguar—my second one this week."

Ron sat up straight.

Finally, a spark of interest. At least I know you're awake.

Edward put his hands on his knees to stand up. "Come on. I'd like to show you what she can do."

"Come out," Ron shouted.

"I beg your pardon?" Edward leaned toward Ron and looked him in the eye, puzzled.

"I'm not talking to you, Edward. I'm talking to the demon of pride that's taken up residence."

Edward jumped to his feet. "Oh, gimme a break. Surely you're not going to start with that garbage, just when we were hitting it off so well."

Ron stood too. Eye to eye within twelve inches of Edward. "I said *come out*, in the name of Jesus Christ!"

Edward backed away momentarily, then lunged forward in Ron's face.

"Leave us alone." The voice didn't sound like Edward. It didn't sound human.

Casey and Indi were preparing coffee when the men began shouting.

"It's time I get in there, Casey." Indi put the lid back on the coffee canister. "It's begun."

"Should I come?" Casey dried her hands on a dishtowel.

"Oh, girl, that's up to you. It could get rough. But you'd probably get some insight into what Edward's been up against. Might help you understand the bad stuff that's taken place between you."

"Okay, I'm coming." Casey hung up her towel and grabbed Indi's hand.

Together they said a quick prayer of protection. Then, hand in hand, the girls marched bravely into battle.

Indi slipped to the front door and turned off the porch light. Then closed the blinds on the big window that faced the front yard. "No more trick-or-treaters tonight."

Edward was baring his teeth in Ron's face. Casey's stomach tightened. No one but she had ever seen that side of him.

Red-faced, Edward advanced on Ron. He had a good physique, but Ron was more muscled out.

Ron refused to budge. "Who are you? In the name of Jesus, tell me your name."

Edward doubled over and grabbed his belly. Between groans, he rasped in guttural tones. "The Big Five. Pride, Lies, Greed, Jealousy, and Violence. And we're not done here. Leave us alone."

The words came from Edward's mouth and his face displayed pure rage, but his eyes . . . his eyes . . . reflected terror. Casey searched his face and covered her mouth with both hands. She was overwhelmed with a wave of compassion. *Oh, Edward.*

He's trapped inside his own body in the presence of the very essence of evil.

Without thinking, she cried out. "Oh, Jesus, help him."

Edward's body convulsed backward.

Steadying himself against the doorway, he searched out Casey's compassionate gaze. In the split second their glances met, she saw the terror vanish. To be replaced by the consummate hatred she'd seen so often before. He was completely entrapped. Helpless to resist as an evil entity assumed control over his entire being. He glared at her and the intensity of his loathing sent her heart to the pit of her stomach.

He took a step forward to regain his stand against Ron.

"We are here to bring down the Very Reverend Edward McAlester."

"Is the demon of addiction in there with you?" Feet planted firmly and powerful arms at the ready, Ron was keeping his cool.

"No, but he will be soon. He's working his plan." Fingernails on a chalkboard. "You can't stop him. And your puny God can't either. He can't save this pitiful wretch. Beelzebub rules."

Indi took Casey by the hand. "Casey, I've never seen anything like this in a saved person. I don't see how Edward could have a personal relationship with Jesus and still host these demons."

"Indi, don't say that. Witt said the same thing. Edward's the pastor of the fastest growing church in the county. He knows the Scriptures better than anyone I've ever heard."

"Listen to yourself, Casey. You know better. That's no assurance of salvation. Even *Satan* knows the Word. We've got to get these demons out. Then we *must* lead Edward to the Lord. If he won't accept Jesus, the same demons and many others will pounce on him like a duck on a June bug. Pray for him . . . and for us, Casey. Pray, girl, like you've never prayed before."

Edward's arms were flailing about. "If we get our hands on the sleaze bucket who sicced these fanatics on us, we'll break him in two. Slice him with our talons, tear his heart out, and feed it to the vultures."

Their dreadful utterances assailed Casey's ears in unison, yet each ominous voice pierced her heart with its own peculiar portent.

The threat was meant for her.

Ron's eyes followed the pacing maniac. When Edward swept close to him he'd say that name. "Jesus."

And each time it threw Edward into a more severe frenzy. Casey knew from experience that at any moment Edward would gain new strength. He may attack Ron—or worse, Indi. And they'd call the police. She'd always managed to keep it from going that far. But they were egging him on. Casey hardly knew these people. She hadn't known Witt very long.

I was a fool to let him talk me into this.

What had she gotten herself and Edward into?

Suddenly she became fearful for Edward's life. Ron was so powerful. What if he had to defend himself and killed Edward?

"Please don't hurt him, Ron."

He smiled gently at Casey and shook his head. "Don't you worry. He'll be fine. He'll be a new man soon." Ron touched her shoulder. "You need to step back so *you* don't get hurt."

"Take your hands off h-e-e-e-r, you vermin. She's mine." Edward lunged at Ron. He heaved his clenched fist at his face. Ron blocked him and defiantly called on Jesus again.

Edward buckled, regained his balance, then reached for a lamp. Ron grabbed his hand and forced it behind him. "You will not break another thing in this home. You will not threaten another person in this home. In Jesus's name, your time here is finished."

Edward bellowed like a wild animal in pain.

Ron didn't release him.

Edward's eyes scanned the room. "For the last time, stop calling me Eddie. I'll show you who's a real man." He hurled his free hand in the air, first grasping behind himself for Ron's hair, then trying for Indi's. Ron caught his free hand and pulled it behind his back with the efficiency of a trained officer of the law.

Edward screamed foul curses.

"You're hurting him. Stop." Casey jumped on Ron. With both hands she tried to pull him off Edward. "Enough. Leave him alone and he'll be okay."

Indi pried Casey's fingers from Ron's arms. "Casey. He's not going to hurt Edward. It's the demons who're screaming. They don't want to leave. Please, Casey, please. Let us do what must be done."

Edward began pleading in his own soothing voice. "Make him let me go, baby. Call the police. We don't really know these people. Who knows what they'll do to *you* after they've finished with me?"

But he wouldn't make eye contact with her.

Casey gulped each breath. She didn't know who to believe anymore. She gripped her head in her hands. "Oh, what have I done? Edward, I'm so sorry I let them talk me into this."

His head snapped toward Casey. Brittle hatred pounced from his eyes. "So, it was you. Of course . . . you'd like to be rid of us, wouldn't you?"

The voices spewed malevolence like spume from a boiling cauldron.

"No, Edward. Don't say that. I could never . . . I mean I only want . . ."

He lunged toward her, but Ron held him at bay. Casey jumped backward and Indi was there to steady her. Enfold her in her arms.

Casey didn't know how to defend herself. She didn't want him to be hurt, but she didn't want him near her either.

Edward screeched. "Why didn't you just stab me in the heart? It would have been kinder."

Voices on all sides of the house wailed in response. From the garage the Jag engine revved and whined. Straining engine belts screeched their empathy with Edward's plight. Thuds against the windows. Cracking windowpanes. The smells of engine oil and sulfur seeped into the room.

Writhing in Ron's viselike hold, Edward flopped around, trying futilely to free himself. His mouth stretched across his face in a gruesome, humorless grin. His eyes seized Casey's and bound her gaze to his. "Take a good look. You did this. This is all your fault." He snarled, "Don't think I'm ever going to forgive . . . or forget!"

Casey recoiled in horror.

A rock came crashing through the window and grazed Ron's head. Indi ran to him, but he shook his head. "I'm okay. Get the drapes."

Indi rushed around, drawing the drapes on all the windows.

A trickle of blood ran down Ron's temple.

"You've gone too far. Time's up." He released Edward's arms and grabbed him by the shoulders.

With one quick move he forced him to the floor and moved his grip to Edward's forearms with lightning speed. Edward let out a feral squall that froze Casey's blood in her veins, but Ron held him fast. He sat on him and repeated, "In the name of Jesus Christ of Nazareth, I command you to come out."

Edward grappled. He kicked. His eyes bulged and his face looked like he was going to explode. His fingers curled viciously, seeking flesh to tear.

Casey stood, whimpering, her back against the wall. Her handsome husband had morphed into a grotesque monster.

Oh God. Oh God. Please make it end.

Edward squirmed and screamed and cursed Ron, Indi, Casey, and every other person he knew who loved the Lord. The voices raked the air. Their din was deafening. Ron and Edward were both soaked in sweat and hoarse.

"Pray for me, Indi," Ron pleaded. "He's as strong as a bear. And he's wearing me down."

Indi closed her eyes but for a second before she quoted the needed Scripture. It flowed effortlessly from her spirit. "Isaiah 40:29. 'He gives strength to the weary, And to *him who* lacks might He increases power.' Father, I call on a thousand angels to come to his rescue, in Jesus's name."

Casey was in awe of Indi's presence of mind. A visible surge of power ran through Ron's body. He renewed his grip on Edward and commanded one more time, "Come out in the name of Jesus!"

His voice was louder and deeper than it had been.

In wonderment, Casey looked from Indi to Ron and back.

Father in heaven! You heard and answered.

Instantly Edward stopped struggling. He grew very quiet. Then he arched his back high, opened his mouth wide, and emitted a horrendous sound. Like the scream of a thousand jackals. A black vapor sifted from his body like smoke from a pile of smoldering leaves. It hovered for an instant, then split and departed in five directions through closed windows and doors.

Casey smelled the same odor that had filled her car one evening. It dissipated along with the malodor of sulfur and motor oil.

Edward's eyes rolled back in his head and he collapsed onto the floor. His eyes closed and his head lolled to one side.

Casey slid to the floor without taking her eyes off the still figure of her husband.

Indi knelt beside Ron and Edward. "Oh, mercy, Ron, did you *kill* him?"

"He's good, Indi. He's good." Ron smiled and slowly extricated his fatigued body from his position over Edward.

"And *they're* gone."

"That's the toughest I've ever seen you get, Ronnie. I don't believe you've ever *sat* on anyone before. Is that your new technique?" Grinning, she pulled him down beside her and examined the laceration on his temple.

"A bit unorthodox, I know, sweetie, but they were the toughest I've ever come against. If I'd stayed passive, I don't think we'd have seen a victory. And the next time they'd have been even tougher." He turned toward Casey. "Are you all right?"

She hadn't moved. She nodded without taking her eyes off Edward. "Are you sure he's okay?"

"Positive."

Looking back at Indi, Ron let out a deep sigh. "Don't you know we'd have had to run for our lives if we hadn't been successful? Have you ever seen such a barbarian in your life?"

Nauseated, Casey pressed her fingers over her mouth.

"Give him time, Casey." Ron put his arm around Indi and held his hand out to Casey. "I couldn't have lasted were it not for your prayers and the intervention of the Holy Spirit. That wasn't me fighting Edward at the end. It was an Angel of the Lord, whoo-pin' up on Satan, through me. Just like Satan's demons were fighting through Edward."

He pulled Indi closer. "Baby, I actually felt my strength increase when you invoked His Word. What a trip."

Indi beamed. "His Word is so powerful. He brought the Scriptures to mind. And fulfilled them when I cried out to Him."

Indi put her hand over Casey's. "I'm looking forward to get-ting to know the real Edward McAlester. It's hard to believe he's the gentle, humble man you described BS"—she smiled at Casey—"before Satan."

Casey didn't return Indi's smile or take her eyes off Edward. "I wonder if the real Edward McAlester is still in there." Her heart was pounding. She didn't know what she'd do if he woke up and tried to touch her.

Edward groaned and tried to sit up.

Ron grabbed a pillow off the couch and tucked it under his damp head. "Take it easy for a moment, my brother. Then we have some im-portant things to discuss."

Edward's fine clothes were wet and rumpled. He didn't look like a male model anymore. But he smiled contentedly and lay back on the pillow.

Ron and Indi knelt at Edward's side and began praying. They thanked the Lord for the power of His holy name. Ron quoted from His Word.

"Now when the unclean spirit goes out of a man, it passes through waterless places, seeking rest, and does not find it. Then it says, 'I will return to my house from which I came'; and when it comes, it finds it unoccupied, swept, and put in order. Then it goes, and takes along with it seven other spirits more wicked than itself, and they go in and live there; and the last state of that man becomes worse than the first . . ."

Indi prayed, "Lord, we ask Your help in leading Edward to You before the return of these demons and their accomplices. In Jesus's name, we ask for Edward's salvation."

Eyes still closed, Edward listened. Tears filled his eyes, squeezed through his closed lids, and ran down his temples, making wet spots on the pillow. A light came on in his spirit and he realized they were right. He'd never really trusted the Lord as his Savior.

He always had a great love for people. In high school he'd ministered to friends and classmates. A natural at leading others, he'd neglected his own salvation. When the Spirit urged him for some one-on-one, he would step up his works for the Lord. Don't actions speak louder than words?

A Bible student, he crammed his mind with facts and memorized Scriptures. He never told the Lord of his love, except from the pulpit. Never repented. His sins seemed so minor compared with those he heard every day. He didn't lie facedown on the floor and cry out to the Lord when the Holy Spirit spoke to him. That was so "holy roller" and didn't seem necessary. Wasn't he doing a good work for the Lord?

But the Scriptures plainly state, "Not by works, but by My Spirit."

Edward knew what he had to do. Now . . . tonight.

His belly hurt.

He hurt all over. But his belly hurt the most. Like something deep inside had been ripped from his body. He sat up and shook his head.

He smiled at Casey. She forced a pallid smile, but didn't reach out to him.

"Gads, Ron. You sure know how to get a fellow's attention. I'm aching, but I feel ten pounds lighter. They're gone, aren't they?"

"Yes, they're gone, Edward. Half the job is done."

"The hardest half, my brother. I've been lying here listening

211

to you pray. And I say, let's get on with it. I'm ready to do what I should've done thirty years ago, before accepting my first pastorate."

Without waiting for Indi and Ron to join him, Edward closed his eyes, raised his hands, and began praying. He prayed the sinner's prayer he'd led so many through. He asked for forgiveness of sin and implored the Lord to heal Casey's heart from the damage he'd done. Then he asked the Lord to fill him with His Holy Spirit, leaving no room for Satan's ghouls to ever find a home in him again.

Tears flowed like a refreshing, cleansing river. He felt the un-fathomable warmth of God's love drench him to the marrow of his bones and knew his prayer had been answered. He was, at last, a child of the living God.

He stretched out, facedown, and worshipped the Lord with all his heart.

Casey felt like a visitor in her own home. She knew she should be an integral part of what was happening to her husband. But her senses were messed up. Ron and Indi kept looking at her, their eyes filled with concern. She should be jumping up and down, hugging them. Instead she sat there, speechless, running her hands up and down her upper arms.

She'd watched the miracle unfold before her eyes. These two wonderful people, whose authority in Jesus she'd dared to doubt, had snatched her husband right out of Satan's clutches.

They'd prayed fervently for his salvation. And the next thing she knew, Edward was praying the prayer of repentance.

Tears gathered in her eyes when she heard him ask the Lord to heal *her* heart from the damage he'd done. They plummeted down her cheeks when she saw him turn and stretch out on the carpet and begin to worship. Her old Edward was back.

Why wasn't she rejoicing? Why was she still fearful? And why did she have the vague feeling she'd just lost something?

23

Casey walked into the master bedroom with a stack of fresh towels.

Edward was flipping through his closet. "Let me find you a shirt, Ron. I'm afraid we've messed yours up." He pulled out a checkered sport shirt. "How's this?"

Ron grimaced. "Kinda small, Edward. Sorry."

"Oh, that's right. You've got some pretty big upper arms. Let me see. A T-shirt. That's the answer. Honey, would you get one of my T-shirts for Ron? My other shirts are all too small in the upper arms." He grinned and shrugged his shoulders.

His honest self-deprecation tugged at Casey's heart. But talk of loaning his shirt brought a vision of Witt sitting at her kitchen table. A blanket over his broad shoulders. His shirt in her dryer.

Her throat tightened. Casey clamped her eyes shut and rubbed her forehead.

What's wrong with you? You're married.

"Soap's on the shelf in the shower, Ron. Make yourself at home. I'll be down the hall." Edward grabbed one of the towels from the stack, touched Casey's cheek, and winked at her as he left the room and strode down the hall, whistling.

She stiffened and a sob escaped her lips.

"Casey, are you all right?" Ron put his hand on her shoulder. "Casey. Look at me."

She shuddered and looked up at Ron, eyes brimming. "I . . . I'll be okay." She got a T-shirt from Edward's drawer and handed it to Ron. "I'd better get back to Indi. I'm being a terrible hostess."

And a terrible wife. I don't know if I can do this. Nothing's the same.

"Shall I make that coffee now?" Indi smiled at her as Casey entered the kitchen.

"Yes, I imagine the guys could use some. And I have dessert in the refrigerator." Casey felt comfortable with Indi. "Bear with me, Indi. This is all new territory for me."

Indi put her arm around Casey's waist. "No secrets between us, okay, girl? I know you've been through a lot and you'll need to talk it out. There's nothing to be embarrassed about. We're going to be good friends . . . for a long time."

Indi put the coffee on and Casey took a homemade cheesecake from the refrigerator and set it on the table. Then they sat down to talk and wait for the guys.

Ron and Edward burst into the kitchen laughing.

Ron held up a key. "Edward had a great idea. He bought a bunch of liquor last week and he'd like to get rid of it tonight. We thought we'd have a mass funeral." He wiped a mock tear from his eye.

"Because Ron's the strongest among us, he'll be the pallbearer and carry the deceased in from the living room. And since I've had practice at this sort of thing"—Edward cleared his throat and straightened his collar in jest—"I'll say a few words over each bottle. And you girls can 'bury' it at sea." He nodded toward the sink. "What say?"

"Sounds like a plan." Casey forced a smile and directed it at Ron.

"First things first." Indi put the cheesecake back in the refrigerator and pulled Casey over to the sink. "I'll open them and you can do the honors. Okay?"

They assumed their positions and Ron began bringing in the "corpses."

Edward cleared his throat. "Dearly beloved, we are gathered here . . . oh no. That's for a wedding."

"Hey, show a little respect." Ron hit Edward's shoulder with his fist.

Indi looked down the drain. "Are you ready down there?"

Casey laughed. "Hope there are no little fishies at the other end of this drain." She flourished a paper towel and wiped the drain with it. "We're ready to receive."

Edward smiled at her and winked again. Casey dropped the paper towel and leaned over to pick it up. As long as she didn't have to face him, she could do this thing.

What will I do when Ron and Indi go home? I'm his wife. He's going to expect to make love.

Thirty minutes later, with all the liquor down the drain, and Casey and Indi in the guest room clucking over a quilt she was working on, Edward called Ron aside and led him back into the master bedroom.

There was a box on the chest of drawers. Edward had gotten it from under the bed to retrieve the key while Ron was in the shower. He lifted the lid and Ron peered in.

"Whoa. Where did you get *that*? That's a civilian Colt Third Model Dragoon."

"Is that what it's called? I inherited it from my granddad, Ron. I don't know a thing about it. Don't even know if it works. I hate to get rid of it, but I have other things that mean more to me. His Bible, for one." He held up a well-worn Bible from the bedside table.

Granddad was the first to tell Edward about Jesus . . . reading to him from this very Bible.

"This revolver looks like it's in mint condition, Edward. What are you planning to do with it?" Ron gingerly examined the piece.

"I was hoping you could help me out there. Do you think it's fine enough that a museum would be interested? I don't want anything for it. Just want it out of the house." He walked to the door and looked down the hall, then closed the door behind him.

Don't want Casey walking in on us.

"Having it around would upset Casey. I won't be entertaining any more ghouls, Ron, but when I think of how dangerous it was for me to have a gun in the house, in my condition, it blows my mind. Could you take it with you to get it out of the house, for her sake?"

"I'll do whatever you'd like, brother, but this beauty could be worth some big bucks. It's got super sharp edges and the grips are about perfect. It doesn't look like it's seen much use. The museum in St. Michael would love to have it. But you could sell it for a pretty good chunk of cash." With his handkerchief, Ron wiped his fingerprints from the handle and carefully placed the gun back in the box.

I just got rid of the demon of greed. All I want is my marriage back the way it was.

Edward replaced the lid. "You never cease to amaze me, Ron. Where'd you learn so much about guns?"

"Oh, my dad was a firearms aficionado. He could never afford anything like that, but he dreamed about it a lot and pored over the magazines. I guess a little of the knowledge just rubbed off on me. I've never been one to collect things, though."

"Let's give it to your dad."

"Thanks, Edward. But he's gone to be with the Lord. Years ago."

"Well, I'd like for it to go to the museum then. Would you mind handling it for me? Anonymous donation. That okay by you?"

"Consider it done. They'll be thrilled out of their skulls."

"Thanks. I owe you a lot, Ron. Hope someday to repay you for all you've done for us."

"No payment wanted, brother." Ron held his hand up for a high five and Edward reciprocated. "But I would like to eat Casey's cooking from time to time. Indi's an astounding woman—but a cook, she's not."

Edward stifled a laugh. "I think I can speak for Casey that she'd love to cook for you two anytime. I hope the four of us spend a lot of time together from now on." He picked up the box and handed it to Ron. They walked out of the room together and Ron excused himself to take the gun to the car.

When he returned the table was set again. Coffee and cheesecake.

They laughed and talked and prayed and celebrated with great joy . . . until the minute Edward and Casey walked Ron and Indi to their car.

Edward wasn't prepared for the sudden change in Casey's countenance after they waved good-bye to their new friends. They walked back into the house in silence, Casey in the lead by several paces. She stopped at the kitchen door and turned stiffly to face him. Her gaze flitted to their bedroom.

Overjoyed at her gesture, Edward approached her with open arms. "I guess it's time for us to hop into bed, darling."

She turned abruptly and walked into the kitchen. "There is still a little bit to clean up in here. I'll be along in a minute."

He followed her as far as the door and leaned against the facing. She was at the sink with her back to him, trembling like a leaf in the wind. Edward longed to put his arms around her and assure her of his love.

It's settled in the spiritual realm but it looks like the natural is going to take a little longer.

He moved a little closer and saw her shoulders tense up.

She's frightened. His heart wept for her. He'd done this to her. *Father, I ask for nothing more than the chance to win her love and trust. Help me.*

He took a step backward. "Well, I'm exhausted, sweetheart. I know you won't mind if I hit the sack. We'll talk more in the morning. I love you."

Casey's shoulders relaxed and she turned to face him. "God is so good, Edward. Welcome home." She smiled briefly before turning back to the sink, but her eyes were dark and clouded.

Edward waited until Casey was asleep before he slipped into the hall bathroom. He opened her overnight bag and was appalled at what he'd done in anger. He took out her makeup items, replaced the lids, and wiped them off before placing them in the drawer. He rinsed her toothbrush thoroughly and placed it in the rack. All he could do with the soiled clothing was to put it in the laundry room. And the overnight bag was such a mess he decided to buy her a new one. Very soon, he'd take her shopping and replace *everything* of hers he'd destroyed.

She was still asleep when he slipped back in bed.

Eight hours of heavenly sleep left Edward ready to take on the world. Delivered, saved, and rested, albeit a little sore, he wanted to make things right with his beloved Casey.

And he could hardly wait until his next opportunity to address his congregation.

Should he dump the whole thing on them at once or break it to them slowly? Some wise counsel from Elder John was in order. So he wouldn't mention it in this morning's service.

When he did, he had to be completely truthful. If they couldn't accept it, then perhaps it was God's will he move to a smaller church. That would mean a big pay cut. But Casey always said she'd be happy living in a tent, as long as they were together. He hoped she still felt that way.

He could certainly live with a lot less. He'd begin by dropping his club membership. Then he'd give the diamond ring and the Jaguar back to Brother Mike. Whatever financial loss Mike suffered, Edward would sign a note to even things up.

It wouldn't be easy. So why did he feel so good about it?

He looked at his beautiful wife, asleep next to him, and his emotions overflowed.

He reached over and gently touched her tousled hair, whispering, "I'll give it all up, darling. All I need is you."

Casey was dreaming about Witt. A gentle dream in which he held her close. He was protecting her from some unknown danger, his hand shielding her eyes from even the sight of evil. She had fairly melted in his arms. Then he melted too and they blended into one.

In that half-asleep, half-awake state of euphoria, she could hear him murmuring about what he'd give up to win her love. He touched her hair and she turned to face him. She raised her eyelids in anticipation of his kind blue eyes.

Edward!

Had she talked in her sleep? Said Witt's name?

Casey's body stiffened and she braced herself for his blast of fury.

Edward smiled. A melancholy smile. "Wake up, sleepyhead. We'll have some coffee together before we get ready for church."

He seemed calm enough. Maybe the nightmare really was over.

If he wants to hold me, I've got to let him. He's my husband. I took a vow. If he wants to kiss me and . . . oh no. I just can't.

She turned away from him. Would it ever go away? Or would she forever look at Edward and see the monster who'd hated her with a vengeance? His terrible threats. The look in his eyes. And the last words he spoke to her before the demons came out: *Don't think I'm ever going to forgive . . . or forget.*

Everything had been good when Ron and Indi were here, but when they left they took the spirit of joy with them. She should call Indi and tell her she was still afraid of Edward. That she recoiled at his touch. Indi was wise. She'd know what to do.

But it wasn't Indi she wanted—it was Witt. She ached for his comforting touch. Longed for the reassuring sound of his voice.

The dreadful reality of it crashed into her mind like a runaway train.

Her beloved husband of twenty years was in bed beside her, delivered and saved. Pleading her forgiveness. And all she could think of was Witt. A man she'd met less than a month ago.

Cold creeps fluttered beneath her skin.

God, have I crossed over an invisible line that separates the faithful from the adulterous?

24

His eyes on the entrance, Witt sat in the booth he and Casey had shared the day they met.

Now that it's done, will I ever see her again?

The last time he laid eyes on her was in the early morning hours after Edward's accident, when he'd reluctantly left her with *him*. She called him later that morning to let him know Edward was leaving soon for his office. Speaking quickly. In a whisper. It did little to alleviate his anxiety.

Now he had only Ron and Indi's report that the deliverance was a success and she was all right. He dare not press them for details lest his feelings for Casey be revealed.

"I have no say in this, God. And I'll make no attempt to contact her. But You know coming here has been my routine for years, so if she walks through that door, I'll assume it's part of Your plan. Where will You take us from there? Will I be the one to end the friendship, and if so, on what grounds? I can't bear to think of hurting her."

Who am I kidding? Tomorrow night will be a week since Edward's deliverance. She's no doubt still on cloud nine.

To take his mind off Casey, he tried to read the morning newspaper. An unseasonably warm breeze blew through the coffee shop. The very atmosphere was charged. He knew when he looked up, he'd see her.

She was wearing the gray lamb's wool cardigan she'd worn the day they met. Draped casually over a pale-yellow blouse, it could be discarded easily if the day grew warmer. A pair of soft-gray pants and low-heeled pumps that clicked when she walked. Her small dangling gold earrings made her look delicate and feminine.

She was the loveliest thing he'd ever seen—thirty years ago and still.

"Hi, Witt." She approached his booth.

"Case. Come sit down. I guess you've been really busy since the big night last week. I'm happy for you. Tell me all about it. How's Edward?"

As pleased as he was to see her, his heart was heavy. This *had* to be the last time. God wasn't going to allow him the luxury of loving another man's wife. Witt had known His plans for them from the beginning.

Casey slid into the booth across from him.

"Edward's fine. He's planning a big day on Sunday. Going to tell the congregation exactly what Satan's been doing *to* him, and *through* him, for the past three years. He's very anxious about it. Spending a lot of time in prayer. He's prepared to resign if the people don't receive it kindly."

Mae brought a cup of coffee for Casey and warmed Witt's cup.

Witt looked up at her smiling face. "Thanks, Mae."

He dragged his eyes back to meet Casey's. It was hard to look at her and not speak his heart. "Sounds like he's back on track."

"Uh-huh."

They sat in silence for a moment. Witt fidgeting with his cup and Casey picking at her nails.

"So, how's Barrett?"

"Oh, he's doing fine."

Drat this stilted conversation. When are we going to settle into our comfort zone?

Witt tried to read Casey's expression. Her eyes were vacant. She seemed ill at ease. Maybe the friendship had already cooled and he wouldn't have to worry about how to end it.

He'd been on a spiritual high, being an important part of her life with God's blessing. Now he had no excuse to see her again. Although he should be . . . well, *was* . . . happy God got the glory in Edward's life, he was let down by the awkwardness between himself and Case. They'd been so connected. He'd hoped the memory of that connection would carry him through the rest of his life.

Casey was comforted by the sight of him. At the same time, uneasy being so close. She was sure she was failing God by coming here. But she felt trapped, with nowhere else to turn. The one thing she knew to be God's will for her—a continued relationship with Edward—was too frightening to contemplate.

She wanted to tell Witt about her dream and ask if he ever dreamed about her. But she couldn't bear it if he were to look at her with disapproval.

"He's already given the Jaguar and the diamond ring back to Brother Mike. And dropped his membership at the country club." Casey looked down at the third finger of her left hand. She hadn't worn her wedding ring today. She wondered if Witt noticed.

"Giving the stuff back to Brother Mike wasn't easy. He was offended at first, but Edward convinced him he'll understand after Sunday. Did Ron and Indi tell you about the big liquor party we had after the deliverance? We poured out *all* of Edward's alcohol."

"Yes, they did. I'm so glad for you, Case. Glad things are going so well." Witt sighed and rubbed his forehead.

I shouldn't have come. I'm chattering like a magpie and he's bored.

Babbling about happenings. She wanted to talk about *feelings*. Hers. His. Theirs.

Please, Witt, say something to bridge the gap between us. Rescue me.

Witt leaned against the back of the booth. Shaking his head, he scanned her face for a long moment.

Casey squirmed in her seat. He looked upset.

He's getting ready to tell me he's meeting someone and I'll have to leave.

She could feel her face getting hot. Tears approached the surface. She reached for her purse and set it on the table in front of her. Holding her breath. Ready to bolt.

Witt put his hand over her hand and her purse. "Case, you told me once you were a terrible actress. You're right. You are. What's going on? Is it Edward? Are the demons back?"

She expelled her waiting breath and hung her head. Squeezing the bridge of her nose between her thumb and forefinger, she tried to stop the tears. But a few escaped to trickle down her cheeks. "Edward's fine, Witt. The demons aren't back . . . yet. But I . . . I'm not doing very well. I'm afraid of him. And I'm afraid they'll come back. They're very angry at me."

The floodgates were opened and it all came rushing out.

"He's trying so hard. But God forgive me, I don't want to be around him. I can't stand for him to touch me. And I am so very frightened of him. I feel like the man I married died. I may as well be a widow living with a terrifying stranger."

Witt squeezed her hand. "Oh, Case. Why didn't I see this coming? Of course. You've been through so much."

"It's been a week, Witt, and he's been a perfect gentleman. So repentant. I've tried to forgive him. Accept his affection. But he made the most horrible threats before his deliverance, and I can't help myself. I keep waiting for the other shoe to drop.

"And I've tried to not think of you—" She covered her mouth.

Witt released her hand like the wrong end of a branding iron.

I shouldn't have said that.

But it was in the open. She may as well spill it all.

"Honestly, Witt, that's the hardest part. Not thinking of you. Your gentleness and the peace I feel when I'm with you. It's like I've stumbled across some invisible line and I don't think I can find my way back." She nibbled at her index fingernail. Then put her hand in her lap, suddenly ashamed she'd not worn her wedding ring.

Maybe I really am a wanton woman.

She was puzzled by his long silence and the odd way he was looking at her. His jaws were clenched and the emotion in his eyes was nearly tangible, but she couldn't read it. Was he pleased with her confession or upset with her? Had she said too much?

224

"How long since you've been on a picnic, Case?"

"Huh?" *What kind of a question is that?*

"You know, fried chicken, potato salad, corn on the cob, checkered tablecloth spread on the grass next to a babbling brook. The whole ball of wax. How long, little lady?"

He had to have heard her heartfelt confession. He was simply letting it pass.

Casey didn't know whether to be relieved or hurt.

Well, at least he isn't upset with me. A picnic?

Their connection was restored.

He couldn't imagine why *that* idea popped into his head. But it must be God, so he'd run with it.

"Now that you ask, I don't think I've *ever* had the whole ball of wax, Mr. Impetuous." Casey smiled. "It's always lacked the babbling brook. And I've never owned a checkered tablecloth."

"Well, I do. And I know where to find the babbling brook. This unseasonably warm weather isn't going to last. We need to take advantage of it."

"That would be so much fun." Casey wiggled in her seat like an excited child.

He raised his hand to get Mae's attention. "Mae, what are our chances of getting six or eight pieces of fried chicken, some corn on the cob, and some really good homemade potato salad to go?"

"Chances are great, Dr. G." She headed his way. "I'll get right on it."

"We're going on a picnic. Can you believe that?" He gave Mae a quick hug. "Oh, put in a couple pieces of your famous strawberry pie. Okay?"

After making arrangements to pick up lunch later, Witt and Casey were walking briskly—she was nearly skipping—to the Jeep.

"Where's the babbling brook, Witt? Close by?"

"A little ways. We'll have to run by the ranch to pick up the tablecloth while Mae's getting lunch ready."

"We don't need to go by the ranch. That's a long way to go to pick up a tablecloth."

"It's not that far. And Mae needs a little time, anyway. For the record, the tablecloth is red-and-white checkered. Required picnic colors. You said you'd never had the whole ball of wax and I'm going to see that you get it once in your lifetime. No work, no worry. Just enjoy."

He smiled down at her.

My good-bye gift.

He put his hands on her waist to help her into the Jeep. Magnetic forces surged from his fingertips to his heart. *Whoa.*

Why had God laid the idea of a picnic on his heart? There must be a plausible explanation. Perhaps He was giving Witt time to figure out how to break the news. Or maybe He was letting him have one more wonderful day with the only woman he'd ever love before their inevitable parting. Witt would find out in God's good time.

Whatever Your reason, God, please don't leave me alone with her.

Casey rested her hand on the edge of the bench seat.

She's not wearing her wedding ring.

He wanted to touch her hand. Trace the pale circle where her ring belonged with his finger. No, he wanted to reach over and pull her close.

A pale circle . . .

Where the ring belongs.

He kept both hands on the steering wheel.

Witt pulled into the driveway. Casey unclasped her seat belt. "May I come in with you? I love your place. It's so homey."

Witt hesitated. Sarah had taken the day off. He couldn't let Casey come in and put his already-weakened willpower to a trial by fire.

"I won't be long." He sprinted toward the ranch house.

Casey shrugged and refastened her seat belt.

He came back out, tablecloth and a couple of fresh horse blankets in hand. He tossed them on the backseat. "You ready?"

He noticed she'd brushed her hair while he was inside. And she'd spritzed on a little fragrance.

Everything you do, Case, makes it a little harder for me to follow orders.

226

She smiled and patted the driver's seat. "Hop in. I'm ready. Hope Mae's had enough time."

The food was packed in a big wicker picnic basket. One rose in a dainty bud vase poked out the top. Mae had winked at Witt as she handed it to him.

Witt wanted to explain to Mae they were only friends, and Casey was married. But that might give the girls the wrong idea about Casey, so he let it slide. Someday he'd explain.

They were almost to the Jeep when Witt had an idea. "I think we should take both vehicles. The spot I have in mind is a long way from here, in the direction of Sugar Bluff. It would be a shame to drive all the way back to get your car. Besides, it would take up precious time we could spend picnicking."

It would be best if they each left the picnic in their own vehicle after they'd agreed to end their relationship.

"Drat. I'm a natural in the Jeep with my hair like this." Casey pointed at her disheveled hairdo. "In my car, I'll look like I got my finger stuck in the cigarette lighter."

Laughing, Witt set the picnic basket in the back of the Jeep.

"Well, you can drive the Jeep if you want, but we both know you can run a brush through your hair and look as beautiful as ever." His tone was alarmingly tender.

Watch your mouth, Witt.

He bowed low, gesturing to both vehicles. "So, what'll it be? Jeep or Jetta?"

"Since you put it that way, kind sir, I guess I'll brush my hair and drive my own little jitney. Somehow, I can't picture you driving the Jetta, anyway. It's so . . . uh . . ."

"*Small* would be the technical terminology you're grasping for. I may get in, but I don't know where I'd put my legs during the actual driving process."

He opened the driver's door of the Jetta. "Well, hop in, little lady, and follow me. We're going to take this road for about a mile." He pointed the direction both cars were headed. "Then the road will Y. We'll take the left leg. After that, it gets a bit twisty. I'll drive slowly so I don't lose you. Oh boy, you're going to love this."

Witt kept a close eye in the rearview mirror on the little Jetta. Like everything else she did, Casey was an excellent driver.

I could kick myself for not forcing my way into her life thirty years ago. I had nothing to lose. Who knows, I might have beat Allen out of the picture. But I can't change that now. All I can do now is set her free . . . from me.

He prayed a simple prayer. "Please give me the words to say, Lord. And *make* me say them, because I sure don't want to."

They came to the last turn before the picnic spot and the quaint covered bridge beyond it. He wanted Casey to see the bridge, so he drove past the little lane that would take them to the brook.

Because of recent freezing rains and heavy runoff up north, the river was roaring violently beneath the covered bridge. Witt pulled onto a wide spot, jumped out, and pointed to a parking place about twenty yards away for Casey. He ran to her car and helped her out. Taking her hand, he led her toward the bridge. He hadn't been here since Faith's kids were little. It used to be a popular picnic spot. But today the river was dangerously swift.

A battered picnic table, mangled from hitting the rocks, gushed by in the rampant waters. Then a rowboat, its broken tether whipping behind it in the turbulence.

Casey raised her eyebrows. "I hope this isn't the babbling brook."

"No, I wanted you to see this old bridge. The brook is back that way a couple hundred yards." He nodded in the direction from which they'd come. "I hope it still classifies as a brook or we may be picnicking on the tailgate of the Jeep."

I did so want her to enjoy today.

"I'm sorry, Case. I've never seen the river this violent. I didn't realize what the recent weather had done to this area. I really wanted this to be special for you. I guess we'd better go check on the brook. Let's leave the Jetta and take the Jeep."

"It's already special, Witt." She reached up and tweaked his earlobe. "Why don't we walk from here? It's not far, is it?"

She looked away. But not before Witt saw the pink creep into her cheeks.

Lord, are You sure this is where You want us? I thought there'd be a crowd.

"Sure. If it's too wet to walk, it'll be too wet to picnic. We may as well find out." He ran to the Jeep and grabbed the basket and the tablecloth from the backseat.

Approaching Casey, he noticed her little gray patent shoes again. "Are you sure you want to walk? What about your shoes?"

Casey reached out for the tablecloth and smoothed it out across her arm. "You go first, Witt. If you sink to your ankles, it's too wet."

The ground was dry and the brook was everything Witt had hoped. Gentle water trickling over large flat rocks. Looking around, Witt was glad to see other picnickers enjoying this splendid day. *Praise God.* On the grassy slope overlooking the brook, a weeping willow touched the ground on all sides, forming a little hideaway. The sound of the boiling, rampaging river just a couple hundred yards away didn't fit into this picture.

It's grown since I was here with Sis and the kids.

"It still qualifies as a babbling brook. Thank You, Jesus, for the small favors, as well as the big ones." Witt was pleased. This was his last chance to give Casey some small pleasure.

They found the perfect spot to spread the tablecloth under some majestic pines. Witt set the basket down and began to unload the goodies. A feast fit for a king.

"What a glorious day." Casey lifted her hands to heaven and whirled in a circle. "Thank you, Lord." She was radiant.

Witt's heart snapped another shot of her. To go with the one he'd saved all these years.

They ate and talked and laughed. Cherishing every moment, he was putting the sad news off until the very last. After the meal, Casey cleaned up the scraps and loaded them into the basket. Witt took it back to the Jeep and returned with the horse blankets.

Spreading them about a foot apart on the grass, Witt made a sweeping gesture. "Lady Casey, princess for a day. Your choice of fine textiles, milady."

Casey executed her best royal curtsy and chose the smaller blanket. She settled onto nature's mattress. Witt sat down about three feet from her. Three feet farther away than he wanted to be.

Time was growing short. Oh, that he could put it off forever.

It's in Your hands, Lord. Tell me when—and be with me.

They lay on their backs, looking at the great fluffs of cloud drifting by and talked about life. Mostly childhood.

Long nights of worry and early morning risings had exhausted both of them. The comfort of each other's company freed them to yield to total relaxation. With but a short lull in the conversation, they both fell asleep.

Witt was awakened by Casey's small hand in his. She'd reached out to him in her sleep. He listened to her slow soft breathing. Dapples of warm November sunlight filtered through the dense pine needles and danced on her cinnamon-and-sugar locks. He ached to touch her hair. But that could start him down a path he wasn't free to follow. So he just loved her and watched her for what he knew would be the last time.

And grappled with the conversation they inevitably had to share.

Shortly, God quickened Witt's spirit to awaken her from her restful sleep. The hour had come for them to face the bitter truth. Their friendship was for but a season and that season was at an end.

"Case."

His heart hurt.

Casey smiled at the sight of Witt's face. Sleepy-eyed and content, she waited for him to continue.

"Case." The words were heavy. His voice husky. "Lovely Case, today has been a beautiful day. And it's marked the end of the most meaningful relationship of my life."

Casey was savoring that exquisite, sleepy feeling when all seems well with the world. It took a split second to sink in. She hastily rose up on one elbow. The delicious feeling was suddenly, irrevocably, concluded as the weight of the world fell onto her shoulders.

"What on earth are you talking about, Witt?"

"I'm talking about us, Case. We can't see each other anymore."

If this was a joke, it wasn't very funny. "No, Witt. No. Don't talk like that. Why would you say something like that?"

He was sitting cross-legged on his blanket, looking at her. She swung her legs around and sat up to face him. Their eyes met and they were both struck silent by the aura of ardor that yoked them.

After a long poignant pause, Witt broke the silence. "Case, am I important to you?"

She answered without hesitation. "More than anyone else in the world."

"*That's* why. I can't hold that position in your life. I'm supposed to be only your friend. My ranking should be well below your husband's. I simply cannot *be* the most important person in your life." Looking down, fingering a blade of grass. "*God* doesn't want it that way."

"Oh, Witt, please, don't do this. Remember, back in town I told you I was afraid of Edward and I don't even want him to touch me? I've got to leave him, Witt. And I can't do it unless you're there to hold me up. You're my strength. I sometimes wonder what would have happened if we had met under different . . ."

Witt reached over and put his fingertip to her lips.

"Sweet Case, don't you remember? I told you in the beginning, God put us together only for me to help you."

"Yes, but why must you leave me *now*? I still need your help. Now more than ever."

I'm more afraid of him now than I was before. You're all I have.

"Your husband's restored and your marriage can be too. Deep in your heart, you know that's true." Witt cast his eyes skyward and ran his fingers through his hair.

He's hurting. He doesn't want this any more than I.

"What about the fact that I'm afraid of him? How can I live in fear of my husband? Would God really want me to live that way, Witt?"

The words tumbled from her lips. She searched his face for a sign of yielding. In his gaze was absolute tenderness, but no surrender.

"Think back to the gargoyle. The demon of fear isn't willing to let you go, Case. He's hanging on for dear life. Still trying to come between you and Edward and his ministry. Have you forgotten how to get that demon out of your life?"

"Maybe I don't want to remember. Maybe I just want to be happy with someone I can trust." *Maybe I just want you.*

"You can trust Edward now. Think of him the way you did when you first married him. Forget the bad times. *Forgive* him, because it wasn't really him. Please don't let Satan have the last word after the Lord has gone to so much trouble to restore your marriage. I think He has very big plans for you and Edward in His service."

He held out a strong hand.

She loved his hands. They were hardworking and calloused, but so gentle.

"Give me your hand please, little one."

Casey laid her trembling hand in his palm. He closed his fingers over it and, leaning toward her, held it to his face. For a lingering moment his eyes closed, and he rested his lips on her fingertips.

Casey fought the desire to put her other hand behind his head and pull him closer.

But he might lose his balance and fall against her. A shiver ran through her.

He raised his head and tears brimmed his eyes. "This is good-bye, Katherine Cecilia Morgan McAlester. I will never forget you. Now, go and do the Lord's will and don't let Satan defeat you."

Casey gently extricated her hand from his.

How can we put this back in the box, close the lid, and pretend it never happened?

She pulled herself to her feet, her heart still in his grasp, and looked down at him. "Witt, I'm going to go, only because I don't know what else to do. But I refuse to let you disappear from my life."

Witt stood. "Case . . . please try to understand."

"I understand you're my best friend. And I'm losing you." She turned her back.

In silence, they gathered and folded the blankets. He walked her to her car.

Casey stopped next to her car. She turned and threw her arms around him. "Oh, Witt, I can't. I just can't," she sobbed.

He laid the blankets on top of her car and pressed her head to his chest, stroking her hair. "We must, little lady. It's the only way." For a long moment they swayed to the music of the billowing river. Casey clung to him. Finally, Witt put one hand on her shoulder and one under her chin. "Kick the demon of fear out, Case. Go back to Edward and allow God to bless you with a long and happy life together." He released her and opened her car door.

Casey slid in and stared at the dash. Tears streamed down her face.

Witt knew something now he hadn't known as a young man living in San Antonio.

Grown men *do* cry.

He made no attempt to restrain his tears. But remained strong in his resolve that he would not give in to his love for Casey. He reached around her and fastened her seat belt, his face so close to hers. Then he grabbed the blankets from on top of her car. One last wistful look and he turned to go. About halfway to the Jeep he looked back at Casey and swung his right leg out in a punting gesture. *Kick the demon out, little one.* He strode to his Jeep.

"Lord God, You're going to have to take a hand in this. I'm at the end of my rope. Should she call me, I'd be helpless not to run to her rescue. And what will I do if I run into her in St. Michael? I'm so weak where she's concerned. You must know what agony this is for me. Still my greatest desire is to please You. Father, help me remain loyal to You above all else."

He tossed the blankets on the backseat. His hand was on the door handle of the Jeep when he heard the scream.

25

Casey glanced in her rearview mirror for one more glimpse of Witt before turning the corner. He was running toward the covered bridge. Running hard. The bridge shuddered and dropped a few inches. Billows of dust curled around the screaming child who clung to the splintered railing.

She braked and slammed the car in reverse. Scouring the roadside for a place to pull off, she glanced briefly at the road ahead. She looked behind her again.

The bridge was gone.

Oh, dear God. That poor child.

Picnickers were running from all directions to where the bridge had been. People yelling and children crying. She searched the crowd for Witt. Fear gripped her heart. She couldn't see him.

Jamming the car in park, she jumped out with it in the middle of the road and raced toward the bridge.

People were pointing down at the raging river. But no one was doing anything. One man attempted to descend the steep embankment, but he almost took a tumble and scrambled back up.

Casey reached the river's edge.

Witt looked like a discarded G.I. Joe doll lying on the rocks amid the shattered bridge timbers.

Oh, Jesus, please let him be alive.

"He saved my baby! He saved my baby!" The child's mother clutched her son to her bosom and peered down the embankment. "Help him, he saved my little boy."

"Someone call 911," Casey shouted into the crowd.

A man waved to her from beside his pickup. He was already dialing.

She started down. All she could think of was getting to Witt. She couldn't see any movement.

Oh, Jesus, please let him be alive.

Her foot slipped and she slid four or five feet before she could steady herself. She had to slow down to keep from plunging to the bottom.

Oh Jesus, please let him be alive.

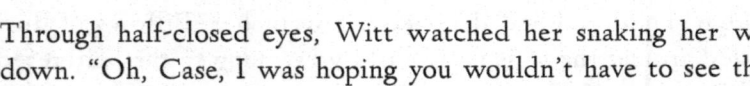

Through half-closed eyes, Witt watched her snaking her way down. "Oh, Case, I was hoping you wouldn't have to see this. Slow down, little one, you're going to hurt yourself. I'm not going anywhere."

He felt no pain, but he couldn't move his arms or legs, and he could feel his strength ebbing. It wasn't frightening. It was a peaceful feeling. His thoughts lapsed into prayer, one that must surely be his last on this side of heaven.

"God, I assign a couple of your mightiest angels to Case. She's got on those little pumps, not meant for rock climbing. Please guide her and keep her from falling."

She slipped and his heart leaped in his chest. She righted herself.

"Thank You, Jesus. But, Lord, why do You have her here instead of in her Jetta on the way home? It's going to hurt her to see me like this."

She wants to say good-bye, son. Remember?

"Oh yes, I remember. Father, may I tell her I've always loved her?"

Yes. When her heart has mended, it will free her to love Edward again.

Witt wanted to wipe his eyes, to clear his vision. But his arms were as heavy as treated four-by-fours. He concentrated on Casey.

On either side of her was a mighty angel, descending the steep incline with her. The celestial beings shone clear and perfect. They were more than twice her size and their impregnable wings encompassed her, protecting her from harm.

"I knew I couldn't go on loving her without offending You. So You're taking me home . . . in the nick of time. Hallelujah."

The banquet table is ready for your arrival.

It was getting harder to see. Witt closed his eyes for a moment.

I gotta save what's left of my sight to see Case. Hope she gets here in time.

When he opened his eyes again he'd see either Jesus or Case. It was a win-win situation.

More than once Casey lost her footing and somehow regained it before falling. It was as though someone caught her and set her back on her feet.

As she got closer, her heart sank. Bloodstains covered Witt's shirt. His eyes were closed and his head was bleeding from a deep gash. His long legs lay limp across a jagged rock. Around him, huge bridge timbers had fallen in jumbled disarray like a giant game of pick up sticks.

She wanted to rush to him, but approached cautiously, not to cause him pain.

She wanted to cry, but if he were alive, he'd need her presence of mind.

And she wanted to blame someone. But whom could she blame? Witt was doing what Witt did. Helping others.

She knelt beside him. He had that slight curl to his lips that usually preceded a smile. "I thought I told you . . . to wait in the car," he quipped.

"Oh, Witt. Praise God. You're alive. Help will be here soon. Don't try to talk."

"Little one, it's . . . doubtful I'll be alive when . . . they get here."

"Shhh. Don't say that, Witt. You can't die. What would I do without you?" Casey caressed his face and gently plucked a small splinter of wood from his cheek.

He can't die. Why would God take him and leave people like me or Edward?

"Case, I've seen . . . the angels. Some things . . . I must tell you. I've cleared it with . . . Jesus."

Casey nodded patiently. "What is it, Witt?"

"I've loved you . . . all my life, Katherine Morgan."

He's delirious.

"I don't understand, Witt. We've only known each other a month." *And why would he call me Katherine?*

His voice was so weak. She leaned closer.

"San Antonio . . . your mother, Del."

Casey pulled back to look at his face. His eyes were fixed on the heavens.

"God brought us together again. You . . . needed my help."

Overwhelmed, Casey put both of her hands on his face, gently touching his lips with hers. When she drew back, his eyes fastened onto hers. He seemed to be trying to tell her more than words could say.

"*Now* I've been . . . kissed by you." He sighed. "And I'm satisfied." His lips curled into a small grin. "Ready to go home."

"Oh, Witt. I'd be so lost without you. You've got to hang on and stop talking about going home. They'll be here soon. You're *not* going to die."

"Case . . . to stay and covet you would be . . . a sin. It's His perfect answer."

Casey couldn't recall him from San Antonio. But she loved him. In one short month she'd learned to love him in a way she didn't comprehend.

Panic crept into her voice. "Oh, Witt. I can't lose you. No, please."

"Case . . . this is our chance . . . to say good-bye. He's doing that . . . for *you*."

He seemed so calm. So sure—and so pale.

Oh, dear God. He really is going to die.

Casey held his hand in both of hers. She had to make him know he was loved in return. "I'd have left Edward to be with you."

He gave her a feeble wink. "No, Case . . . you'd have come to your . . . senses."

Casey began caressing him. His face, his arms, his shoulders. Like she might be able to store up the feel of him and call on it later when devastation overtook her.

Witt smiled. "Defeat the demon of fear, Case. Promise me . . . before I go."

"I'll do my best. For *you*, Witt."

He'd loved her all his life. But never competed with Edward for her love.

What a man of God to put the Lord's will before his own. And what agony the last few weeks must have been.

I was his for the taking.

Casey's throat ached from restrained tears. She didn't know how much longer she could hold them back.

"So tired, Case."

He's asking to go home. With my blessing.

She'd never have another chance to be strong for him. Casey looked to heaven.

Father, give me the right words.

"To be absent in the body is to be present with the Lord, Witt. God will bless you richly when you come into His presence. And you'll be a part of my life for all eternity." Her tears would no longer be denied.

His eyelids fluttered and closed. "Don't cry, little one. I'll see you in the . . . the morning."

His body relaxed.

Instantly, Casey's entire being was engulfed in a quivering warmth. Mighty angels hovered over them in brilliant, breathtaking magnificence. There were not just a few. But *hundreds*. Wing tip to iridescent wing tip, their splendor overwhelmed her senses.

The crowd on the shore, the noise of the raging river, and the rocks gouging her knees were gone. They were floating above it. The magnificent angels, Witt, and Casey. Surrounded by incredible radiance. Celestial music soothed her world-weary ears.

Witt's face was glowing. He looked at her and smiled. His eyes were dancing. He was free of wounds and a resplendent white robe had replaced his bloodstained shirt.

Soft cords of agape love pulled them upward into the glorious light. Casey's spirit was soaring with the angels. Her eyes partaking wondrous sights. Thousands of rejoicing angels awaited their arrival on the other side of a magnificent gate. Witt was right. Death is beautiful. *But when did I die?*

Witt reached the gate first and turned to wave to Casey.

She lifted her arm to wave back and the cord slipped from around her. Glory dissipated.

Sharp rocks dug into her knees. The awful noise of the crashing river and the crowd were augmented by the woeful sound of sirens. Witt's lifeless body lay before her.

In the blinking of an eye God's angels had come to collect his spirit. In their great compassion for her shattered heart, they had allowed her to see him received into glory.

Casey lifted his hand and held it in hers. A cascade of fresh tears washed her cheeks and dropped onto Witt's peaceful face. She knew he was with God. But that didn't quench her pain.

Several uniformed men stumbled the last few feet down the embankment. Ropes around their chests tethered them to the safety of the upper shore. An officer gently removed her hand from Witt's and helped her to her feet. He stood beside her, supporting her.

A paramedic checked for vital signs. Casey wanted to tell him Witt was already with the Lord, but she kept her silence and let him do his job.

"I'm sorry, ma'am," he muttered without looking at her. "He's gone. You did all you could. A lot more than most people would've done for a perfect stranger. We'll take it from here."

They lifted Witt onto a gurney and covered him from head to toe with a white sheet. By the grace of God, Casey was able to keep standing. They struggled with their tethers, and Witt's body, up the steep slope. Battling to keep the gurney level.

Casey watched their every move.

Don't you dare slip and let him fall.

He no longer occupied that shell, but it was the precious vessel that had housed his dauntless spirit for so long. She wanted no more harm to come to it.

The gurney slid silently into the waiting ambulance. The doors slammed shut.

Casey whimpered and collapsed into the attending officer's arms.

26

Edward followed the desk clerk to a tiny room in the police station.

"Your wife's in here, sir."

From his vantage point he could see Casey before she saw him. He gazed at her for a long time, tenderness for her welling up in his heart. She looked like she was weathering a pretty bad storm.

"She must be a very special lady, sir. She shimmied down a steep embankment in those fancy shoes to try to save him. And comforted him in his last moments." The officer shook his head and smacked his lips. "But I'm afraid she's taking it too hard. She did all she could. I doubt the EMTs could have saved him, had they been there when it happened."

Edward put his hand on the young man's shoulder. "Thank you for looking after her. Exactly what happened out there, anyway?"

"Sir, as far as we can determine from eyewitness reports, your wife was in her car headed toward the highway. It's a shortcut through there from St. Michael to the highway south. Anyways, the deceased heard a scream. The covered bridge was shivering like it was going to collapse. River's been really rough . . ."

Edward nodded patiently. "And?"

"Anyways, there was this little kid on the bridge, 'bout four years old. His mom's screaming up a storm and he's a-screaming too. And this gentleman, a vet from St. Michael, might have been in these parts on a house call. Anyways, he was about to get in his Jeep, but he took off for the bridge without hesitating."

The officer leaned in close to Edward. "A beam was working its way loose right over the boy. The doc grabbed the beam to keep it from falling on the kid, kinda like Sampson in the Bible, and yelled, 'Run, son, run.' The little boy ran to his mom, but before the doc could leap to safety, the bridge caved and fell into the river. He was close enough to the edge that he didn't hit the water. Hit the rocks." The corners of the young man's mouth jutted down. "Bad stuff. Might have survived if he'd hit the water. Then again maybe not." He shrugged.

"How awful." Edward rubbed his forehead, wondering how much of this Casey had witnessed. "Did he have a family?"

"A niece and a nephew, sir. They've been notified. I imagine they've taken care of all the details at the morgue by now. Last name's Gregory, in case you want to check the obits."

"And you say my wife was just passing by?"

I wonder where she learned about the shortcut.

"Looks that way. She evidently saw it all. Left the car running in the middle of the road and shouted to the crowd for someone to dial 911, before she headed down the embankment. It's a miracle she didn't fall and get hurt too. Is she a nurse, sir?"

"No, just a very caring person."

"Anyways, she did what she could. He was a goner from the get-go. She's a good woman, sir. Did more than most would do for a perfect stranger. But after it was over, well, she was too shook up to drive."

Casey, Casey. Why would you risk your life like that? What would I do if you'd been hurt? Sometimes I wish you weren't so tenderhearted.

"Yes, watching helplessly while a man died would take its toll on her. But if she was able to make his last moments easier . . . well, that's what she's all about.

"I think I should let her know I'm here now, Officer. She needs the comfort of home and family. Did you have her car towed here?"

"Yes, sir. Well, that is, an officer drove her here in it. Said she cried and didn't say a word the whole way, except to thank him for his kindness, that is."

Edward shook his head. "That's so unlike her. She's really quite outgoing. May I leave the car here until we can pick it up?"

"No problem. It'll be right here in the precinct parking lot. Snug as a bug in a rug."

"Need money for gas? You said she left it running."

"No sir, someone in the crowd moved it off the road and cut the engine after a couple minutes."

"Thanks again." Edward shook his hand and walked into the room where Casey was waiting.

She looked up at him, eyes red and puffy, but didn't reach out or smile. There was blood on her yellow blouse and dirt on her cheek. Edward was at her side in two strides. He knelt in front of her. Her gray pants had been ripped at the knee and an angry red welt was exposed. Edward took her hand. She twitched at his touch, so he made no attempt to hold her close, though he longed to. He waited for her to speak, praying under his breath.

"He's dead, Edward. It happened so fast and now he's gone. What'll I do?"

"It's all right, darling. There was nothing more you could do. Perhaps he's with the Lord, even as we speak. We'll have to believe he made it to heaven."

"He's in heaven. I'm sure of that. I saw . . ." Casey turned her head toward the wall. "There's no doubt he's in heaven," she concluded flatly.

Of course she would have talked to him about the Lord. Maybe even led him to the Lord in his dying moments.

Edward helped Casey to her feet and led her out of the room. She stopped to thank the officers. Holding each one's hand, she prayed for his safety. A room full of tough cops with teary eyes watched the dear lady leave with her husband.

Edward took her to his modest Dodge minivan and held the door open for her. "Do you want to talk about it, baby?"

Casey's hands were shaking. She sank into the seat and tried unsuccessfully to fasten her seat belt. Dropping her head, she began sobbing.

Oh, Jesus, what can I do? If I try to hold her, I'll scare her. But I can't bear to see her like this. Why is this hitting her so hard, God? Have my actions pushed her over the edge? Please help me. Let me be her pillar of strength. Let it be like it used to be.

Casey cut her eyes toward Edward and saw his lips moving. Lately it seemed he prayed without ceasing. Like Witt. He reached across her to fasten her seat belt. She wanted to pound on him with her fists. *No! Don't you dare horn in on my memories of Witt. He does that for me.*

She swallowed the bile that rose in her throat. Edward was here with her, doing his best. And Witt was gone. Oh that the angels had taken her the rest of the way with him. All the way to heaven. Through that magnificent gate. She wanted to be with Witt and Jesus.

Then she remembered his last request. And her promise to him. She had to honor his memory. And that meant she must keep her promise.

Her gaze followed Edward as he walked around the front of the van. She purposed to look at him through God's eyes. He was a good man. A changed man. And he was trying very hard to make things right. He opened the door and slid into the driver's seat.

Looking over at her. "You okay, honey? Ready to go home?

It was sad to see him sitting behind the wheel, anxious to know if she was comfortable before he started the van. Like she'd break if he didn't do everything just right. Such a bright and spiritual person. A leader among men. But her fear of him had reduced him to a shell of a man in her presence.

Looking into her husband's sad eyes, she saw his concern. His love. She sighed. Her heart lacked the will to beat. "I'm ready."

Help me, Witt. How can I keep my promise and give my heart back to him, when you took it with you?

27

For Casey, the timing was all wrong. She was still grieving Witt's death.

But Edward went ahead with his plans to tell the church about his deliverance and salvation. It went well for *him*. Devoted parishioners pledged their continued support and undying love.

Woodenly, Casey nodded and smiled at each of them as they filed by. Some apologized for not being observant enough to realize their pastor and his wife were in trouble. Occasionally a teary-eyed lady hugged her and murmured words of sympathy. Casey allowed herself to imagine they were mourning her loss of Witt. More than once she broke into tears. But evidently no one suspected her tears had nothing to do with Edward's demon possession. They'd hug her a little tighter and cry with her.

Edward and Casey drove home in silence, Edward looking at her repeatedly, his brow furrowed.

"It was good, wasn't it, honey?" he asked after they'd settled in at home. "Not as hair-raising as I'd expected."

He had his feet propped up on the hassock, his Bible on his lap. Casey was in front of the big window that overlooked the mountains in the distance . . . in the direction of the river—where it had happened.

"Yes, good." Her mind dwelled on her grief.

"Casey, *where are you?* I feel like we're living in different universes. I need you, darling. Please come back."

She turned to face him. "I need to go to the funeral."

Edward groaned and removed his glasses. "Honey, you're taking this too hard. I know it was very traumatic to watch helplessly while this DeWitt Gregory fellow died. But you went beyond what any other person would've done." He laid his Bible on the end table, his reading glasses on top of it, and swung his feet to the floor. With his forearms on his knees and his fingers clasped, he leaned toward Casey. "This man . . . this stranger . . . had a family, darling. And friends . . . lots of them. You saw his obit. It's not as though he were a homeless man. There's no point in torturing yourself. I can't forbid you to go. But I wish you wouldn't."

Casey had read Witt's obit. Over and over. This morning while Edward was in the shower, she had repeatedly run her fingers across Witt's picture. And wept.

She took a step toward Edward. "I know he had lots of friends." She was about to plunge in headfirst. But she couldn't live a lie. Edward would have to understand. If he was truly a changed man, he'd somehow learn to accept it. If he wasn't, there was no point in trying to keep her promise to Witt. It would never work, anyway.

"I know he had lots of friends," she repeated. "Because I was one of them."

Edward's mouth fell open. He leaned back in his chair and blinked. "I beg your pardon?"

"DeWitt was a family name. He liked to be called Witt. I don't know all his friends, but I've met some of them. He had a close relationship with the Lord. Serving people was his joy."

She turned to look out the window again, her back to Edward.

"He wanted a big family but never married. So he made the whole town of St. Michael his family." She hastily wiped a tear from her cheek. "An honorable man. Completely devoted to his grown niece and nephew. He liked to be called Witt."

She stopped abruptly, realizing she was rambling and repeating herself. And trembling.

Edward was standing behind her now. He put his hands on her shoulders and turned her around to face him. She drew her body tight and waited for his outburst.

But he was looking at her through troubled eyes, shaking his head as though she'd lost her mind. "How can this be?"

He tilted his head to one side and ran his tongue over his lips. "Where'd you meet him? And how long have you known him?" A new deep crease furrowed his brow.

Before she could answer, he took a deep breath. "Casey, what's going on?"

There was no anger in his eyes. But profound hurt. He looked older, and more vulnerable, than Casey had ever seen him. Instead of fear, she felt pity for him.

Talking about Witt, even to her husband, filled Casey with a strange elation. It made him *real* again. Not some wonderful dream she'd had. But a real, live, loving person who'd come into her life and changed her forever.

She touched Edward's cheek. It was warm. Flushed.

"Nothing's going on, Edward. I've lost a good friend, that's all."

She spoke as to a child who must be made to understand something very important. "We owe Witt a debt of gratitude. He saved your life. And your ministry and . . ." She'd intended to include their marriage, but she wasn't sure about that yet. "There's so much to tell about him I don't know where to begin. But I hope you'll believe me when I say we were just friends. We didn't have an . . . an inappropriate relationship."

She couldn't bring herself to say *affair* because to speak of their alliance in carnal terms would be to blemish it. She'd have to choose her words very carefully. She didn't want to lie to Edward. But neither did she want to hurt him. Not when there was the slightest chance of recapturing everything good they'd ever had.

It would serve no purpose to confess her heart had entertained thoughts of a life with Witt. A man of such tremendous wisdom and kindness, with whom every day would've brought new pleasures.

And no reason to say she and Witt had a point of connection the two of them hadn't achieved in twenty years. Once spoken, those words would live in Edward's heart and destroy any chance of restoring their marriage.

Edward leaned against the door facing and crossed his arms in front of himself. His face was ashen. His features sagged. "Casey, I need some sort of explanation, other than you were friends. You've never kept secrets from me before. Why now? How do I know you weren't having an affair?" His eyes pierced the air between them.

Casey bit her lip. He was so calm. It was an act. He'd explode any moment.

Oh, Jesus, I'm afraid he'll kill me if I tell him Witt loved me.

Recalling the beauty of death, and who she'd see when she got there, she drew in a ragged breath.

"This is hard, Edward." She closed her eyes—a long pause and a deep breath to gain control of her trembling heart—and opened them. "Witt was in love with me."

He winced. And drooped like a deflated balloon. Pain filled his eyes, but still no anger.

"He'd loved me since we were quite young. But I never knew it. I didn't remember him. I still can't place him from my past . . . even now."

"Witt was in love with me?" You tell me how wonderful he was and then stand there and say those words to me? Do I look like I'm made of steel?

Edward grabbed the door facing on either side and brought his head down between his hands. He wanted to bash his head against it, scream, cry, hit something. He looked back at Casey and groaned. "What else do you have for me in your little bag of surprises?"

Casey stepped back—farther away from him. "He fell in love with me in San Antonio and I left *there* when I was twenty-one." Her gaze dropped to the floor.

Suddenly Edward had a fifty-pound weight strapped to his chest. "That's thirty years ago!" He ran his hand across his face, stopping at his mouth. He might have to vomit.

He reached for his glass on the coffee table and took a drink of water. "How did you happen to run across each other again? Has he been stalking you all these years?"

San Antonio was before his time. He knew only what Casey had told him about her past. He'd always trusted her. Was his trust misplaced?

"Heavens, no." Casey shook her head vigorously. "We met last month, quite by accident, when I was in St. Michael having the Jetta serviced. You and I had one of our really bad evenings and I wasn't in very good shape." She fiddled with her wedding ring, pulling it back and forth across her knuckle. "Witt and I literally ran into each other in the doorway of a little antique shop. And I burst into tears."

Edward looked away. *Really bad evening.* Guilt added another ten pounds to the weight on his chest.

Casey kept plowing through his heart, like a runaway bulldozer. "He asked if I'd like a cup of coffee. And I accepted. We just talked. It was all so innocent. And even though I felt odd having coffee with a strange man, I was in no condition to refuse. I'd have probably collapsed into a puddle of tears, had someone not taken pity on me. I just thank God that He sent such a good person. I was pretty vulnerable."

Yeah, a good person who just happened to be in love with my wife.

"Sounds like a pickup to me." He spoke through clenched teeth.

"Edward, he was an on-fire Christian, I couldn't help but like him. You'd have liked him too. I didn't know we'd met before. In fact, neither did he, at first."

"When did you find *that* out?" He rubbed his neck at the base of his skull and winced.

"I'm not sure when he did. I suspect that first day. But I didn't know until the moment he was dying." Casey blinked. A lone tear found its way down her cheek. "He discussed the situation with the Lord—like he did everything—and came to the conclusion God let our paths cross again so he could help with our marriage. And your ministry."

The more she talked, the harder his heart beat.

"When he was dying, he confessed to loving me all his life. There

251

wasn't enough time to tell me where we'd met. Only that my mother was his friend."

Edward stomped into the kitchen with his empty glass and came back with more water.

"Edward, is this bothering you too much?" She was looking out the window again.

The more she stared out the window, the less likely it was that she and DeWitt Gregory were only friends.

"Oh no. I'm good. I love hearing about some guy being in love with you." He held up the morning paper and rattled it over his head. "I've seen his picture, Casey. This was one good-looking fellow. I was acting like an . . . ass. And you're telling me you felt *nothing* for him?" He tossed the paper down.

Casey didn't answer.

And the more questions she ignores, the worse things look for us. I've been shot out of the saddle . . . by a dead man.

"How tall was he?" He had a reason for wanting to know.

Casey looked at him askance. "I don't know. Tall. Six three, six four, maybe. Why?"

He didn't answer. He swung around, his back to Casey. His stomach heaved with nausea and sweat beads popped out on his forehead.

He wiped his forehead on his sleeve and turned back to her. He had to ask, but he wasn't sure he wanted to know. "How many times did you see him? And where did you meet? Never mind. I don't want to know . . . yes, I . . . no, I don't."

Casey stepped closer and looked pleadingly at him. "You have to remember, Edward, he was keeping his feelings to himself. I'd have been an easy target. Had he not been so honorable, he'd have tried to get me to leave you."

Edward tilted his head to one side and shook his index finger skyward. "*This* is where I have a little problem, *Mrs. McAlester.*" He began pacing around Casey. She turned with him. "*No one* is that honorable. When I fell in love with you, if I'd found out you had an abusive husband, I'd have torn him limb from limb—not tried to patch up your marriage."

Casey stomped her foot. "Stand still. This is what I've been try-

252

ing to tell you. He was not like anyone I've ever known. We prayed for you. For your deliverance. *He's* the one who connected us with Ron and Indi."

Edward had wondered why someone in the deliverance ministry suddenly dropped into his life. He was thankful, but curious how God had arranged that so-called coincidence.

Casey continued, "In answer to your question, we met several times, usually on Friday, and almost always in downtown St. Michael. I went to his ranch once, but we weren't alone."

Edward made a stabbing motion to his heart. "Oh, that's a comfort." He pulled the imaginary knife back out and looked at Casey, his eyes brimming with tears.

"Edward, had I been meeting a woman, no one would've thought a thing of it. But a pastor's wife can't have a man for a best friend, can she?"

"Seems like you could've found a woman to talk to. What about Indi?"

"I didn't know her yet." Casey averted her eyes and fidgeted with one of her earrings. "Anyway, it was his intention we say our final good-byes Friday. Said his mission in my life had been accomplished. But I wasn't willing to end it. I was losing the best friend I ever had, simply because he was a man. I didn't know he was fighting a different battle than I. He'd promised the Lord he'd help me and not covet me. And there I was, heaping on the coals."

Edward heaved a deep sigh and plopped back into his chair. "Well, you're heaping them on *me* now." He clenched his fist and hit it against his palm. "How am I supposed to compete against a dead man?" He was immediately sorry at his lack of sensitivity. He dropped his head into his hand and rocked forward.

Casey whimpered. "Edward, he worked so hard at getting our marriage restored, and your life back on track. You've simply got to appreciate that."

His head was reeling. It was unbelievable that *his* Casey could have her head turned by some guy on the street. How close had he come to losing her to a stranger? Would this hero of hers come between them, even now?

Seeking some reassurance of her feelings for him, Edward stood up and moved close, reaching out for her. "What are . . . were . . . your feelings for *him*, Casey?"

She jumped backward and bumped into a floor lamp.

He put his hands up, palms toward Casey. "You don't have to answer that. I don't think I want to know." His hands dropped to his sides.

Casey opened her mouth, hesitated, and didn't answer.

Edward stewed. No answer was not a good sign.

"He bathed our friendship in prayer every day—many times a day. I think his prayers were the only thing that kept him in line. And kept me from giving up on you."

Suddenly Casey grabbed her forehead with one hand and pressed the other to her chest. Her shoulders curved forward and she rocked, looking like she might lose her balance at any moment. "To think such a person would waste his whole life because he loved me."

Edward knew he should put his arms around her and comfort her. But she was mourning another man. Anyway she'd just draw away from him and make him feel worse.

His insides were churning. He could blame Casey, but this was *his* fault. Had he been her priest like he should have been, this wouldn't have happened. Apparently God had arranged it all to get him back on track. And it cost a man his life. Ooof. *Another ten pounds of guilt.*

How would this have played out if Witt hadn't died? What if they'd met in St. Michael ten years ago? Would Casey still be his wife? *Are there any other good-looking guys out there who love her?*

You've got to get a handle on this, Edward. The demon of jealousy would love to have another crack at you. Don't let him in.

Edward sat down and grabbed his Bible and glasses again.

He opened the Bible and looked up over his reading glasses. "I want to go with you to your friend's funeral, Casey. I'd like to pay my respects too. That is, unless you don't want me there." He put his head down and began flipping through the pages.

Her answer would tell him a great deal about her true feelings. And their future.

Casey stared at the top of Edward's head. She'd be in Witt's tranquil world this one last time. Edward was up to no good. Why would he want to go except to cause trouble?

Yet to refuse might bring on World War III.

"I'd like that." She forced a smile. "I'll be meeting Megan, Mark, and Zach for the first time. It would be great . . . for you to be there with me."

Did I sound sincere?

When he looked up at her, his square jaw was clamped tight and he had a faraway look in his eyes. She'd taken too long to respond. Casey had banished the demon of fear many times. But it was a tenacious beast that kept popping up when least expected.

Edward was rubbing his chin. "So, that rascal, Ron, was a friend of Witt's. And Witt set up the deliverance deal. Do you suppose Ron really likes me, or am I one of his pet projects?"

Glad to be off the subject of her relationship with Witt, Casey breathed a sigh. "Ron and Indi are our good friends, Edward. Yes, he likes you. A lot. Indi told me so."

Dreading what she must do next, Casey sat down on the end of the couch with her hands folded in her lap and cleared her throat. "Satan has dealt us a cruel blow, Edward. I've been honest with you about Witt. Now I've got to be honest about *our* relationship."

Edward visibly stiffened.

This is it, Edward. You've lost her. You fool!

She looked so prim and proper sitting there. How could he have accused her of having an affair? Yet—

She studied her folded hands. "Edward, I dream often of the terrible things the demons caused you to do. The loathing in your eyes. The threats to 'tear my heart out' you made right before deliverance.

255

In my subconscious I'm waiting for the other shoe to drop." She lifted moist amber eyes to meet his gaze. "I'm frightened of you, Edward."

Edward hung his head. He hadn't known he'd said *anything* to her on that awful night. But he should've known the demons would arrange to have the last word.

He looked up and put his hands together—prayer style. "Casey, please forgive me for whatever I said. I really don't remember any of it. You've got to know I'd never hurt you."

"I'm trying to believe that, Edward." She rubbed her fingers across her shoulder. "But you *did* hurt me. I can't make any promises. Not yet."

Oh, Jesus, have mercy. I remember now. I put a pretty nasty bruise on her shoulder.

Since the demons left, Edward had been trying to recall the things he'd said and done while under their influence. Until now nothing would surface, except for one vague memory that plagued his heart and mind. It tormented him every time he passed by the hall bathroom.

It was there—reflected in the bathtub cold-water knob—he'd been shown the vision of Casey and a *tall* man walking together . . . into the woods.

28

Indi had one elbow on the table, resting her chin on the heel of her hand. With the other hand she used her straw to chase ice cubes around in her tea glass. "Do I believe in soul mates? Good question." She clicked her tongue and raised her eyebrows. "Well, yes I do."

She dropped the straw into the glass and leaned way back in her chair. "But I think the world—Hollywood, in particular—has made the blending of soul mates far too common a thing."

Casey tilted her head to one side. "Meaning?"

"Well, meeting a soul mate doesn't always mean you're going to end up marrying him. Doesn't even mean you'll be together." She shook her head. "And you certainly can't travel through time and space to find him, like in the movies."

Casey wrinkled her brow and sighed. "I guess you're right."

"You look disappointed. Do you have a special reason for asking, Casey?"

"No, I was just thinking about that very movie. The one where a guy traveled through time to find his soul mate. We watched it a couple of months ago. I wondered if . . . oh, it's nothing. Just romantic stuff. It touched me and I wondered if it really happens that way. That connection between two people. And if it happens for everyone, or just a few lucky ones."

"About that movie, that's my point exactly, Casey. Very few people ever meet a soul mate. Even fewer marry them. We fall in love. And with God's help, we work out our differences."

Indi had come across the mountain to see Casey while Edward was at the church, studying. Specifically to give the two of them a chance to talk about the recent traumatic events. When they talked yesterday Casey mentioned all was not well between her and Edward, but she didn't want to discuss it on the phone.

She knew Casey needed ministering to help her get over Edward's horrific behavior and the shock of his deliverance. And the terrible thing that had happened to Witt. He'd been a good friend to Casey. After she'd known him for such a short time, he was gone.

Indi had canceled an appointment to be here for her. And with so much on Casey's mind, Indi thought it odd she wanted to talk about trivial matters like movies.

Maybe that's how she keeps her sanity.

Indi changed the subject to something more pertinent. "Are you going to Witt's funeral tomorrow?"

The color left Casey's face. She hopped from the table and raced to the sink. But not before Indi had seen the change in her demeanor.

"Would you like more tea, Indi?" Her voice was tremulous. She didn't turn to face her.

Indi started to repeat her question about Witt but decided against it. She'd let Casey make the next move. "Not now, thank you."

Indi didn't know the whole story about Witt being in love with the same woman since his youth. But she'd overheard a few things said about it between Witt and Ron a year or so ago. And took it for granted that whatever the situation was, Witt had a handle on it. He had stuff together.

But he'd been acting differently for the last few weeks.

For years it had been their habit to get together at least once a week for supper and games. But since meeting Casey he came over only to pray. They prayed for Casey and Edward, and for confirmation regarding how Witt was handling a situation that weighed heavily on his heart. But he shared no details. And he told them about an awesome time he had with the Lord in his prayer closet. But he picked his way around the story, trying to share the excitement without divulging any details. The whole thing was very unlike Witt. He was usually so open. So transparent.

Indi pondered this. Could it be that Witt and Casey had a history?

She put two and two together and concluded Casey could be the one he'd loved all those years. What a dilemma it would have been for Witt to meet her again and not be able to share his feelings.

Ron called her a hopeless romantic.

But when Witt talked about Casey's problems his eyes shone with unshed tears. They'd assumed he was touched by this lady's grievous situation. Now it seemed entirely possible he was suffering—because he loved her. He never would have allowed himself to become romantically involved with a married woman. So he coveted their prayers but dared not reveal the problem. How sad for Witt.

Indi didn't know Casey's feelings or the relationship they'd shared. Knowing Witt, she was sure it was an honorable one. Now Witt was gone. His loss had wounded Indi and Ron very deeply.

And Edward showed the promise of becoming a great man of God. But he needed Casey by his side if he were to continue in the ministry Witt had worked so hard to preserve. Her love and support would mean the difference between victory and defeat.

What a tremendous burden for Casey to bear, if she'd fallen in love with Witt.

Lord, if this is so, please put the words in my mouth that will free her to talk this out and arrive at Your solution.

Indi slipped away from the table and approached the sink.

Casey still had her back to Indi, her whole body quavering. Indi laid her hands on her shoulder blades.

Words poured from her lips. "Casey, we're truly blessed if our soul mate touches our lives, however briefly. But we can't let the depth of that connection between two mortals cause us to lose sight of our real purpose in life as Christians: serving our Spirit Mate, Jesus Christ."

Casey's trembling subsided. Her tense body relaxed. "Thank you, Indi. You're right."

She reached over her shoulder with one hand to touch Indi's fingertips. Turning to face her, she took both of her hands. "I need your wise counsel to set me straight." She looked down at their clasped hands. "But I'm afraid of losing your friendship."

"Casey, Casey, I'm your friend for life and your sister in Christ. There's nothing you could say or do to lose my friendship." Indi pulled Casey to her and wrapped her arms tightly around her. She ran her hands up and down Casey's back as she whispered a prayer for God's blessing on their friendship.

Finally, Indi pulled away and searched the face of her petite friend. "Let's sit down."

Indi sat first and patted the closest chair for Casey to sit in. Casey wiped the table and freshened their iced tea before sitting.

You seem to be stalling, girl.

"So talk to me, Casey. Whatever the problem is, God has the answer."

Casey crossed her arms on the table and looked at Indi through misty eyes. "Did you know Witt had been in love with the same woman since he was young, but she was unaware of his feelings?"

Indi's throat tightened. She nodded. It looked like she was right about Witt and Casey.

"I was that woman, Indi. I learned of his love as he was dying in my arms. I wanted to shake him and make him come back to tell me more. I knew there was something special about our relationship from the first time we met. I cherished the time we spent together . . . too much. He was my rock here on earth."

Casey looked toward the window, avoiding Indi's steady gaze. "But when he told me he loved me, oh, God forgive me, Indi, I think I fell in love with him—and lost him—in one heartbeat."

Indi gently turned Casey's face toward her and pulled her hands down to the table. She covered them with her own. "Casey, look at me."

"Oh, Indi, what am I going to do? I miss him so much." The tears that had been building up behind her lower lids overflowed the spillway, splashing onto her freckled cheeks.

Indi handed her a tissue. "Casey, you know Jesus Christ was Witt's first love. You and he and Edward will always have *that* in common, along with me and Ron, and a multitude of saints we've yet to meet. We'll all be together one day. One family in glory."

Indi moved her chair closer to Casey so she could put her arm around her. "Keep that hope of glory in your heart and be true to the mission God has given you here on earth. You'll never forget Witt. Couldn't if you wanted to. And you'll always love him in Christ."

Casey was shaking her head. "But my heart, Indi. Edward broke it. And Witt mended it. Then he took it with him." She whimpered. "I don't have anything to give Edward."

"Casey, you loved Edward for twenty years. You've ministered together and raised a son together. You surely have some love in your heart for him. Give him a chance to make you happy again."

"I've been trying, Indi. I know if I don't honor my marriage vows, Witt will have died for nothing. He made me promise I'd forgive Edward and mend our marriage. But I can't seem to shake the fear. I've rebuked the demon of fear again and again, but it keeps coming back. Every time Edward touches me, I'm consumed with terror. Then from the recesses of my mind comes the memory of Witt's gentleness and I melt with grief because I've lost him."

Indi leaned back in her chair. "The grief will lessen as time goes on, Casey. More quickly if you'll stop to appreciate how the *Lord* used Witt in your life." She pulled back up and placed her face right in front of Casey's. "The demon of fear is just that . . . a demon. Not of God. We're not going to let a demon defeat us, Casey McAlester."

Casey wrenched her hands together and looked unblinkingly at Indi.

No reply to my challenge, eh? Well, I've got more ammo, my friend.

"How is Edward doing? Did the congregation accept his confession?"

"His congregation loves him. And he was doing great until I told him about Witt and me yesterday. Everything except how much I miss Witt. I didn't want to hurt him."

So you do care about Edward.

"Oh, that must've been really hard on both of you. How'd he take it?"

"Not too well. He's not convinced Witt and I weren't having an . . ." Casey lowered her head and whispered, "An *affair*." She looked up at Indi, shaking her head. "And he wants to come to the funeral with me. I'm afraid he's devised a plan to hurt me. And Witt's family will be the ones to suffer."

"Casey, I'll get in touch with Megan. We'll all pray the spirit of revenge away from the services. And ask God to touch Edward's heart with compassion. For you. For Witt. I know you'll be praying with us.

"If you don't remember anything else I say today, remember this: it wasn't Edward, but Satan, who did those terrible things to you. Forgive your husband, Casey, and don't cheat either of you out of the blessings of a happy marriage. Start today. Tell Edward you love him. Just say the three words. Let them soak into his spirit. And God will take care of tomorrow. What a future He must have planned for you and Edward, for Satan to be so determined to destroy it."

Casey pulled away to look into Indi's soulful dark eyes. "That's exactly what Witt said."

Indi grinned. "Witt was a wise man."

Casey shook her head and smiled. "Indi, I don't know what the future would've held for us, had Witt not died. We had that connection. Now I realize why he said it was best for him to go home. He knew the heartache we'd have faced denying that connection—or acknowledging it and being out of God's will."

Indi hadn't heard the whole story about the day Witt died. She wouldn't rush Casey. In the weeks and months to come, she'd need a friend to talk to, to work it all out.

One day at a time, sweet Jesus!

Indi could feel her smile growing. She knew if she let go, it would cover the whole bottom half of her face. "Isn't it something, the way God works? You have your husband back, a trusted new friend—that would be me—and Edward has a good friend in Ron. And it's all because of Witt. You had none of these things one short month ago. Praise God."

262

"Thank you, Indi, for making me look at it from God's point of view. I'm not going to let Satan have the victory. I promised Witt and now I'm promising you."

"Now *that's* the Casey I know and love." Indi leaned over to pat her hand. A car door slammed in the drive.

Casey ran to the window. "Oh no, Edward's home early. What if he wants to know why you're here? What'll I say?"

"That's a no-brainer, Casey. I'm your friend." Indi held her hand out to her. "Girl, there are two things you need to do—no, three—let Edward know he's loved, boot out the demon of fear, and give Witt back to God. You only had him on loan."

Indi wasn't worried about Casey's safety. She knew a successful deliverance when she saw one. That man was delivered *and* saved.

The restoration of Edward and Casey's marriage may be a long, arduous one, but it would happen if Casey would get a handle on her fears and release Witt. And if Edward could come to terms with Witt's feelings for Casey. A tall order.

Dear God, please speak to his heart. Don't let him destroy everything You've given him.

Indi and Casey were at the front door saying good-bye when Edward walked in.

"Hi, Indi." Edward put his arm around her and bussed her on the cheek. "Don't leave just 'cause I'm here."

Indi patted his cheek and smiled to herself.

No demons in him, girl. He's just your garden-variety hardheaded husband.

"Gotta get across the mountain before nightfall, Edward. Good to see you." Indi grinned. "We're gonna see you two on Friday night, right?"

"You bet. Give Ron our love." Edward smiled and closed the door behind her.

"You're home early, Edward." Casey smiled cautiously. She was trying to screw up the courage to tell him she loved him. Was it a lie because it was only partially true?

"Finished early." Edward's tone and expression were wooden.

He picked up a Bible and his reading glasses from the end table and fell onto the couch. He began reading, ignoring Casey's presence.

"I . . . I love you." She forced the words out.

Edward marked his place with one forefinger and closed the Bible. Peering over the top of his glasses with dull eyes, he scrutinized her for a few seconds. He reopened the Bible and resumed reading. "Yeah."

29

Edward awoke with a dull headache.

Today he'd meet his wife's lover. Postmortem.

Nothing he'd learned in seminary had prepared him for the occasion.

He'd never adhered to the belief you should act happy and victorious when your life is falling apart. "Claiming the victory," they call it. Jumping for joy when you should be lying on your face, begging for mercy.

Like it or not, that was his plan for today. He could hardly announce to the world that his wife had fallen in love with another man while he was busy abusing her. So he'd go to the funeral with his lovely wife on his arm and pretend he thought DeWitt Gregory was wonderful.

Nausea gripped his guts as he passed the hall bathroom on his way to the kitchen. He fought the tears that kept trying to surface. The last thing he needed was for Casey to see him crying. He didn't want her pity.

He wanted to go to the church, lie on his face in the upper room, and throw himself on God's mercy. Stay there until he had an answer. But others may come in to pray. He didn't want their pity either.

Casey was already in the kitchen having coffee. "Good morning, Edward." She smiled without parting her lips.

"Morning." He poured his coffee, stirred in two spoons of sugar, turned, and left the room.

The church marquee read "Join us in a celebration of the life of Witt Gregory." Edward and Casey filed in with a group of eight or ten others. Edward had a pasted-on smile. Casey's upper lip was quivering. He had a perfunctory hand on her shoulder to guide her through the crowd.

It looked more like an Easter service than a funeral. No somber attendants. None of the usual pomp and circumstance. And apparently standing room only.

Witt's niece, Megan—large with child—was in the sanctuary, mingling with the congregation. Her eyes were misty, but she was smiling. Fair skin and natural blonde hair, shoulder length and shining. Next to her Zach, her brother, was hugging an elderly lady.

Megan saw the two strangers enter and tapped Zach's shoulder. Looking up, he followed her gaze to Casey and Edward. He gently extricated himself from the senior citizen's grip. Together, he and Megan excused themselves and hastened to greet the McAlesters.

"You've got to be Miss Casey." Megan's pale-blue eyes gleamed as she hugged Casey. "Uncle Witt talked so much about you. He wanted us to meet, but the time was never right. With Zach studying at State and me pregnant, it seems like life is stuck in fast-forward."

Zach stood there, smiling pleasantly, azure eyes—that obviously ran in the family—peering through tortoiseshell glasses.

Megan turned her attention to Edward. She opened her mouth to speak . . . and hesitated.

He put her at ease by introducing himself. "I am so sorry I never got to meet your uncle. Casey thought the world of him. And she'll miss him terribly." He gagged on the words.

Megan released an audible sigh and held out her hand.

Edward took her hand in one of his and reached out for Zach

with the other. "And you're Zach. God bless you both. If we can ever help you in *any* way, please let us know."

How am I doing so far, God?

Megan waved at someone across the room. A large, muscular young man with a quick, disarming grin quickly made his way through the crowd to greet them. Copper-red hair in a buzz cut, if he took a deep breath, his chest might burst right out of his shirt.

"This is my husband, Mark," Megan said, with obvious pride. "Mark, I want you to meet Casey and Edward McAlester. Casey was a dear friend of Uncle Witt's. Well, of course, you know that. She was with him when the Lord called him home." Her face reddened. With a pained expression, she cut her eyes to Casey.

It's all right, little mother. The big, dumb husband already knows.

Edward's lips were numb from maintaining the fake smile.

Mark pulled Casey to him in a big bear hug. He held her tight and squeezed her gently. Then it was Edward's turn. Edward gritted his teeth and received Mark's hug.

This is harder than I thought. I gotta get away from these people. They all know about Casey and their uncle. They must think I'm the biggest fool in the world.

Edward excused himself and sauntered into the crowded sanctuary. He noticed Casey cast a worried glance his direction and shrugged it off. Everywhere he turned some smiling mourner cornered him, wanting to know about his relationship to Witt.

This is ridiculous. If they loved him so much, how can they be so happy?

He spied the closed casket off to one side, waiting to be wheeled in, front and center, at the right moment. He headed for it. Most of the folks wouldn't see him over there. If they did, they wouldn't expect him to chitchat when he was paying his respects to the deceased.

He looked around, then opened the casket lid. The remains of a man who loved Casey. An empty shell that would rot away in a grave.

His spirit's still alive. He'll always love her.

Edward groaned.

"Jesus, help me. I know it's a sin to hate a brother in Christ. But what can I do? He made an adulteress of my wife. He trashed my marriage and ruined my life. How can You ask me to *love* him?"

Edward glanced at the pews. Casey was seated on the front row. The family row. *Now she's a part of his family. How much more of this can I take? I hate this man.*

He swung around and glared back into the casket. His knees buckled. He stuffed a fist in his mouth to stifle the primal sound erupting from his innermost parts. And clutched the edge of the casket lest he collapse.

Lying there, cushioned by quilted white satin, was the Reverend Edward McAlester.

His head swiveled back to Casey. "Nooo!" Witt was sitting next to her. That wife-stealing, no-good lothario had his arm around her.

Her hair glowed incandescent under the bright lights. *Her beautiful hair.*

Casey dabbed her eyes with a tissue and snuggled into Witt's chest. He pulled her closer and touched her hair with his lips.

"Take your filthy mouth off her," Edward bellowed. But he made no sound. "That's my wife." No one heard him or turned a head.

I'll yank him out of that seat and pulverize him.

But he couldn't move. All he could do was watch as Witt touched her face. Blotted her tears. Caressed her and whispered comforting words in her ear. Slumped shoulders lurching, Edward sobbed, "That's my wife . . . she's *mine.*"

He gouged his fists into his eyes and rubbed. But when he opened them, nothing had changed.

"Oh, Jesus, why is this happening? I can't be dead. Please speak to me, Father."

But for the obedience of my servant Witt, this is the way it would be. You drove your wife into his arms. He protected her, even from his own desires, to return her to you, pure and holy.

An enormous weight bore down on Edward's shoulders and he dropped to his hands and knees.

His head drooped to the floor. "What about my vision, Father? They were walking into the woods together. That doesn't look so pure and holy to me."

You didn't look closely enough, my son. Lift your head. I have something to show you.

God gave Edward the same vision the demons had given him. But not in a small chrome faucet handle. No, God's version filled the sanctuary. Edward was right behind them, following them into the woods.

What do you see in my servant's right hand?

"A Bible, Father."

Let's follow them for a moment, son.

Casey and Witt walked into the woods to a small bench surrounded by wild clover and honeysuckle. Edward could smell it. Witt opened the Bible and read a few verses. Then with his hands raised to heaven he began praising the Lord and praying. Hands folded demurely in her lap, Casey bowed her head and prayed. For Edward.

Their prayers reached My throne, Edward. Casey's marriage vows are intact. And you are her priest. Let it be, according to My Word.

The weight lifted from Edward's shoulders. He wiped his wet cheeks with the back of his suit sleeve.

The pastor happened by and offered Edward his hand. "Brother, don't weep. Witt's with the Father. We can celebrate."

"Yes, Pastor. I know." Edward rose. He reached over and put his hand on Witt's cold, lifeless hand. "Thank you, my brother." He gently closed the casket lid and slipped out a side door to regain his composure.

The pianist began playing "The Trumpet of the Lord." Those who weren't seated started milling toward the pews. Mark and Zach found seats on the front row, flanking Casey, leaving room for Edward. Behind them were Ron and Indi. Indi reached across the pew and squeezed Casey's shoulder. Indi's friendship was so precious to her. Casey grabbed her hand and squeezed back. She leaned back in her seat and bowed her head to pray.

Six men rolled Witt's casket into position about fifteen feet in front of her. And opened it. People began to praise the Lord. Casey looked up.

Fresh grief caught her off guard. A boulder in silent freefall fell on her and crushed her. Tears gushed from a bottomless well. Debilitating weakness overcame her and she struggled to breathe.

Then she heard Witt's reassuring voice. "Don't cry, little lady. I'll see you in the morning."

His presence was all around her. Her skin prickled and her breath came in soft gulps. Had anyone else heard him? Casey perused the chattering crowd. All were oblivious to his presence. He'd spoken only to her.

The pastor walked to the podium and belted out the song being played. Witt's favorite. He wouldn't sing it for Casey, but he often recited the words from this scripture song.

"For the Lord will come from Heaven with a shout.
With the voice of the Angel. The trumpet of God.
And, the dead in Christ shall arise, and we which
are alive and remain . . .
Shall be caught up together in the clouds,
To meet our blessed Lord in the air . . ."

The pastor stopped singing. "Did you hear that, folks?" he shouted. "Did you hear *that*? Witt is going to rise first and we which are alive and remain shall be caught up together, to meet our blessed Lord in the air. Hallelujah! Lead the way, Witt. Lead the way."

The congregation rose to their feet as one. "Lead the way, Witt," they shouted in unison. "Lead the way."

Edward was walking down the aisle to the front row. He joined in the chorus. "Lead the way, Witt." His hands stretched heavenward. His face tear streaked.

The pastor delivered the eulogy. It was short, considering how much Witt had done for the Lord. "Witt wouldn't want his victories for the Lord listed. They were many and they are impressive. He was humble and he'd be embarrassed if I carried on too much. But he surely wouldn't mind if his friends and family shared what's on their hearts."

Casey could still feel the closeness of Witt's spirit. Then, as though on cue, she felt a cool breeze ruffle her hair like gentle fingers. And his spirit departed. Even in death, he was too humble to accept praise.

"See you in the morning," she breathed softly to his departing spirit.

Edward found his place between Casey and Zach. His hand sought out hers. He took it in both of his hands and held it firmly against his chest. She could feel his heart beating. Excitedly. Casey tried to tug her hand out of his grip, but he clutched it tightly and smiled down at her. A strange smile. He leaned over and touched his lips to her temple.

Why the sudden public display of affection?

Oh, God, what is he up to?

Mae was the first to stand. She shared Witt's strawberry pie addiction and got a hearty laugh. After that, she related how he'd led her to the Lord, right there in the coffee shop.

Sarah, Witt's housekeeper, stood next. "I only worked for Dr. G., but we were family." She paused a moment to collect her emotions. Then told about squeezing her ample body into the little prayer room where Witt led her to the Lord.

There was some muffled laughter from the congregation.

"Hey, it's okay to laugh. This is happy stuff. Dr. G. and me, we laughed about it all the time. Why, folks, I was thinkin'—if I ever gets in here will I ever get out again?"

Her eyes squeezed shut. "Turns out I didn't care if I ever got out. God was waitin' for us, y'know. Maybe that's why I had such a tough time gettin' in, 'cause our God is *big*.

"After me and Jesus settled our business, Dr. G. left me alone with Him. I don't know how long I basked in His love. But when I came out, Dr. G. had fixed supper for me. Now it was supposed to be the other way around."

Dabbing her eyes with a dainty white hanky, Sarah sat down. She bounced back up like a rubber ball. "By the way, Dr. G. was a wonderful man, but he wasn't much of a cook."

That brought the house down.

Many of Witt's friends spoke, and laughter was in no short supply.

When Casey saw Edward preparing to stand, her heart froze midbeat. He knew nothing of Witt except the horrible things he'd imagined. A hush fell over the congregation and all eyes were on

271

him as he stood. He had an air about him that caused people to sit up and take notice.

Casey sat paralyzed. A tight band of panic across her forehead cut the blood off from her brain. She tried to blink away the blurriness that plagued her vision.

Dear God, don't let him do anything to hurt Witt's family.

Pinching his lower lip between his teeth, he looked down at her through a veil of tears. He was still gripping her hand. Too tight. He pulled her up. On legs of Jell-O she rose to her feet.

From behind, Indi grabbed her other hand. Casey knew she was praying.

"My name is Edward McAlester. This is my wife, Casey. Witt was *her* friend. I never met him. But . . ." Edward's eloquent voice cracked and he stood silent for a moment. Rubbing his free palm against his thigh. His face contorted as though in pain.

Edward, please don't do this.

He cleared his throat. The words burst from his lips. "But I can thank him for saving my marriage, my ministry, and my life." He released Casey's hand and put both of his hands over his face. From all over the sanctuary, hands were stretched out to him in compassion.

Edward regained his composure. "He did for an undeserving stranger as Jesus would have done. I'm looking forward to meeting him when I go to be with my Savior."

Like a rag doll, Casey sank into her seat. Drained. But relieved. Edward hadn't taken his anger out on Witt's family.

God, what just took place? Was he sincere or was that for show?

Ron stood up and put his hands on Edward's shoulders. "He forgot to mention Witt brought our two families together in a lasting friendship. I suspect there are going to be so many jewels in Witt's crown he's going to need help from the Lord Himself to stand up after it's on his head." He clapped Edward's shoulder. "Love ya, buddy."

The pastor announced that after the viewing there'd be coffee and strawberry pie, in Witt's honor, in the fellowship hall—compliments of Mae and Georgie, who'd stayed up all night baking pies. Folks began forming a single line down the center aisle to pay their last respects to their good friend.

Casey chose to not view Witt's body. She'd been there at the moment of his death when the angels came to collect his spirit. And she'd felt his imperishable presence next to her before the service, as though God had allowed him to return for a short time to check on her. That which was lying in the casket was his earthly dwelling. He no longer lived there.

Megan motioned to Casey to wait up. Witt's niece was everything he'd said and more. How sad for her and Zach that they had no more family. When Megan was able to break away, Casey was waiting with open arms to fold her to her heart.

"Miss Casey," Megan began, "I want to get you to myself for a minute. I hope you don't mind. I need to talk to you. Would your husband object if we walked over to the fellowship hall ahead of the others?"

I have no idea anymore what he's thinking.

"I'm sure he wouldn't, Megan. Are you okay?" The baby appeared to be due any day.

"I'm fine, Miss Casey. *We're* fine." Megan massaged her protruding belly with both hands. "The doctor says any day now." She pressed her index finger just below her eye to catch a tear before it could smudge her makeup. "But I need to talk about Uncle Witt with the one person he loved the most."

30

Casey watched as Witt's niece checked each room.

Oh, Lord, Megan is being so secretive. Edward will make another mountain out of a molehill if he walks in on us.

The first group of people to arrive for refreshments walked in as Megan was leading Casey into a small anteroom. She closed the door.

Just inside the room she turned to Casey, wide-eyed. "Miss Casey, I don't want to cause any trouble for you and your husband, but Uncle Witt shared a lot of things with me. He and Mom were close. After she died he turned to me." Her pale complexion tinged pink. "He told me some things I think you should know."

Except for being fair-haired, Megan and Zach favored Witt. The same blue eyes. And the same hint of a curl at the corners of their mouths. They felt like family.

Casey held her hand up, palm toward Megan, and closed her eyes momentarily, bidding her to listen. She took a moment to pull herself together.

"Please call me Casey. Miss Casey sounds so formal. And, baby, I think I know what you're going to say." She walked to the window. She could see the main building. A smattering of people were sauntering in their direction. "Your uncle told me in his dying moments he

loved me. I'd known there was something special about our relationship, but he never allowed it to be anything but platonic."

Megan walked up behind her. Casey turned and took her
hand. "He could've taken me from Edward in a heartbeat. I was so
vulnerable. Megan, your Uncle Witt was the most honorable man
I've ever met."

"I'm glad you heard it from him, Miss . . . uh, Casey. He loved
you so much. And when he found you again, after all those years, it
thrilled his socks off. I guess you know he'd been praying for your
salvation all his life. Just knowing you were saved blessed him more
than you can imagine."

Now I know why he was so elated when I told him I was a Christian.

"I needed prayer, Megan. And it may have been *his* prayers that
clinched the deal. He probably pestered the Holy Spirit to distraction."

"Yeah." Megan chuckled. She held her hair up off her neck and
fanned herself. And took a turn looking out the window. "Oh, pooh.
Your husband's coming. I was hoping we'd have more time." She
dug in her purse, pulled out a rubber band, and peeked into a little
side pocket.

"But I guess we'd better get back to the dining room. Your
Edward seems like a doll, but Indi said to walk on eggs around him.
I sure don't want you to get in any trouble." She held the rubber band
between her teeth and pulled her thick hair into a ponytail. She se-
cured it and gave it a shake. "I hope you don't mind Uncle Witt's sharing with me. He knew it wouldn't go any further."

She's adorable. No wonder Witt was so crazy about these kids.

"I don't mind at all. He told me you were his confidante."

Reaching for the doorknob, Casey stopped and turned to Megan.
"I hope Edward's coming today didn't upset you."

Megan smiled. "He was a perfect gentleman. And his testimony
was very moving."

Casey drew a deep breath and let it out in a whoosh. Her
shoulders sagged. "I just wish I knew whether he was being honest or putting on an act. Megan, I don't know if our marriage is
going to survive."

Megan looked puzzled. "He seemed awfully sincere to me. He'd have to be a pretty good actor to pull that off. I was hoping everything would be okay now."

Someone turned the knob from the other side and Casey jumped from in front of the door. Edward stuck his head in. "They told me you were in here. Is everything okay, girls?" His eyes were hooded. His voice saturated with concern.

Casey heaved another sigh. A mixture of aggravation and a generous portion of fear.

I guess I've had my last private conversation. He's not going to give me the chance to grieve. And certainly not the opportunity to talk to anyone about Witt.

Megan spoke up before Casey could respond. "I was just talking with Casey about Uncle Witt. I brought her in here. I'm sorry." She shook her head. "Please don't be mad at her."

When Edward stepped into the room and closed the door behind him, Casey backed up. With a somber expression, he looked from one to the other. Finally resting on Megan.

Casey balled her hands into fists. A mother bear, ready to defend her young.

If you lay a hand on her . . .

Edward revealed an anguished smile and echoed Megan's head shake. "Mad at her? Oh, Megan, I'm not mad at her." His voice broke. "I love her. But I've not been there for her—for a long time." He took Megan's hand. But his green eyes, dusky with emotion, were cast on Casey. She cut her eyes away. "I'm just praying she'll give me another chance to prove how *much* I love her."

Casey eyed him suspiciously. Her fists relaxed.

Then Edward beheld the lovely child-mother before him. "As for *you*, young lady, I could never take your Uncle Witt's place. But I owe it to him to be there for you kids. How about letting me be your honorary uncle?"

Casey stifled a gasp and surveyed his face.

You'd better not be toying with her, Edward McAlester. I'd never forgive you.

"You really *mean* it?" Megan grinned at him and then Casey. "That would be super."

"Of course I mean it. Look at you. You're going to have a baby any day, and there are no grandparents in sight. Casey and I have longed for a grandchild. Barrett's a little slow out of the starting gate. Not even married yet."

Like an exuberant child, Megan stood on her tiptoes and threw her arms around Edward. Looking over his shoulder, she smiled at Casey. "Can we call you Aunt Casey?"

Casey swallowed hard. "Nothing would make me happier."

I'd never forgive you, Edward. I mean it.

Edward turned to Casey. "Uncle Edward and Aunt Casey. Sounds good, doesn't it?"

Casey nodded. "Sure does." All she could manage were a half smile through clenched teeth and a glaring look.

Never.

Edward walked to the door. Then turned to Casey. His eyes beseeched her. "Please forgive me for thinking . . ." He glanced toward Megan. "For doubting you. I should have trusted you. But Casey . . . I can't wait forever." He opened the door.

"Edward, I . . ."

Don't pressure me.

"Only till the day I die," he concluded with an endearing smile. A pleading glance in her direction and he backed out the door. "You girls take as long as you like. I'll save you a piece of strawberry pie." The door clicked shut.

"What'd I tell you, Casey . . . Aunt Casey? He's sincere. I know he is. He's so sweet . . . and he's a *hunk* too. You just gotta give him another chance. Uncle Witt would want you to."

A hunk who's dragged me over the coals.

"I don't know, Megan." Casey stared out the window at the narrow stream of chattering people strolling over from the main building.

Father, I don't know what to do. Seems like every time I turn around Edward has a different personality. I'm too tired to deal with it anymore. I wish I could come home to You. Everything's happening too fast. I don't have time to think.

The approaching people froze where they were. A bird in flight hung in the air as though from a wire, wings extended.

278

Casey gaped. She turned to look at Megan. She was staring at her through blank eyes. Her mouth open as though she were speaking. Her hands behind her head to adjust her ponytail. Still as a stone. Like a childhood game of statue.

Silence. No conversation from the next room. The ceiling fan stopped short overhead. The second hand on the clock was stuck between two little marks.

A soft breeze ruffled Casey's hair and the smell of wild clover and honeysuckle hung in the air. She jerked her head around frantically. "What's happening, Lord?"

I'm giving you time to think.

Her brain felt drained of blood. She dropped to her knees. "Oh, God, help me."

Tell Me, daughter, who is for your marriage?

Her lips quivered and her throat constricted. "You are, Lord," she squeaked.

Who else?

"Witt. Edward . . . and I'm sure if he knew we were in trouble, Barrett."

And?

"Ron and Indi. Megan."

Probably everyone who loves you . . . right?

"Yes, Father."

And who is against your marriage?

"Uh . . . Satan . . . and . . . uh . . . a handful of demons."

What is there to think about?

Suddenly she was back on her feet. Megan was speaking. The fan droning. Activity outside the little room bustled. A shudder rippled through Casey. She was seeking an invitation to heaven. But she'd been issued a warrant to battle. Ire for Satan rose in her spirit.

Where's your backbone, woman? How long are you going let the powers of hell direct your life?

She straightened her shoulders and smiled at Megan. "I'm sorry, what were you saying?"

"Just trying to talk you into giving Uncle Edward another chance."

Casey pulled up two folding chairs. "Let's sit down, Megan. You shouldn't be on your feet so much. And I want to tell you a story."

Megan deserved to know about Witt's reception in glory.

"Oh, how wonderful." She was clapping when Casey finished. "You should've shared that with the whole church, Aunt Casey."

"No, Megan. You're the only person I've told. It was a sacred moment and it belongs to me and Witt. I don't think I'm going to tell anyone else just yet. You see, my feelings for your uncle go . . . went . . . further than I'm willing to share. But the angels knew."

"It's awesome to know Uncle Witt's love was returned, if only for a little while. Not for the world to see . . . but for the angels in heaven to witness." Megan's face was aglow.

Casey brushed a stray hair from Megan's soft cheek. "You know he believed only his constant prayers kept him in line."

"Yes, I know." Megan nodded.

"I don't know if he realized they were keeping me in line, as well, so I'd be able to return to Edward with my vows intact. Megan, God has made me see the best way to honor Witt is to follow his example of putting the Lord's will first."

"You mean you're going to . . ."

"Yes, I'm going to *make* my marriage work." Casey took a deep, determined—if rather shaky—breath. "Looks like you've got yourself a brand-new aunt and uncle."

Megan put her hands around her belly. "I'd jump up and dance, but I don't think I'd better. Oh, Aunt Casey, that's an answer to so many prayers."

Casey kneaded her hands in her lap. "There's one thing that bothers me, baby. I wish I could remember Uncle Witt from our youth. I think it would help me deal with what's taken place. I can't believe someone so extraordinary could love me and I'd be unaware of it."

Megan hesitated. "I have something for you. I was afraid I wasn't going to be able to give it to you when Uncle Edward showed up. I hope it helps and doesn't cause you more problems, Aunt Casey."

She opened her purse again and reached into the side pocket. "I found this note in Uncle Witt's personal belongings. He'd want you to have it."

She handed her new aunt a small, tattered piece of paper, folded into a tiny square and worn at the edges. A piece of cash register tape. Witt had obviously unfolded and refolded it many times.

Casey opened it carefully. She recognized her own handwriting, from when she was young.

The note read:

You have a nice smile. Thank you for your kindness to my mother. You've been a true friend. I hope we meet again sometime in the future.

Love,

Katherine

The word *love* was smeared as though Witt might have run his fingers over it more than a few times. Down in one corner in Witt's easy handwriting was the date: 08-30-63.

Thoughts of the "nice boy," as she'd called him, flooded her remembrance. When she wrote that note, she was wrapped up in Allen and didn't realize how special the young busboy was. She couldn't even remember his name.

But his amazing blue eyes would light up every time she spoke to him. He was thin. And she had to look up to him. Way up. Never without a warm and ready smile, even when he was weary.

Casey hung her head.

Oh, my Jesus. I remember now where I've seen that little curl at the corners of Witt's mouth. How could I have forgotten?

His thick, dark locks, often in need of a trim, curled over his white uniform collar in defiance of the hotel dress code. No wonder. He was working full-time and putting himself through college. But he always found the time to do little favors for Del.

Casey took a deep breath and whimpered as she released it.

Megan lifted Casey's chin to look at her through compassionate blue eyes—identical to Witt's. "Are you all right, Aunt Casey?"

"I will be, Megan . . . now." She held the note up. "Thank you so much for this."

She touched the paper to her lips. "The circle is complete."

In slow motion, she folded the note back into a small square, just as she'd done thirty years ago. She unzipped the cover of her Bible and opened it to 1 Thessalonians 4:16 . . . "For the Lord shall come from

Heaven with a shout . . ." Reverently placing the note between the pages, she closed her Bible and zipped the cover.

Smiling through her tears, she reached out to pull Megan to her. They embraced for a long time. Megan finally found the release to weep for her beloved uncle as Casey held her tight and stroked her back.

Don't cry, precious one. He's with the Father.

Casey's heart ventured back to just one month ago . . . the first time Witt embraced her. While she was yet a stranger.

It was that day he made her laugh with his awful impersonation of Paul Harvey. Several times in the weeks to follow, he raised her spirits with his one and only impersonation.

She'd tell Megan about it when her tears subsided. It would make her smile again.

Was Witt doing his impersonation right now . . . in glory?

I know he is. He wouldn't pass up this opportunity.

Trying to keep a straight face. His mirthful blue eyes betraying him. She could hear him saying, "And now you know . . . the rest of the story."

31

For Christmas Edward had wanted to take Casey somewhere special. Somewhere they'd never been. Sort of a second honeymoon. But Casey's battle with the demon of fear was still an ongoing problem. She slept in the guest room every night. Other than that, their life was taking on some semblance of normalcy.

Barrett was coming home for Christmas. But he had to work Christmas Eve day and wouldn't get in until ten or eleven that evening. So they opened one present each and sat around the fireplace by the light of the Christmas tree and the crackling fire.

Casey had given Edward a beautiful new golf shirt, and he was anxious to try it on. "I'm going to take my shower first, honey. Then try on my new shirt."

He returned, wearing his pajama bottoms and a T-shirt. "Where's the shirt?"

Casey held it out to him and smiled. "Hope it fits." She was dressed in the silky green lounging pajamas he'd given her. Her hair glinted in the soft glow of the fire.

His heart leaped in his chest. *Let's try again.* "Please stand up, darling. Put your arms around me. For one minute. I won't ask any more of you."

Casey dropped the shirt on the arm of the couch and rose. He put his hand out to her and rebuked the demon, as he'd learned to do each time they touched. Head down, Casey took his hand. He gently pulled her close.

She froze.

"No. I can't, Edward. Please." She yanked her hand from his.

"Listen to me, Casey. You've got to buck this demon. You've got to *do* the very thing you're frightened of—if you're ever going to be free of it."

Her chin was quivering. "I've tried, Edward. What more can I do?"

"Teamwork. I want to help you." Edward stretched his arms out to each side, palms up, shoulder high. "Touch me, Casey. I will *not* touch you unless you ask me to. But I want you to put your hands on me.

"Demon of fear, don't come near her. Now put your hands on me, baby."

"This is silly, Edward." She started to turn from him.

"It's not silly. It's warfare with a demon and we've got its number."

Reluctantly she put a hand on his chest. And one on his rib cage. She was shivering.

"That's good. That's good. Relax. You can trust me."

God, give me the strength to not touch her. Make me worthy of her trust.

"Now slip your arms around my waist. And hang on, no matter what it says to you. We're going to beat this demon . . . together. Demon of fear, I rebuke you. You may not come near my wife. She's *my* gift from God."

Casey hesitated.

"Come on, baby. I won't touch you. I promise."

She did as she was asked. Awkwardly trying to span his body without touching him.

"You're doing great, sweetheart. Now lock your fingers behind my back."

Casey whimpered and clasped her hands together.

"Lean into me, baby. Lay your head on my chest."

You have only to lower your arms to embrace your wife. That's what you want, isn't it? Do it. She might struggle a little, but she'll come around. She needs to know you're a real man.

The hair on the back of Edward's neck prickled.

She's trusting me. The demon doesn't like that.

His eyes probed the room. "I rebuke you, in the name of Jesus."

Casey looked like she was about to bolt.

"Steady, Casey. I've got your back. Rebuke it with me, darling. Come on. 'Demon of fear, I'm holding my husband. And you can't do a thing about it.' Say it, darling."

Casey moaned. Her fingernails dug through his T-shirt into his flesh.

"You've got to say it, baby. It'll get easier. 'Demon of fear, I'm holding my husband . . .'"

Casey repeated the words. First timidly, then a little bolder.

Her warm breath lapped at his chest and the fresh fragrance of her hair teased his nostrils. Molten tears imbued his T-shirt.

Your arms are getting tired, Edward. Rest them for a moment. She'll understand.

His own tears bathed his face and his knees were about to buckle. His heart was a bass drum. Again and again his outstretched hands curled into tight fists and back out, but he did not lower his arms.

She tightened her embrace and buried her face in his chest. He bit his lower lip to keep from sobbing. His body shook. She clung to him. "I'm holding my husband . . . I'm holding my husband . . ."

The back door slammed shut. "Mom! Dad! You home? It's dark in here. Didn't you pay your electric bill?"

Casey scampered to the hall bathroom. Edward dove for the couch and wiped his face on his new shirt. "In here, Barrett. We're enjoying the Christmas tree and the fire."

Casey's heart hurt for Edward. He was unusually quiet. She knew last night had left him confused. She was confused too. After Barrett had gone to bed, she and Edward went to their own beds.

285

She didn't sleep. They'd gotten so close. Together they'd stood against the demon of fear. She wanted to creep into the master bedroom and cuddle her husband. But had they really won the battle? Barrett's ill-timed arrival left some doubt. She didn't want to climb into bed with Edward only to give the demon another victory.

The drive to the ranch was filled with excited conversation about Barrett's recent promotion and his move to a new apartment. Casey filled him in on who would be at the celebration.

Witt had left the ranch to Megan and Zach. It was big enough for two families. Sarah stayed on to help Megan and Mark with their new baby girl, Catherine Cecilia II. They'd changed the spelling of Katherine, to avoid confusion.

Zach pinned the moniker "CiCi" on her before she had her first diaper change.

Enjoying coffee after a wonderful Christmas dinner, seated around the big pine trestle table Witt had built, were Nana and Granddad (formerly known as Aunt Casey and Uncle Edward), Barrett, Zach, Megan, Mark, Ron, Indi, Sarah, and Sadie Anderson. *What a family they did make!*

They raised their coffee cups in a toast to Witt for bringing them together.

When little CiCi whimpered from her crib, Edward jumped up to check on her. Carrying her to the rocking chair, he rocked her and sang to her.

Casey observed the others at the table. How they loved one another. Had they known each other under the right circumstances, Witt and Edward would have loved one another. Her gaze drifted to the nursery doorway. She could see Edward and the baby.

He was softly singing "Jesus Loves Me" in his rich baritone voice.

Casey had spent a little time in the prayer room right before the meal. Asking the Lord to hug Witt the way he used to hug her and tell him she'd never forget him. She hoped this Christmas Day prayer would finally release her to love Edward completely.

The Lord was answering her prayer. The hollow ache had at last subsided and she could think of Witt with great fondness. A loved one gone on to be with the Lord. A dear friend who'd always be sorely missed. The purity of her feelings for him was a refreshing balm to her spirit.

Her heart was open to receive Edward. Her husband of twenty years. Last night he'd called her "his gift from God."

Father, I want Edward back. In him I see a gentle man of God. My priest. My husband, with whom I can trust my life . . . and my heart. But I don't want to invite him back into my life, then hurt him by rejecting him—again.

You're healed, My daughter. The time is nigh.

Casey's anxious heart took flight. She slipped out of her chair and walked to the archway between the dining room and the living room.

Where the mistletoe hung.

She stood under it, waiting. Expectant.

Indi saw her first. A big smile slowly formed on her generous mouth. She nudged Ron, and his eyes lit up.

Finally Megan looked up and giggled. "Granddad," she called out in a singsong voice, "I think Nana's trying to tell you something."

Edward looked toward the table. Casey smiled as his eyes swept the large room and stopped when they met hers. Igniting the span that separated them.

His voice broke and he lost his place in the song. Still humming, he stood up and carried the sleeping baby back to her crib. CiCi didn't stir. Edward closed the nursery door.

With his forefinger to his lips—trying to hush the hooting and hollering from the guys at the table—he approached Casey. Timorously, he put his hands on her waist. And gently pulled her to him.

She placed her hands on his neck, just below his strong jaw, and drew his face close to hers. He looked older—and more vulnerable—than he used to. But he was still her handsome prince. And her knees grew weak at the thought of their lips touching.

He put his mouth close to her ear. "Are you sure?" His husky voice faltered. "We haven't kissed one another for a very long time."

Casey stood on her tiptoes and brushed her lips against his forehead. Then his temple. And the scar on his jaw from when he fell off his bicycle as a little boy.

A little boy. Now her husband and lover. Protector and priest. *Her* gift from God.

Thank You, Father, for Your gift to me. I'll treasure it forever.

She caressed his face. "That's a real problem, Edward McAlester. And there's only one way to deal with it. We're going to have to kiss one another *for a very long time.*"

Softly grazing his mouth with hers, she kissed the scar again. Edward released his grip on her waist. With a wry smile he held her face between his hands and claimed her lips.

THE END

Coming soon . . .

WINNOBY CABIN

1

Casey stood at the banister, biting her lower lip.

"Edward, can you come out here for a moment?"

"What is it, honey?"

"Bring your coffee and come out. I want you to listen to something."

Edward finished pouring his coffee, sugared it, and began stirring as he walked out onto the deck with Casey, who was still in her robe.

"Okay, I'm here. What do you want me to hear?" he asked good-naturedly.

"Just listen." She looked up at him.

Edward stood, head cocked. "I don't hear a thing. It's as quiet as a tomb."

"Yes, it is. Eerily so, if you ask me. It's a bright spring morning and there's no sound of birds. Look at the feeder. Normally, they'd be crowding around, clamoring for a spot on the perch. But this morning there's not one feathered creature in sight. Don't you find that a bit strange?"

"Let's sit here a moment and see if they come."

Edward pulled a chair up close for Casey, then reached for one for himself.

"More coffee before we settle in?"

"Yes, please." Casey's brow creased as she handed him her nearly empty cup, pondering the weird feeling in the air. A shudder ran through her body.

She was looking out over the distant landscape when Edward returned with her coffee.

"Look down there." She pointed to their magnificent view of the valley. "In the mornings, we almost always see several deer in the meadow. But there are none this morning. Nothing. Not even our little indigo bunting has come by to serenade us."

Edward sat down next to her and raised his cup to his lips.

"Let's just sit back and enjoy our coffee for a while, baby. The birds will be back, and you'll be fussing about how fast they go through their food."

But the longer they sat, the heavier the silence became, until it was a lead weight on their spirits. Not a blade of grass moved. Not a sound was heard. Edward put his hand on his wife's arm. "Casey, I had a strange dream last night."

"Was it somehow related to this ominous silence?"

"Well, I'm not sure. How 'bout you be the judge? I dreamed a magnificent angel of the Lord came to me and told me to get my family out of Winnoby. When I tried to question him, he started to fade from view. I cried, *Please don't go.*

"His image solidified once again, in all his brilliance. *Why do you question me?*

"I told him I thought the Lord had a job for me to do here.

"To which he replied, *Who do you think sent me? Some jobs are done more quickly than others. Who knows better, you or the Lord?*

"With that, he disappeared. Then I woke up—if indeed I was asleep. I had the strongest feeling it was not a dream. But after

290

dozing off again and awakening this morning, the reality of it has faded somewhat."

Casey laid her coffee cup on the banister and put her hands together, prayer fashion. "Oh, honey, I believe it was a real angel. The Lord's trying to tell us something. You know we've both wanted to leave for quite a while, but felt like we'd be letting the Lord down. Maybe it was His intention we leave when our congregation dwindled and those remaining began to fight every move we made. Perhaps He thought we'd have the good sense to act when your life was threatened. Twice, if you count Ward. Since we didn't, He's had to resort to sending an angel to talk some sense into us."

Edward leaned way back in his chair, his eyes avoiding his wife's intense gaze. "And you think this relates to the absence of wildlife this morning?"

Casey didn't answer right away. She was afraid he'd find her answer silly. But it had been percolating in her mind since she first noticed her beloved birds were AWOL on such a gorgeous morning. Finally—hesitantly—she spoke.

"Yes, especially since you've shared your vision. What I think is this: He's called out every innocent creature and He's going to leave the ungodly inhabitants of this valley to their own devices. Think about it, Edward. The last child moved from this valley over a month ago when the Petersons left. The school bus doesn't even come to Winnoby anymore."

Edward shifted in his chair and stared at his feet. Casey plunged on.

"The Lord took Miss Millie home in December. And poor old Andy a month before that. The Borgers were blessed with an opportunity to serve Him in Arizona. The Simpsons inherited a house in Florida. Janie Dunson married a wonderful Christian man she met in Houston. You know each story. We've tried to figure out why only the faithful were leaving. Doesn't it seem like more than a coincidence that, one by one, they've all been removed from our congregation? Not by some whim, but by a blessing from the Lord. We've been left with a group that doesn't want to hear about the blood, was glad to see the children go, and thinks a baptistery would be too messy."

She glanced over at Edward. His jaw was clenched. His eyes clamped shut. She knew he wasn't happy to be reminded. It made him feel he'd failed the Lord.

Yet she continued. "I overheard Jean Anne saying we need to be more particular who we invite to our services. And Lucy Stern insisted I stop advertising in the *Hortonville News*. *Those people don't belong over here* is how she put it." Casey leaned back in her chair and sighed. She'd said her piece. It would take the Lord to make Edward see the light.

After a moment Edward broke the silence. "Has God revealed this to you? Because if not, it's certainly not our place to decide who needs the Lord and who's already rejected Him for eternity."

"I know. But it *is* our place to listen when He speaks. If I'm interpreting His voice correctly, He's saying essentially the same thing to both of us. That being the case, whatever becomes of those who remain is strictly between Him and them. I don't think last night was a dream or a trick of your subconscious mind. If you need any proof He wants us to leave, look around. He's removed his beloved creatures. He's called out all of His faithful. And He's given us a release from this place in our hearts."

Edward sat up straight. Looking stern, he counted on the fingers of his left hand. "Okay, Casey, number one, we'd have to decide where to go. Two, we'd have to sell our place, and three, we'd have to buy another house before we could move."

"Is that what the angel said, darling? *Sell your house, buy another, and then leave Winnoby.* No! He said to *get out* of Winnoby. That sounds pretty urgent to me. We don't have much money tied up in this cabin. We may be able to sell it later—or even return to it—when we see where the Lord's leading us. For now, I think we should do as we're told. He'll fill us in as we go along."

Edward sat shaking his head. "I wish I could be more sure. It's such a major decision."

Casey sighed. The sigh of a loving, but frustrated, wife. Edward could hear so clearly from the Lord when he was preparing a message to deliver to needy ears. But he had a tendency to drag his feet when it came to such as this. He was so concerned he might leave behind just one soul who needed to hear the message of salvation.

She scooted her chair closer and leaning toward him, she took his hand. "Honey, just three weeks ago you brought a message to that little group in Hortonville. The Nike message, remember? In a nutshell, you said, 'If you get an order from the Holy Spirit . . . just do it!'"

They came from every direction to join the tight, close formation. Flying wing tip to wing tip. Had they been of the natural world, their presence would have blocked out the light of the sun as they passed between it and the valley below. But the darkness created by these vultures of the spirit world could be seen only with spiritual eyes.

"Snake-Eyes, when is the master going to give us physical bodies, like he promised?" a smaller demon called Slug asked the ghoul to his right.

"Shut up you fool, lest the master hear you and give you what you want. Don't you know how cumbersome a physical body is? You can't do *this* with a physical body." He dove downward, out of formation and out of sight before the sound from his words had reached the ears of the foolish one. In a nanosecond he reappeared, coming from overheard.

Slug ducked his head. "Impressive, but how can you frighten humans when they can't even see you?"

"Our assignment isn't to *frighten* them, you idiot. They do a good enough job of *that* to themselves with their wars and weapons of mass destruction. We're to infiltrate their lives and destroy them from within. It's a time-consuming process. If they're already Christians, the best we can hope for is to get them to put their God on the back burner . . . not always an easy task. But we can consider our work a partial success if we sidetrack them to the point they can do no service for their King.

"If they're *not* Christians, the master expects us to harden their hearts and bring them into submission to him. Severe punishment is meted out to anyone who fails to convert a likely candidate."

"How? How do we do it if they can't see us?" Slug blinked and his flimsy wings quivered. He began to lose altitude. Palpable fear shot from his eyes.

"Cut that out, wimp!" Snake-Eyes snagged one of Slug's wings and yanked him back into formation. Tender membrane ripped and the tip of Slug's right wing flapped uselessly in the wind.

"Listen and learn. A whispered suggestion can do wonders. Ever heard of Grazzo?"

Slug shook his head.

"No? Well, he's only the meanest man in Winnoby. And probably for a hundred miles in any direction. Well, that's how I got him when he was a very young man. A whispered suggestion." With a smirk, he whipped his scaly tail to the left and scraped some slimy hide off his companion.

Slug veered off course. Then, licking his wound, he pulled back into formation. "Ow. Why'd you do that?"

"To shut you up. No more questions. I don't want to miss out on today's activities because of an ignorant slimeball like you."

The smaller demon looked confused, but didn't speak.

"You don't know what today is, either?" Snake-Eyes groaned and with his magnificent, translucent wings he made a wide sweeping gesture. "What do you think this is all about?"

"Don't know." Slug kept his head down. His eyes straight ahead. His spiny wings flapping at full speed. "Just following the crowd. This is my first day."

"Just my luck. A probie. Well, El Stupido, we're going to *eliminate* that Christian couple that's kept everything in an uproar for our master for so long. It's the same pair of Goody Two-shoes who got us in deep stuff with the master in Sugar Bluff, Arkansas, several years ago. This time they've wandered into his chosen hometown to stir up trouble. Christian idiots! That's what they are."

Snake-Eyes disappeared again. He returned in a heartbeat with an oak leaf impaled on one fang. "Winnoby's become so noxious, their God can't even look on it, so they have no backup. They're toast."

He howled. "Dog food."

He stuck a talon down his scaly neck to provoke a gagging reflex. "Dead meat."

Sniggering, he flipped over to fly upside down. "But not before we've had some fun. All their believers have deserted them. It's game time. We're going to make believers out of *them*. It should be quite a show."

"You got a leaf on your fang," Slug ventured and then ducked.

"Mind your own business, Probie. I'll get rid of it when the time is right."

Some time later Snake-Eyes noticed they were directly over the mountain road. Through the heavy foliage, he could see the top of an SUV working its way down the mountain. When it broke into the clearing . . .

He spat and the leaf fluttered to earth.

Edward opened his mouth to continue his argument but stopped short when he spotted the first live creature of the morning. It appeared out of nowhere. They'd never had any snakes on their place, which was nothing short of a miracle. Why would the first serpent—and a very large one, at that—choose this particular time to make its appearance? Edward didn't believe in coincidence. He reached over, took Casey's hand, and gave it a little squeeze. When she looked up at him, he nodded toward the reptile. Casey drew in her breath but didn't scream.

As they watched, it opened its slit of a mouth. One fang pierced an oak leaf that was lying on the ground before the reptile disappeared before their eyes.

"I think you're right, Casey. Gather all of our valuables we can carry in the car. We'll head for St. Michael immediately. If we leave soon enough, we can be there by lunch."

They were both aware that if they left their few family heirlooms, like the grandfather clock and the cedar chest, behind in Winnoby, they may never see them again. Thievery was rampant among the weekend homes and family cabins here in the mountains. But obedience is of the utmost importance to the Lord. They'd follow His lead. If it was His desire they have these treasures back in their lives, He'd preserve them.

Quickly and wordlessly, they loaded their vehicle.

Casey made another pot of coffee in the old tin percolator Edward had bought her when they first married. She poured two large cups and cleaned the pot to take along. Edward finished his packing just as she was squeezing it in between two boxes. The whole process had taken them only thirty-five minutes, plus another five for Casey to slip into a pair of jeans, her tennis shoes, and a lightweight sweater.

They were both antsy and ready to move out. The Lord hadn't given them a time frame, but He seemed to be impressing upon them that time was of the essence. Before they climbed into their small SUV, Edward enclosed Casey tightly in his arms and said a prayer for both of them that they were correctly interpreting His instructions.

Then he held her hands while they looked around at the place they'd put so much love and effort into making their home. They'd thought it was going to be their haven until the Lord called them to their eternal home. Edward's eyes swept over the little gravesite where Soupy, Casey's beloved pet possum, was buried. He knew it was traumatic for her to leave like this, but they could only trust God had even better things in store for their future.

From the depths of the wooded area encircling their home, several pairs of human eyes were watching their every move. Shrouded behind a covering of camouflage netting, Ward and his cohorts were indiscernible from their surroundings. As Edward and Casey stepped into their vehicle, there came the eerie sound of a coyote howling, followed by another farther away, and yet another even more distant howl.

They're on their way. Set the trap.

Goose bumps prickled Edward's arms.

With a renewed sense of awareness the McAlesters pulled down their long drive and out onto the blacktop highway, still searching the skies and the fields for any sign of life. There was none. Not even a breeze to ripple the silent treetops. The passing scenery could have been a gigantic oil painting—a stage backdrop—so still it was in its breathtaking beauty.

They snaked their way down the narrow road, the sun now blotted out by overhanging trees on both sides. At the bottom of the mountain, where the trees thinned and the road began to level off, a single leaf fluttered from the sky and drifted to the windshield. Leaf met glass with the sound of lightning splitting a mighty oak tree. The windshield shattered beneath its weight. Edward skidded to a stop and jumped out to survey the damage. Puzzled, he picked up the leaf and examined it. It was slimy . . . and bore a single small hole.

Spiritual darkness closed in around them, and a tuneless funeral dirge droned in their spirits. They were alone in enemy territory. Ahead, the only exit from this little hamlet was blocked by a stalled, fully loaded log truck, the front wheels almost touching the café patio.

Jesus, where are You?

Half of the remaining men of Winnoby were milling around the cab of the stalled truck—beer in hand at 9:00 a.m.—taking turns peering under the hood. They hadn't gotten an early start. It had become a twenty-four-hour-a-day pastime to hang out in the streets, drinking beer and wreaking havoc. Napping when it suited them and bathing seldom. Profane language rose over them like tendrils of smoke from a foul flame.

Looking up at Edward's approaching vehicle, there was no surprise in their eyes. They were expecting him.

"Oh, lookie, if it ain't the pretty preacher man come to help us," one of them sneered in Edward's direction.

Edward pulled to a stop ten or twelve feet from the truck. "Stay in the car, darling. I'll see if there's anything I can do."

"Please don't go over there, Edward. What could you possibly do that they couldn't?"

He was already on the outside of the SUV. "I have no choice, Casey. There's no other way out of town. It's best I remain friendly. I may catch them off guard and they won't act on their dislike for me. Besides, I can't let Satan turn me into an uncaring fool because these men taunt me. The Lord will deal with them in due time. In the meantime, I've got to remain true to my calling." He leaned in and touched her cheek. "There may be one among them who would still receive the Lord."

Casey sank in her seat and cast him a worried look.

Walking closer to the group of men, Edward felt the presence of the demon of violence. Its nearness brought a wave of nausea over him as it surrounded and suffocated him.

It's looking for a way back in.

Silently, Edward called on Jesus with every breath, to keep the evil at bay. But he felt no satisfaction his prayers were being heard. Pity for these men filled his heart. He looked from one to the other, searching for some sign of a salvageable soul in this wretched group. But pure evil emanated from every stare, as they visually dissected the approaching servant of God. Their hearts had long since been seared over by hell's dreadful flames.

There, but for the grace of God and the intervention of caring Christians, go I.

"Good morning, gentlemen." He smiled genuinely. "Is there anything I can do to help?"

"Well, if it isn't Mr. Rogers come to welcome us to the neighborhood," one of them snickered. Another laughed out loud. Then another. Soon they were all howling with laughter.

The filthiest man in the group extended a greasy hand. "Yeah, you can shake my hand, *neighbor.*"

Edward boldly clasped his hand into the filthy one and shook it vigorously.

The malefactor bellowed over his shoulder to his cohorts, "Hey, preacher man and me are big buds." He slapped his other huge hand on Edward's back and rubbed affectionately, wiping grease and grime all over his fresh shirt. "Mr. Rogers wants to be our friend." He guffawed, revealing pointy yellow teeth and gaping black holes.

Others followed suit. Surrounding Edward, they rubbed grubby hands all over his shirt. Some stepped to the exposed engine to get more grime on their hands before approaching him.

They reached around one another, clamoring to wipe a filthy hand on his clothing. Eight men closed in on him. Laughing, jabbing, and spitting.

"Oh, we're getting him *dirty*, guys. Here, let me clean you up a bit." Grazzo poured his bottle of beer down Edward's chest and fell back in sidesplitting laughter.

"Rub-a-dub-dub." The one called Rankin goaded in a singsong voice as he jabbed repeatedly into Edward's chest.

Edward struggled with the spirit of anger. He might be able to overpower one of them, but if he gave in to his feelings of rage, he'd be opening the door to all the demons of the past. Besides he'd most likely be beaten beyond recognition by this gang of hoodlums.

That may happen, anyway!

He looked at Casey. She was holding her screams in with both hands, and the terror in her eyes was tangible. It dawned on him that were he to be killed by this gang of thugs, she'd be helpless. He *had* to think of a way for them to get past this truck.

Several of the men seemed to lose interest in the game and walked away to retrieve their beer. Grazzo gripped Edward's shoulder but kept averting his gaze in Casey's direction.

Rankin punched Edward's chest one more time. "Hey, pretty boy, where are you and dollface going, all packed to the gills? You're not thinking of leaving us, are ya?"

"Just taking a little time off, guys." Edward replied through clenched teeth.

"A little time off, huh? Must be nice. What all you got in that fancy jitney besides your fancy-lookin' dame?" Grazzo dropped his hand from Edward and started ambling toward the SUV.

Edward moved to step in front of him, motioning for Casey to lock the doors.

Grazzo lifted his hand over his head and snapped a finger. Two men grabbed Edward's arms from behind.

The look of horror on Casey's face as she punched the door lock sent a chill down his spine. How could he have allowed her to be put in such danger?

His captors yanked him backward, slamming him against the cab of the truck. A third man brought a vicious knee to his groin before climbing on the hood to drink his beer and watch Grazzo's show.

Edward sagged against the side of the truck, straining to keep his eyes open, his head erect.

ABOUT THE AUTHOR

Lynne Wells Walding spent more than twenty-five years in the full-time Christian ministry with her pastor husband, Dee. She wrote many of the praise and worship songs for their services, and served as pianist, co-worship leader, and minister to women.

They're now retired and live in the Piney Woods of East Texas with their dog, Sarah. There they enjoy frequent visits from children, grandchildren, and great-grandchildren. Not to mention daily visits from two squirrels named Elmo and Faye, a couple of Lynne's wildlife rescues, whom she raised from infancy.

She writes a blog called "The Battle is Real" . . . an exposé of Satan's bag of tricks. And she's a member of ACFW (American Christian Fiction Writers). Drawing from her years in the ministry, her greatest passion is writing novels to demonstrate the spiritual battle we all face daily and the power of Jesus Christ to overcome the Enemy.

You can e-mail Lynne at lynne@lynnewellswalding.com—or visit her website at www.lynnewellswalding.com, where you'll find a link to her blog, *The Battle Is Real*.